Bella Abzug

Bella Abzug

How One Tough Broad from the Bronx Fought Jim Crow and Joe McCarthy, Pissed Off Jimmy Carter, Battled for the Rights of Women and Workers, Rallied Against War and for the Planet, and Shook Up Politics Along the Way

An Oral History by

Suzanne Braun Levine and Mary Thom

Farrar, Straus and Giroux / New York

Farrar, Straus and Giroux
19 Union Square West, New York 10003

Distributed in Canada by Douglas & McIntyre Ltd.
Printed in the United States of America
First edition, 2007

Library of Congress Cataloging-in-Publicaton Data

Levine, Suzanne.
Bella Abzug : how one tough broad from the Bronx fought Jim Crow and Joe McCarthy, pissed off Jimmy Carter, battled for the rights of women and workers, rallied against war and for the planet, and shook up politics along the way / by Suzanne Braun Levine and Mary Thom.— 1st ed.
p. cm.
Includes bibliographical references and index.
ISBN-13: 978-0-374-29952-1 (hardcover : alk. paper)
ISBN-10: 0-374-29952-8 (hardcover : alk. paper)
1. Abzug, Bella S., 1920–1998. 2. Women legislators—United States—Biography. 3. Legislators—United States—Biography. 4. Political activists—United States—Biography. 5. Social reformers—United States—Biography. 6. United States. Congress. House—Biography. 7. United States—Politics and government—1945–1989. 8. United States—Politics and government—1989- 9. United States—Social conditions—1945- I. Thom, Mary. II. Title.

E840.8.A2L485 2007
328.73092—dc22
[B]

2007009120

Designed by Jonathan D. Lippincott

www.fsgbooks.com

1 3 5 7 9 10 8 6 4 2

I've been described as a tough and noisy woman, a prizefighter, a man-hater, you name it. They call me Battling Bella, Mother Courage, and a Jewish mother with more complaints than Portnoy. There are those who say I'm impatient, impetuous, uppity, rude, profane, brash, and overbearing. Whether I'm any of these things or all of them, you can decide for yourself. But whatever I am—and this ought to be made very clear at the outset—I am a very serious woman.

—Bella S. Abzug

Contents

Preface:
What Would Bella Do?

There was standing room only at the Riverside Memorial Chapel on April 2, 1998, as friends and admirers gathered to celebrate the life of a woman who believed she could nudge, inveigle, and wrangle the world onto a path of social justice. The speakers evoked a heady era of political possibility as they told "Bella stories"; they implored each other to preserve her legacy and carry forward her agenda. They began asking each other, as colleagues and admirers still do today, nearly a decade later, What would Bella do?

One of the first speakers was Geraldine Ferraro, the only woman to appear on a major party presidential ticket, as Walter Mondale's running mate in 1984. "If there had never been a Bella Abzug, there would never have been a Gerry Ferraro," she said. Bella "didn't knock lightly on the door. She didn't even push it open or batter it down. She took it off the hinges forever. So that those of us who came after could walk through." Marlo Thomas told how happy Bella was to hear that she was finally getting married and then began to push her to have children. "I said, 'Bella, I got married. Make Gloria [Steinem] have the babies!' " Marlo's husband, Phil Donahue, recalled a gathering of intellectual luminaries at which he sat next to Bella. Minutes into each presentation, she would mumble, "Good. Sit down." The historian Amy Swerdlow marveled at Bella's "brilliance as a strategist" and recalled her appearance impersonating Marlene Dietrich, dressed in a tuxedo and singing "Falling in Love Again." Jane Fonda wore a hat to commemorate Bella's signature symbol. Shirley MacLaine—true to her faith in channeling—spoke "directly" to Bella, and the microphone mysteriously jumped to one side. Speakers recalled the pride she took in her two daughters and the "great love affair" with Martin, her husband of more than four decades, who had died twelve years earlier.

Gloria Steinem, one of the last speakers, tried to sum up this larger-than-life, braver-than-any leader. She described how frightened she was the first time she encountered Bella's outsized voice and aggressive conviction. Then she took note of Bella's independence and unremitting passion and pointed out that she had "come up through social justice movements, not through a political party." In other words, she was beholden to no institution with traditions, trade-offs, and party lines; she was guided by her commitment to the ideas and the groups she believed were working to make society more responsive to the needs of the people.

As a lawyer and a congresswoman, Bella Abzug was an activist and leader in every major social movement of her lifetime—from socialist Zionism and labor in the forties, to the civil rights, ban-the-bomb, and anti–Vietnam war movements in the fifties and sixties; the women's movement in the seventies and eighties; and, in the years before she died, global human rights, as, along with her lifelong collaborator, Mim Kelber, she founded the Women's Environment and Development Organization to promote an international agenda of economic equality and environmental sanity.

She began her life's work as an advocate and organizer, developing policy and legal arguments, making connections between ideas and constituencies. Then in 1970, at age fifty, she ran for office for the first time and was elected to Congress, representing a progressive district in Manhattan. Being on the inside was a new experience for her, but Bella became one of the most respected strategists in the Congress. Friend and foe alike marveled at her mastery of congressional procedure and her innovative approaches to legislation. Moreover, she continued mobilizing pressure on the government, organizing women around the country to participate in lobbying her colleagues, and securing funding and authorization for the First National Women's Conference, which she chaired after she left office. Then she was appointed chair of the Presidential Advisory Committee on Women only to find herself on the outside again, when President Jimmy Carter fired her for the insubordination of insisting that the economy and even foreign policy were women's issues.

With each evolution her career underwent, her core commitment to social justice took on a new dimension. Thus, for Bella, feminism was a natural extension of her years in progressive politics; for many other women, the politics came later, growing out of the frustrating experience of trying to establish an equal footing in the culture. From the beginning she was committed to diversifying and enlarging the reach of any movement she became part of.

No matter how big the job she took on, Bella always made it bigger. As a member of Congress from New York, she became better known in most other districts than the representative serving there. Later, as an international leader and activist, she may have been better known in several other countries than in her own. To this day, women leaders in emerging countries will identify themselves as "the Bella Abzug of Nigeria" or "the Bella Abzug of Mongolia."

Along the way, she ruffled plenty of feathers. But she stood up to all adversaries with fierce conviction, and frequently bested them with her trademark wit. In 1995, at seventy-five and in a wheelchair, she was attending the world conference on women in Beijing, when George H. W. Bush, who was in China on a private visit to give a speech to corporate executives, attacked her as an extremist. "I feel somewhat sorry for the Chinese, having Bella running around," he said. Bella's reply left no doubt as to what she thought of that remark: "He was addressing a fertilizer group? That's appropriate."

For over half a century, Bella Abzug was the standard-bearer for the politics of the powerless and disenfranchised. While others courted interest groups, she gathered her constituencies into a larger and larger coalition. Where did she get the chutzpah? Where did she get the resilience and optimism and tenacity? Where did she get the brilliance?

Most perplexing, where are the contemporary voices of outrage and defiant optimism? In recent years the executive branch of government has reconfigured the relationship of the United States with the rest of the world from trusted alliances to unilateral exercise of power, with barely a murmur from our elected representatives. Until recently, momentous issues were being decided virtually without public debate or accountability from Congress. In the lead-up to the 2008 elections, it is inconceivable that Bella would keep quiet. Even if she couldn't immediately change minds, she would raise the issues—and her voice. She would prod and poke; haggle and debate; educate and galvanize. If she were still among us, what would Bella do? If we are to carry forward her legacy, what should *we* do?

The question is repeated over and over again in conversations with those who knew her personally and worked with her. It is echoed by those who only know of her and long for a resurgence of the kind of fierce outrage and creative stubbornness she stood for. Bella's real legacy may turn out to be the inspiration her life offers us and the model she sets for the kind of leadership we are so desperately looking for today.

Because we both knew and worked with her, we know how uppity and vivid she was, how passionate and loud. We were convinced that the way to bring her persona to life was to build a memoir in many voices from her own testimony and the words of those who knew her. The stories told by fellow politicians, family, friends, *and* enemies evoke one of the most colorful, controversial, effective, courageous—and very cantankerous—women of the twentieth century. The image that emerges has many layers. Her complex relationships with family, friends, and colleagues could generate deep conflict and bitterness as well as joy and appreciation.

No one is able to talk about Bella without reciting a "Bella story," frequently assuming her unmistakable New York accent in the telling. (Norman Mailer, not an admirer, said her voice "could boil the fat off a taxicab driver's neck.") Everyone had a favorite Bella phrase that nailed an issue. The journalist Myra MacPherson singled out a favorite with typical Bella vocabulary: "Abzug even stressed equality for the mediocre, cracking that the goal was not to see a 'female Einstein become an assistant professor. We want a woman schlemiel to get promoted as quickly as a male schlemiel.' "

We assembled a list of people to interview, from those who knew her as a girl growing up in the Bronx through those who were beside her in the historic moments she helped create as well as those who worked for her (now *that* was an experience). We also had access to her incomplete memoir and to oral histories taken at Columbia University. In addition to evoking one of the most audacious and outrageous women of her time, the testimony brings to life many compelling people who shared moments in her political legacy.

We edited those interviews into a "conversation" in which the story unfolds through anecdote, embellishment, contradiction, flashback and flash-forward, asides, commentary, speculation—as if the wide-ranging and ill-assorted cast of characters were gathered around a fireplace reminiscing about someone who stomped into their lives and left an indelible mark. It is not necessary to know who's who to follow the plot, but we have also provided thumbnail sketches of all the speakers. To set the stage, each chapter begins with a short chronology of events in Bella's life and the world at large.

The cumulative testimony speaks to a particularly powerful moment in which vital social movements converged in the second half of the twentieth century, every one of which featured Bella as a catalyst and creative force. It sheds light on how she mobilized followers and used whatever tools were at hand—the pressure of protest, the force of law, the give-and-take of the legislative process—to move forward on a broad agenda. And it gives insight into the personal qualities that fired her courage. Her life stands as an example of those rare and crucial public figures who stand up—and do so again and again, without losing faith—to "speak truth to power."

The Speakers

For those people listed here who were interviewed specifically for this book, the date of the interview is noted in brackets. Otherwise the sources of quotes are listed in the notes section, as are the several sources of Bella's words. Throughout the text, *italics* signify Bella speaking.

Eve Abzug—Bella's daughter, associate director of residential services at The Bridge, a social service organization, and therapist at Maria Droste Services. Cofounder, Bella Abzug Leadership Institute, a nonprofit organization dedicated to leadership training for young women. For three decades she has served as a public policy administrator and advocate working with the homeless, mentally ill, chemically dependent, incarcerated, and people living with HIV/AIDS and cancer. Former director, Kingsbridge Women's Assessment Shelter, a handicapped-accessible women's intake shelter in New York City. Former deputy executive director, Bowery Residents' Committee, a social service organization. Facilitator of support groups for people living with cancer and their families at Gilda's Club, New York City. [Interviewed by Robin Morgan on July 26, 2004]

Liz Abzug (Isobel Jo)—Bella's daughter, head of a nationwide economic development consulting business. Cofounder of the Bella Abzug Leadership Institute. Adjunct professor of Urban Studies at Barnard College. She worked on thirty political campaigns, including ten of her mother's, and in 1991, ran unsuccessfully for a New York City Council seat. Under Governor Mario Cuomo she served as deputy commissioner of New York State's Human Rights Enforcement Agency, vice president of operations at the New York State Urban Development Corporation, and director of New York State's Empowerment Zone Program. [Interviewed by Robin Morgan on July 28, 2004; e-mail February 2, 2007]

Helene Savitzky Alexander—Bella's older sister; music teacher, concert pianist. [Interviewed on March 17, 2005]

Kofi Annan—UN secretary general (1997–2006). Born in Ghana, he joined the United Nations system in 1962. He served as assistant secretary general for peacekeeping operations (1992–1993) and as undersecretary general (1993–1996).

Martha Baker—Women Strike for Peace activist, advocate for women in nontraditional jobs and for equity in education and employment. [Interviewed on October 7, 2005]

Leslie Bennetts—Journalist, former *New York Times* reporter, author of *The Feminine Mistake* (2007).

Judy Berek—Labor organizer, former administrator for the Center for Medicare and Medicaid Services (Northeast Consortium), regional consortium administrator in the New York Health Care Financing Administration. [Interviewed on March 11, 2005]

Barbara Bick—Founding member of Women Strike for Peace; Bella's closest friend in Washington, D.C., and traveling companion. Former associate at the Institute for Policy Studies working for multiculturalism, women's rights, and peace. [Interviewed on June 9, 2005]

Joseph (Joe) Bologna—Broadway and Hollywood actor (sixty-seven films), director, writer. He and his wife, the actress and writer Renée Taylor, were close friends of Bella's.

Erma Bombeck (died 1996)—Author and humorist.

Kathy Bonk—Cofounder and executive director of Communications Consortium in Washington, D.C. U.S. Department of State public information officer (1977), staff member for International Women's Year Commission. [E-mail, June 14, 2006]

Jimmy Breslin—New York columnist and author; husband of Bella's friend and colleague Ronnie Eldridge.

David S. Broder—Pulitzer Prize–winning columnist for *The Washington Post.*

Esther Broner—Writer, pioneer of Jewish feminism. Along with Bella, one of the Seder Sisters, who met for more than twenty years, beginning in 1976, for a women's seder. [Interviewed on November 21, 2005]

Susan Brownmiller—Author of *Against Our Will: Men, Women, and Rape* (1975); cofounder of Women Against Pornography (1979). [Interviewed on November 29, 2005]

Patrick J. Buchanan—Syndicated columnist and broadcaster.

Liz Carpenter—Author and founding member of the National Women's Political Caucus; White House staff director and press secretary to First Lady Lady Bird Johnson. She served on President Gerald Ford's International Women's Year Commission. President Jimmy Carter appointed her assistant secretary of education for public affairs. [Interviewed on August 10, 2005]

Jimmy Carter—Thirty-ninth president of the United States (1974–1978).

Rosalynn Smith Carter—Global human rights activist, writer, former First Lady, vice chair of The Carter Center in Atlanta, founded in 1982 to promote peace and human rights worldwide.

Sey Chassler (died 1997)—Longtime editor of *Redbook* magazine; member of Carter's Advisory Committee on Women.

Shirley Chisholm (died 2005)—First African American woman to serve in Congress (1969–1983). As a member of the New York delegation and a fellow social activist, she worked with Bella on civil rights legislation and women's issues.

Hillary Clinton—U.S. senator from New York, former First Lady (1993–2001).

Alice Cohan—NOW (National Organization for Women) activist, director of National Programs and political director at the Feminist Majority Foundation. [Interviewed on June 9, 2005]

Midge Costanza—Champion of gay and women's rights. Assistant to President Jimmy Carter (1976), special assistant to California governor Gray Davis (2000), serving as liaison for women's groups and issues. [Interviewed on April 6, 2006]

Susan Davis—Adviser, International Labor Organization. Former executive director of WEDO (Women's Environment and Development Organization), a global women's advocacy organization founded by Bella and Mim Kelber. [Interviewed October 14, 2005]

Ronald Dellums—Mayor of Oakland, first elected to the U.S. House of Representatives from California in 1970, the same year as Bella, where he served for twenty-eight years. Author of an autobiography, *Lying Down with the Lions: A Public Life from the Streets of Oakland to the Halls of Power*, and *Defense Sense: The Search for a Rational Military Policy*. [Interviewed on November 1, 2005]

Phil Donahue—Host of the *Donahue* talk show (1974–1996), recipient of numerous Emmy awards, the Margaret Sanger Award, and the Peabody Award.

Robert K. (Bob) Dornan—U.S. congressman (1977–1997). Pro-life advocate, author of legislation to prevent federally funded abortions in the District of Columbia, in military hospitals (both in the United States and overseas), in federal prisons, and on Native American Indian reservations.

Joanne Edgar—A founding editor of Ms. magazine, former director of communications at the Edna McConnell Clark Foundation, writer and communications consultant to social justice foundations. [E-mail, September 26, 2006]

Ronnie Eldridge—Longtime political adviser, colleague, and friend of Bella's. New York City Council member (1989–2001), prime sponsor of the Clinic Access Law that provides protection for women seeking reproductive health care as well as for the health-care providers performing those services, and legislation that sets standards for child care. [Interviewed on August 9, 2004]

Wendy Westbrook Fairey—A Bella poker crony, author of *Full House* and *One of the Family*. [Interviewed on October 6, 2005]

Geraldine Ferraro—U.S. Congresswoman (1979–1985) and first woman vice presidential candidate (1984). Author of *Ferraro: My Story*. [Interviewed August 16, 2004, and October 25, 2005]

Jane Fonda—Actor (more than forty films), author, and activist, Fonda describes herself as a liberal and a feminist. Cofounder of the Women's Media Center. Her autobiography, *My Life So Far*, was published in 2005. [Interviewed by Robin Morgan in September 2005]

Anne Foner—Retired professor of sociology at Rutgers University, widow of Moe Foner. [Interviewed on April 4, 2005]

Henry Foner—One of four brothers, all educators and organizers. Mobilized labor opposition to the war in Vietnam, led his union's participation in the struggle for civil rights, and headed the fur industry's Committee on Wildlife Conservation and Legislation. [Interviewed on April 15, 2005]

Moe Foner (died 2002)—Founder of Bread and Roses, the pioneering labor arts program. Champion of civil rights and civil liberties. Longtime executive secretary of 1199/SEIU, New York's health and human service union.

Betty Ford—Former U.S. First Lady (1974–1977), known for speaking her mind on delicate issues, including breast cancer, marijuana use, premarital sex, and the benefits of psychiatric treatment. In 1982, after her recovery from alcoholism and medical drug addiction, she established the Betty Ford Center in Rancho Mirage, California, for the treatment of chemical dependency.

Betty Friedan (died 2006)—Cofounder of NOW with twenty-seven other women and men, and its first president (1966–1970). Cofounded the National Women's Political Caucus (NWPC) with Bella and others. Author of the groundbreaking book *The Feminine Mystique* (1963), which first articulated "the problem that has no name." [Interviewed by Marlene Sanders on November 29, 2005]

Lesley Gore—Singer, songwriter, Bella's friend and Long Island neighbor. Her first single, at age sixteen, was the number-one hit "It's My Party." [Interviewed on March 1, 2006]

Nadine B. Hack—New York Democratic Party fund-raiser. She served as commissioner general for the United Nations in EXPO 2000, in Hanover, Germany. President of beCause Global Consulting, which advises on cause-related strategies and philanthropic initiatives. [Interviewed on November 3, 2005]

Fannie Lou Hamer (died 1977)—Civil rights leader, founding member of NWPC. She ran for Congress in 1964 and 1965, and was eventually seated as a member of Mississippi's legitimate delegation to the Democratic National Convention of 1968.

Pete Hamill—Brooklyn-born novelist and journalist.

Donald S. Harrington (died 2005)—Unitarian minister and New York Liberal Party leader. He supported progressive candidates and ran for state office himself.

Eric Hirschhorn—Bella's congressional legislative assistant. Deputy assistant secretary for export administration at the U.S. Department of Commerce (1980–1981), member of President Jimmy Carter's staff (1977–1980). Currently a partner in the Washington, D.C., office of Winston & Strawn. [Interviewed on June 9, 2005]

Harold Holzer—Bella's U.S. Senate campaign press secretary, now Metropolitan Museum of Art publicist. One of the country's leading authorities on Abraham Lincoln and the political culture of the Civil War era. [Interviewed on September 21, 2005]

Koryne Horbal—In the early 1970s, as Minnesota member of the Democratic National Committee, she helped lead the movement for gender balance in delegates to presidential conventions. Appointed by President Jimmy Carter U.S. representative to the United Nations Commission on the Status of Women in 1977. [Interviewed on January 4, 2007]

Doug Ireland—Journalist and blogger about politics, power, media, and gay issues. He managed Bella's successful 1970 campaign for Congress. [Interviewed on April 27, 2005; e-mail, March 7, 2007]

Lady Bird Johnson (died 2007)—As First Lady (1963–1969), she started a capital beautification project and was an advocate for the Head Start program.

Barbara Jordan (died 1996)—Congresswoman from Texas (1972–1978). In July 1976, she became the first African American and the first woman to deliver a keynote address to the Democratic National Convention. Gained national prominence as a member of the House Judiciary Committee proceedings on the impeachment of Richard Nixon.

Mim Kelber (died 2004)—Bella's lifelong friend, speechwriter, coauthor, and collaborator on all fronts; cofounder of Women USA and WEDO. [Interviewed in fall 2003]

Edward M. Kennedy—U.S. senator from Massachusetts (1962–). [Interviewed on October 31, 2005]

Peggy Kobernot-Kaplan—Marathon runner, torchbearer at the Houston conference (1977).

Ed Koch—Political commentator and movie critic. Former U.S. congressman from New York's 17th District (1969–1977) and mayor of New York City (1978–1989).

Michelle Landsberg—Canadian writer and feminist activist.

Brownie Ledbetter—NWPC organizer, WEDO board member, Arkansas Public Policy Group, advocate for equal education opportunities for women and minorities. [Interviewed on May 27, 2005, and November 15, 2005]

Eva Lederman—Bella's Walton high school gym teacher.

Judy Lerner—Westchester-based Women Strike for Peace activist and one of Bella's oldest friends. [Interviewed on May 11, 2005]

Rosalyn Levitt—High school friend. [Interviewed May 13, 2005]

Karin Lippert—Press consultant for social justice organizations. She headed *Ms.* magazine's publicity department in the 1970s and organized press conferences and events for various national feminist causes. [E-mail, March 13, 2007]

Wangari Maathai—Feminist, environmentalist, and Nobel Peace Prize winner for her work organizing Kenya's Green Belt movement. Founding board member of WEDO. [Interviewed on December 21, 2006]

Shirley MacLaine—Political activist, actress, author of four books about her spiritual journeys. [Interviewed on January 30, 2003]

Norman Mailer—Novelist, journalist, playwright, screenwriter, and film director.

Marilyn Marcosson—Bella's congressional administrative assistant, currently a vice president and wealth management adviser at Merrill Lynch in Washington, D.C. [Interviewed on June 10, 2005]

Shirley Margolin—Democratic Party organizer and peace activist, delegate to the 1972 Democratic National Convention from New York. [Interviewed on March 31, 2005]

Margaret Mead (died 1978)—Pioneering anthropologist, scientist, explorer, writer, teacher, and activist.

Joyce Miller—President of the Coalition of Labor Union Women (1977–1993), the first woman on the AFL-CIO executive council (1980–1993). [Interviewed on November 1, 2005]

Robin Morgan—Activist, writer, and poet; editor of Ms. magazine (1989–1993); edited *Sisterhood Is Powerful: An Anthology of Writings from the Women's Liberation Movement* (1970). Author of twenty-one books of poetry, fiction, and prose. [Interviewed on January 30, 2003]

Constance Baker Motley (died 2005)—Bella's Columbia Law School classmate, NAACP Legal Defense Fund attorney, New York state senator and Manhattan borough president, first African American woman appointed to the federal judiciary (1966). [Interviewed on June 13, 2005]

Bill Moyers—Broadcast journalist, deputy director of the Peace Corps in the Kennedy Administration, and special assistant to President Johnson (1963–1967).

Jerrold Nadler—New York political activist, holds Bella's former House seat in Congress (1992–). [Interviewed on October 14, 2005]

Joan Nixon—Driver, friend. [Interviewed in fall 2003]

John Oakes—Executive editor of Atlas Books, an independent publisher specializing in short books by distinguished authors. [Interviewed on April 13, 2007]

Maggi Peyton—Member of Bella's U.S. Senate campaign staff; currently senior assistant to Manhattan Borough President Scott Stringer. [Interviewed on May 10, 2006]

Letty Cottin Pogrebin—Author, journalist, lecturer, and social justice activist; cofounded Ms. magazine, the NWPC, the Ms. Foundation for Women, and the International Center for Peace in the Middle East; past president of the Authors Guild and Americans for Peace Now; author of nine books, including *Deborah, Golda, and Me: Being Female and Jewish in America*. [Interviewed on December 22, 2005]

Margot Polivy—Bella's congressional administrative assistant; attorney for the Association for Intercollegiate Athletics for Women (AIAW). [Interviewed on June 8, 2005]

Stanley Pottinger—Assistant attorney general of the Civil Rights Division, U.S. Department of Justice in the Nixon and Ford administrations; *New York Times* bestselling mystery author. [E-mail, April 20, 2006]

Charles Rangel—Chair of the House Ways and Means Committee; represents (since 1970) New York's 15th Congressional District. [Interviewed on March 10, 2006]

Marguerite Rawalt (died 1989)—Attorney, American Association of University Women (AAUW) activist.

Carolyn Reed (died 1993)—Organizer of the Household Technicians of America, a national advocacy group for household workers; member of Carter's Advisory Committee on Women; chair of the New York Women's Political Caucus.

Claire Reed—New York City–based activist. [Interviewed on March 29, 2005]

Ann Richards (died 2006)—Governor of Texas (1991–1995). Member of Carter's Advisory Committee on Women.

Dorothy Goldin Rosenberg—Canadian editor, activist, and feminist; education outreach coordinator for Women's Healthy Environments Network.

Lois Sasson—Bella's friend and political supporter, jewelry designer. [Interviewed on March 1, 2006]

Phyllis Schlafly—Political organizer; known for her bestselling 1964 book A *Choice, Not An Echo*, and her opposition to feminism in general and the Equal Rights Amendment (ERA) in particular.

Eileen Shanahan (died 2001)—Former *New York Times* and *St. Petersburg Times* reporter. Participated in efforts to open the National Press Club and the Gridiron Club to women and in a landmark employment discrimination lawsuit against *The New York Times*.

Ralph Shapiro—Labor lawyer; colleague at Bella's first law firm; Lawyer's Guild organizer. [Interviewed on May 10, 2005]

Patricia Schroeder—Democratic congresswoman from Colorado (1973–1997), first woman to serve on the House Armed Services Committee. [Interviewed on August 25, 2004]

Eleanor Smeal—NOW president (1977–1982 and 1985–1987), member of Carter's Advisory Committee on Women, currently president of the Feminist Majority Foundation. In December 2001, FMF became the publisher of Ms. magazine. [Interviewed on June 9, 2005]

Martha Smiley—Participant in the Houston conference. Member of the board of regents of the University of Texas; member of the board of directors of the Foundation for Women's Resources, the Austin Women's Center, the Texas Rape Prevention and Control Project, the Austin Area Urban League, and the Austin Commission on the Status of Women. Chaired the Austin Women's Political Caucus and the Texas Women's Political Caucus.

Gloria Steinem—Writer, feminist activist, journalist, and women's rights advocate. Political partner and cofounder of several organizations with Bella. Cofounder of Ms. magazine. [Interviewed on January 30, 2003, and August 26, 2006; e-mail, April 28, 2006]

Barbra Streisand—Actor, singer, early supporter; Bella's colleague on the International Women's Year Commission. [E-mail, November 17, 2005]

Scott Stringer—New York Democratic politician and current borough president of Manhattan. His mother is Bella's cousin. [Interviewed on May 10, 2006]

Amy Swerdlow—Bella's Hunter College classmate; founding member of Women Strike for Peace; emerita professor of history, Sarah Lawrence College. [Interviewed on March 9, 2005]

Linda Tarr-Whelan—Carter administration staff member, D.C. policy consultant. As president and chief executive officer of the Center for Policy Alternatives (1986–2001), she helped create five women's economic summits. Member of the U.S. delegation to the UN Fourth World Conference on Women, in Beijing; ambassador and U.S. representative to the UN Commission on the Status of Women under President Clinton. [Interviewed on January 5, 2006]

Ethel Taylor—National coordinator and spokeswoman for Women Strike for Peace; founder of the Philadelphia branch of SANE; Women's International League for Peace and Freedom activist; sculptor; member of Carter's National Commission on the Observance of International Women's Year.

Marlo Thomas—Actor and feminist activist, produced and hosted the TV special *Free to Be . . . You and Me*, founded the Free To Be Foundation, and edited *The Right Words at the Right Time*. [Interviewed on January 4, 2005]

Lindsy Van Gelder—Chief writer for *Allure* magazine, former staff writer for Ms. magazine, and coauthor of *The Girls Next Door: Into the Heart of Lesbian America*.

Carmen Delgado Votaw—Cochair of President Carter's National Advisory Committee for Women; civil rights activist, promoting equal opportunities for Hispanics and women. Director of government relations, Girl Scouts of the USA (1991–1997); director of government relations, United Way (1997–1998); senior vice president, Alliance for Children and Families (1998–2006). [Interviewed on June 9, 2005]

Robert F. Wagner (died 1991)—New York City mayor (1954–1965).

Maxine Waters—Democratic congresswoman (1991–) representing California's 35th District; self-described protégé of Bella. [Interviewed on June 9, 2005]

Faye Wattleton—First African American and youngest president of Planned Parenthood (1978–1992); founder of the Center for the Advancement of Women. [Interviewed on November 2, 2005]

Cora Weiss—Peace activist, cofounder of Women Strike for Peace. Currently president of the Hague Appeal for Peace. [Interviewed on May 13, 2005; e-mail, October 16, 2005]

Sarah Weddington—Argued *Roe v. Wade* before the Supreme Court; elected to the Texas House of Representatives in 1972; special White House adviser to President Jimmy Carter.

Jean Westwood—First female chair of the Democratic National Committee (1972), she worked for the presidential campaigns of Terry Sanford, Gary Hart, and Bruce Babbitt.

June Zeitlin—Bella's congressional legislative assistant, now director of WEDO. Formerly program officer at the Ford Foundation. [Interviewed on July 29, 2004]

Lyonel Zunz—Bella's Columbia law school classmate.

Bella Abzug

1

The Early Years: A Passion for Social Justice

Chronology

1920 On July 24, in the year American women secure the right to vote, Bella Savitzky is born in New York City to Esther and Emanuel Savitzky, both immigrants from Russia.

1932 Twelve-year-old Bella collects money on the New York City subways for the creation of the State of Israel and makes Zionist speeches in front of her father's butcher shop, the Live and Let Live Meat Market on Thirty-ninth Street and Ninth Avenue. Between 1922 and 1940, Jews increase their numbers from 11 percent to 30 percent of the population of Palestine under the British mandate from the UN and, on May 14, 1948, they proclaim the State of Israel, the day before the mandate was to expire.

1934 Bella, along with her lifelong friend Mim Kelber, attends Walton High School in the Bronx, New York.

1935 Eleanor Roosevelt begins writing her syndicated newspaper column, "My Day," which Walton students follow.

1938–1942 Bella and Mim attend Hunter College and in 1941 Bella is elected president of the student government; she is active in the American Student Union, which Joseph

Lash called "the student brain of the New Deal." She also studies at the Jewish Theological Seminary.

1939 The Hitler-Stalin Pact is signed, disillusioning many in the leftist student movement.

1940–1942 New York legislators, in early Joseph McCarthy–like hearings, search for Communist influence on college campuses.

1941 The attack on Pearl Harbor brings the United States into World War II; the pacifist Jeanette Rankin, Democrat from Montana, the first woman elected to the House of Representatives (1917), casts the only vote in the House against entering the war.

1945 Bella graduates from Columbia Law School after being an editor of *Law Review* and marrying Martin Abzug in her final year. She begins her law practice, specializing in civil liberties, civil rights, and labor law.

1945 World War II ends, bringing a halt to price and wage controls and ushering in a period of strikes and union agitation.

Late 1940s Bella joins the law firm Whitt and Cammer. She chairs the Civil Rights Committee of the National Lawyers Guild, a progressive bar association for lawyers and law students founded in 1937.

My parents had the foresight to give birth to me in the year that women got the vote. I was born July 24, 1920, in a South Bronx apartment on Hoe Avenue. All the rooms were on one side of a hall that ran the length of the apartment. Mama and Papa shared a room, as did my grandparents (on Mama's side). Uncle Julius, the youngest of Grandpa's four sons, had a room. He lived with us until he married my gorgeous Aunt Janet. I think I slept in my parents' room. My sister, Helene, slept on the couch.

Papa was a serious man, but not too good at making a living. First he owned a laundry with his brother-in-law Geffen, but down went the laundry. Then he owned a "dry" stationery store—it sold no drinks. That didn't work either. So my mother's brother Hymie set him up in the butcher business. Papa put on a white coat, hired some butchers, and put up a sign over the store that read, "Live and Let Live Meat Market." This was his philosophy, and his personal protest against the imperialist World War I.

Helene Savitzky Alexander When I was about fourteen, Bella's and my father, Emanuel Savitzky, didn't want me to be on the street with boys, so every Saturday, I came down to his store on Ninth Avenue in Manhattan. It was cold, and I would always get burned because I sat at this box with the heater. One of the butchers would give me a ticket, which I stamped and took in the money. Then the butcher went back and got the meat. The box had holes where you would put in the quarters, dimes, and nickels. The bills went underneath. On a Saturday, I would take in a thousand dollars—a lot in those days. Customers would come from across the river in Jersey. Bella was five years younger than I was, and she got so jealous that she started to come down and sell bags for shoppers to carry their provisions. She'd sell these paper bags along Ninth Avenue for maybe a nickel or a few pennies.

We were good kids—nothing like the rebellious kids today. For instance, my father would say to Bella, "Now you were fresh. You go stand in that corner." She'd say, "I'm not gonna stand in that corner!" That was her rebellion. My father was actually a very gentle man.

Papa was a big disciplinarian. When he would tell me to stand in the corner, there was a big struggle between us. "For what reason should I go into the corner?" I'd say. "How will that change anything?"

Helene Savitzky Alexander Bella was a hot Zionist as a young kid—about eleven or twelve. She would get dressed in this gold outfit with an orange tie and go to meetings and come back late. Our mother, Esther Savitzky, never made a fuss about it. She was the disciplinarian of the family, but with Bella, she somehow understood. Bella would go on the subway trains collecting money for Israel, and she wouldn't come back until her blue jar was completely full. When I think back, my mother was remarkable with Bella—very supportive. She never said, "You can't do this." She knew where my sister was and what she was doing, and she understood that this was Bella's interest.

I spent most of my free time with a group called a Kvutzah in Hebrew. We sang songs, danced the hora, studied socialism and communal living and the history of Israel. This was 1931. Few people understood what we meant by the establishment of a homeland for Jews.

Robin Morgan Bella was the first person to ever reposition Zionism for me, by saying, "For Christ sake, it started out as a national liberation movement like every other national liberation movement but it kind of has gone—you know—bad. It's a problem now."

I would go on the subways and make a speech in between stops describing the need for a homeland. This all seemed to irk Papa, especially the late hours. His exasperation reached a peak when I borrowed a dolly and pulled our Victrola and records—including Caruso and Chaliapin—through the streets of the Bronx to the local synagogue because they had no entertainment. I have no recollection of having the Victrola returned. It was then that Papa used his belt.

Papa came and stayed with me the first time they sent me to camp, and I cried and wanted to go home. Papa stayed for a week, and by that time, I hardly had time to say goodbye when he left.

Liz Abzug We have a picture of her on the cover of the camp brochure throwing a ball, and she looks like such a little tomboy.

Helene Savitzky Alexander When our father was in Russia, he worked for his brother, who had a club in Kiev, so he danced very well—folk dancing particularly—and he taught me. We grew up in a large family and had these big weddings where I would dance with him. Bella was younger and in the background. So she always felt that I was my father's favorite.

I played the piano, and he taught me how to sing in Russian, so I would play and sing for his family when they came. Bella played the violin until she stopped and didn't practice anymore. I have her violin now. Of all her things, when the kids asked me what I wanted after my sister died, I wanted that violin. We would play for my father on Friday nights. Bella had a marvelous voice, and when she was young, it was much higher. When I was music counselor at camp, Bella was the soloist in my choir. She was also the camp bugler—she played it by ear. Years later, her friend Judy Lerner would give these great New Year's parties, and they invited me once. I played the piano and they sang all these oldies and the folk songs. Liz is the musical one in Bella's family.

Eve Abzug My mother never said she regretted giving up studying the violin, but she would say, "They paid more attention to Helene." She said they pushed her sister, and then, when they got to my mother, they didn't really pay much attention to her musical education.

Helene Savitzky Alexander Our grandfather was the one who took a cotton to Bella as a youngster, so to speak. He was crazy about her. My grandfather wasn't a religious man when he was in Russia. He owned a saloon there. But he came to this country and had nothing to do—his sons sent him money to live on because there was no unemployment insurance or anything like that. He started taking Bella to the synagogue with him when she was six years old. She became very knowledgeable in Hebrew. Of course, the synagogue was Orthodox, and she went upstairs with the women. They all asked her to point out the place in readings. She would say later that's when she started to be a feminist, because they separated her from the men.

He was my babysitter, and since he spent a lot of time in the synagogue, so did I. He was very proud of me, but after showing off my reading prowess to his cronies, he would dispatch me to sit with the women behind the "mechitzah" [curtain].

Liz Abzug My great-grandfather Wolf, the one who took her to the temple, he would say in Yiddish, "She's an 'oytser'—a jewel!"

Helene Savitzky Alexander I didn't know what the word [oytser] meant until I asked the women at Women's Space here in Great Neck. They said it meant "treasure." There was something in Bella that my grandfather found. And she always kept that part of her—her Jewishness. Perhaps the cultural aspect more than anything else, but she always belonged to a temple. Even when she was in Congress, she would come home for the holidays no matter what. She would tell them, "This is my holiday. I'm leaving."

Eve Abzug My understanding growing up was that Judaism teaches you that Jews care about social responsibility, that you aren't free until every person is free. What my parents stood for instilled in me a desire to speak for those who cannot speak for themselves and has become the foundation for all the work that I do.

Helene Savitzky Alexander Bella was young when our father died. He had hardening of the arteries—today they have all kinds of things they can do for that, but they couldn't help him then. She was very affected by his death. In the Jewish religion, the child of the deceased goes to the synagogue to say Kaddish. Well, they never had women do that. And I didn't do it, but Bella went every day for one year, in the morning before school. When she was running for Congress, one of the volunteers, a man, came in and said, "I will never forget your sister, eleven or twelve years old, how she came to the synagogue every morning."

I stood apart in the corner. The men scowled at me but no one stopped me. It was those mornings that taught me you could do unconventional things. After I had become a congresswoman, I was invited back to speak at that synagogue. [I spoke about securing] the right of women to become rabbis and for women congregants to be able to participate as "persons" in all rituals. The rabbi—perhaps wanting to outsmart his speaker of the evening—said, "I disagree. How would it look if Elizabeth Taylor was walking down the aisle carrying the Torah and the men, as was the custom, in reaching out with the talesim [prayer shawls] to kiss the Torah, one of their hands slipped and touched Elizabeth Taylor?" I replied, "It would be wonderful. The synagogue is always looking for more congregants. This would be, to say the least, an enticement." Later, when I got to know Elizabeth Taylor—she attended my sixtieth birthday party with Shirley MacLaine—she got a great kick out of the story.

Shirley MacLaine I remember when Elizabeth Taylor gave her the little tiny diamond. She wore that thing on a chain that Elizabeth gave her. And the chain got tighter and tighter. It became a choker, but she would not take that diamond off. Wore it for ten years.

It was not until I was in my sixties that I actually was permitted to go up to the bimah—the platform in the synagogue on which the Ark rested—to chant an opening prayer. My actor friends Renée Taylor, who is Jewish, and Joe Bologna, who is Italian, had agreed that their son should have a bar mitzvah, and so began a search for a synagogue that would allow this uncircumcised Italian to accompany his son with his wife to the bimah. We found a conservative synagogue in need of funds and a rabbi who figured out a way for Joe to participate without being circumcised. When I stood up there and started to chant "Baruch atah Adonai"—blessed art Thou oh Lord—the tears came to my eyes. At long last I was considered a human person in my own religion.

Liz Abzug After my mother's father died, my grandmother Esther worked in S. Klein's and another department store so that she could feed her daughters and nurture them and put them in the best of everything. She was short, five feet, but very tough. She was a young woman when my grandfather died, but she never went back with a man. She would say to both her daughters, "You can do anything you want and then some." But she was also very much a mother who would cook and care for them in the traditional way. She had enormous endurance. My mom got it from somewhere!

Helene Savitzky Alexander Bella used to win all the street games from the boys. My mother wouldn't buy her a bike—she thought it was dangerous—so Bella rode every boy's bike in the neighborhood. I have a neighbor here in Great Neck who remembers that she borrowed his bike. Once when we were kids, someone rang the bell and told my mother, pointing at me, "Your daughter hit my kid." Mama said, "You got the wrong daughter."

I never saw a reason why girls couldn't play immies—which were marbles—down the sides of the gutters, or checker games on the sidewalks, which only boys played. Yes, I jumped rope, played potsy—a game like hopscotch—with the girls. I had a doll and a carriage, but I also wanted a real bicycle.

Helene Savitzky Alexander Every night with her supper, Bella would sit in front of the radio for her three programs—*Just Plain Bill*, *Myrt and Marge*, and one other one. I was never interested in that, but I used to read a lot. My mother had twenty volumes of *The Book of Knowledge*. They had everything—including fairy tales—and I read them all. I was a good student and my mother was a frustrated teacher. In those days you would skip grades if you knew the material, and I knew all the multiplication tables because she would drill me as we walked to school. With Bella she didn't do anything like that because she was so tired of doing it with me, I guess. Anyway, Bella was just naturally bright, and she immediately showed it. My sister was born with a sense of herself.

My mother more than any other person gave me self-esteem and self-assurance. She would meet me after school every day, take my books, and give me my Hebrew school books. I attended Hebrew school all during my elementary and high school years. My mother always worried I might become a rabbi. Then, when I became a lawyer, she said it was too much work—I should have been an actress. In my mother's view, an actress led a charmed life, lying around in a beautiful negligee.

Claire Reed One day during the Vietnam War, I'm at a demonstration with Mrs. Savitzky, that's Bella's mother. Mrs. Savitzky is standing next to me, and she's going, "Oy vey. I don't understand. I don't understand." I said, "What is it that you don't understand?" "My Bella has worked so hard against this war, how come it hasn't stopped?" She wasn't kidding! She was totally serious. If you're brought up to believe there's nothing you can't do—which is how Bella was brought up by her mother and father—then nothing can stop you. There was nothing that Bella couldn't do.

Liz Abzug Everything was extreme with her—the sports, the violin, the bugle. How is it that a young girl rose up in the 1930s and knows she wants to be a lawyer when she doesn't even know any lawyers—women or men? How did she come up with that? How did she know that she should go and collect nickels on the subway for this homeland they were trying to create that she didn't even really understand at twelve years old? I don't know.

In my home always there was a fair sense of social justice, based on no ideology—just hardworking sincere people with a tremendous sense of values and standards. They subscribed to philosophical Judaism, which relied on the creed of justice for all. That's one of the reasons I wanted to be a lawyer ever since I was a little kid. I had no role models. But I always thought if I could become a lawyer I could set things straight.

Teenage Organizer for Social Change (1931–1938)

Mim Kelber I'm Bella's oldest friend. We were classmates at Walton High School, and we were polar opposites. Bella was our champion athlete. She always seemed to be bouncing a ball, climbing a rope, riding a bike, running a race, diving into a pool, and making waves literally and figuratively. Walton was an academic all-girls' school in the West Bronx, and they had lots of buildings. Bella used to roller skate around the campus. I hung out in the library and was shy. Bella was not shy. She was elected senior class president—a natural leader. She liked herself too much, but I think you need that. She was very self-confident.

Rosalyn Levitt People came from all over to go to Walton. They had an excellent academic record. And parents liked it because it was all girls. We had a tennis court and played basketball against the faculty. We swam and learned to dive. This was around the time of the first World's Fair in New York [1939], when Billy Rose had the [synchronized] swim team starring Eleanor Holmes, and we did a little of that ensemble swimming—learning how to swim without making splashes and breathe without making bubbles. Bella and I were friends at school but we didn't visit each other's homes. Bella also lived in the Bronx, but not in my neighborhood. You've got to remember, these were apartment houses with a lot of people in them. You didn't have to go anywhere for friends.

Eva Lederman She was a fresh kid. A fresh Jewish kid. She was sixteen . . . I was twenty, looking like twelve. She said, "Who are you?" Just like that! And I said, "I'm your teacher." "You're too young to be my teacher." And I said, "No, I'm very smart. That's why I'm here. And now you shut up." And the next day she met me before class and said, "You're the first person who ever told me to shut up." And I said, "I'm sure I won't be the last person."

If I got into trouble—which I sometimes did in school, being somewhat outspoken—and they would scold me . . . I'd come home upset about it . . . and my mother would go to school and scold the teacher.

Rosalyn Levitt Bella could multitask before multitask was a word. I took Latin with her, and she would be sitting in class, doing her algebra homework. When she was called on, she would pick up the book, do a translation, sit down, and continue doing the homework. If she had not devoted so much time to politics and student government, she probably could have done even better academically, but she did very well.

She was editor of our social studies department newspaper, called *The Outlook*. There must have been six of us in the group that worked on the paper. I guess you'd say we were young radicals, a very idealistic bunch. We were children of the Depression—ready to remedy all the faults in society. We had the advantage of some very good columnists, like Walter Lippmann and Eleanor Roosevelt.

Bella was the leader. In any group she was in, she was a leader. Nobody had to teach her how. She had a certain abrasive quality about her, and not much patience with stupidity. But her personality never bothered us. As a matter of fact, we sort of admired it. Once when she was editing *The Outlook*, I wrote a paper for it and she threw it back at me—literally threw it—and told me it's too superficial. I realized it was not that good, but she sure let me know about it. So I did some research, looked some things up in the library, and rewrote it.

June Zeitlin When Bella was in Congress, in her last term, I did her women's rights and civil rights legislative work. One of the first things I had to write for her was a statement against an amendment to restrict school busing. I wrote it up and thought it was pretty strong. I bring it to her. She looks at it, throws it down, and says, "This is so weak! You expect me to say this? Go back and rewrite it." In my whole career since then, no one has ever sent me back to write something stronger.

Rosalyn Levitt I look back on high school as a very pleasant time of my life. We were introduced to things in literature, music, current events—New York had a lot of advantages. I thought everybody had museums and concerts and the theater. Bella and I lost touch after high school. But once, after I moved to Orlando, I was back in New York on a trip. I turned on the TV and I heard this Bella Abzug talking. It was during one of her campaigns. I said, "That's Bella Savitzky!" And I called a classmate of ours, who laughed and said, "Yes. You spotted her."

Peace, War, and Campus Big Shot (1938–1942)

Mim Kelber Bella and I went from Walton on to Hunter College. It was maybe our second day there when she said, "Quick, we're electing the president of the freshman class." She won. When we got to college, suddenly Bella turned from being a tomboy to wearing hats. She started to dress as if she was on stage all the time.

Amy Swerdlow I was a freshman, sixteen years old. That was the time when, if you had a brain in your head, they skipped you. Bella was a sophomore or junior and already a big shot. I had been in the American Student Union* in high school, and Bella was involved in the ASU, and we somehow hit it off. She would say, "Get that Amy with the braids," and I would do things for her. She had a very close friend by the name of Helen Bierman. I thought they were like twins. The two of them ran the progressive and antiwar activities on campus. Bella was always in charge of something.

We were very peace-minded, hoping there would be no war. But the day the Nazis invaded the Soviet Union, the pro-Soviet faction stopped their antiwar agitation. That turnabout was very troublesome to me, but then, of course, I was Jewish and it was Hitler. You went along with it. Bella claimed later that the reason she was against the war was not that she was influenced by

*At its peak, from about 1936 to 1939, the American Student Union mobilized thousands of students against war and on behalf of a reform agenda, functioning, according to the Roosevelt biographer Joseph P. Lash, as a sort of student brain of the New Deal (http://newdeal.feri.org/students/lash.htm#26).

the popular front and the left, but because she hated Britain and its attitude toward Palestine. I knew that she was head of some Zionist organizations, but I hadn't realized that a lot of where she was coming from was that loyalty to Israel.

Mim Kelber Bella would only eat kosher food when we went out to dinner. We made fun of her, but she was adamant about that at the time.

While I was going to Hunter, Mama would make me what she would call "nutritious" meals for lunch—one pound of calf's liver in between two pieces of bread—to make sure I had enough iron in my system.

Mim Kelber We had a Young Communist League unit at Hunter with maybe ten people in it. Some years later, Bella asked, "Why didn't you ever try to recruit me?" I said, "You don't understand. You were our 'broad element.' " It was the war period, and we were supposed to be working with all kinds of groups—not just party members.

Amy Swerdlow My second semester at Hunter, we moved to the Bronx campus. It was in April—Peace Day—and Bella and I dreamed up this event where we would invite Dalton Trumbo to read from his antiwar novel, *Johnny Got His Gun*. We brought a mimeograph machine outside on the campus and kept running off these flyers announcing the performance. It was like guerilla theater! Actually, we didn't invent it. My friends at Brooklyn College did it first, but we were very enterprising.

We were anti-Franco and anti-Japan because of its invasions of China. We wore lisle stockings and had a lot of demonstrations. We'd get up early in the morning or stay late at night and leaflet every locker, calling on people to come to a rally. We were a politically con-

scious group, although not as much as the City College boys, who were very into anti-fascist activity.

Henry Foner I met Bella when I was at City College and active in the ASU. We were both part of a delegation of people from the various city colleges that went to Washington on some student issue, I think. I remember because it was the first time I ever flew in an airplane, and my fountain pen leaked all over the place because the cabins weren't properly pressurized in those days. I was president of the student council, and she held some student office, and we had many friends in common between Hunter and City College. As a matter of fact, there's a song, "A Pretty Girl Is Like a Melody." The version I wrote went, "A City boy is like a malady that haunts you spring and fall / Pleasing to you / With a perfect IQ / When day is done he's on the run with a Hunter girl or two."

I think Bella and I were in the same class, and I took a young lady to the senior prom at some hotel, and I know Bella was there. Whenever I needed a tuxedo, I'd go to my cousin who was an undertaker, but this night it was being used by another cousin who wore it to the prom. I said to my date, "There but for the grace of God."

When I was in college, I had various relationships with different men. None of it was very torrid, as far as I was concerned. That may be because a couple of the people I went out with were rabbis, and they were preserving themselves!

Moe Foner The ASU was very large . . . It could bring to a big rally, its annual peace rally, fifteen hundred, two thousand, three thousand people. But it had influence among the leaders of the student council, the editors of the publications . . . Bella was like she is now [October 25, 1984], but less so . . . She was always a leader.

Judy Lerner I was seventeen when I entered Hunter College, and Bella had been there for one year. A terror! I ran for president of my class and I had a brilliant campaign. It was a sign that said, "Don't be snooty. Vote for Judy." Bella saw it and screamed from an upper window, "Who is this idiot?" I said, "Bella Savitzky, you don't know me or my politics!" I was already an activist kid in high school. And she said, "Al*right*." Anyway, I won, and we were in the student council together. She became president of the student council and my mentor—it meant everything in the world to me.

There's a whole group from college who stayed friends. One of us, Judy Lerner, her husband died and she had this new man she was interested in. I said one night—at first not in his presence, then I said it in his presence—"Listen here. We have been together for fifty years. You have to please us, we don't have to please you." Poor Judy. But everybody loved my saying that.

Mim Kelber I saw Bella transform in those college years from a short-haired tomboy to a sophisticated, cool young woman who wore suits, high heels, and hats, and who knew Robert's Rules of Order backward and forward. She was always getting into trouble with the college president and deans because of our student demonstrations, but they treated her with respect. They could recognize a formidable opponent.

Judy Lerner It was during a terrible period, politically. *The New York Post* accused Bella of being a leftist, and the president of Hunter came to her defense. I'll never forget him defending her right to be an activist.

Amy Swerdlow She had enormous influence at the school. And she was very gutsy. The left was calling World War II, which had begun in Europe, the "phony war." The Rapp-Coudert Committee* had held hearings in the state legislature on campus activism—a kind of mini-McCarthyism—and we were very unpopular. But it didn't scare her.

I was not influenced by the Communist movement. I was a sympathizer to most progressive causes, but I was an independent. So I had no commitment to the Soviet Union as such. When the Hitler-Stalin Pact happened, I was shocked, but I was more shocked by the people who were trying to justify it. Even as a student, I always said, "Look, my work is to be influential in this country. I'm not going to get involved in bickers internationally. What I'm concerned about is American policy, how to influence it and make it work.

Amy Swerdlow Bella was not kind to stupid people. She just attacked them. "You jackass!" There was a little bit of a sadistic streak—if you really couldn't talk back to her, she could get even more abusive.

Phil Donahue She could spot a phony across a crowded room. Nobody had a detector for pomposity and pretense quite as well tuned. I found myself seated next to her at an occasion that was to be an evening with Abba Eban that evolved into a very thoughtful, somber reflection on the life of Prime Minister [Yitzhak] Rabin. And as the movie stars got up and began to speak, I was instructed as well about her impatience with oration, because sooner or later, four or five sentences into the speech that referred to the man "without whom the future of peace in the Middle East and the region would be unsure for our

*This New York State joint legislative committee, formed to investigate "subversive activities"—including Communist Party membership—subpoenaed and interrogated some five hundred public college students and faculty in 1940 and 1941 (http://www.virtualny.cuny.edu/gutter/panels/panel15.html).

children . . . so that all of us may live in the next century," and her voice would say—for many around her to hear—"Good. Sit down." The next speaker would take a breath about five sentences in, and I would hear her say, "Good. Sit down."

Toward the end of my time in college, when we had entered the war, we spent enormous energy organizing to help the soldiers. We were knitting these masks—I always said I was "Knittin' for Britain and Crochettin' for the Sovietin"—but I pitied the poor soldier who had to try to keep warm with the mask I knit.

Judy Lerner I remember going to a meeting when Eleanor Roosevelt came to Hunter, and Bella and Mim Kelber really connected with her. I got to know Mim better afterwards. She was like a shadow person. She was the editor of the college newspaper, and she did a splendid job, but she never put herself forward.

Mim Kelber Bella shared a platform at Hunter with First Lady Eleanor Roosevelt at a student assembly. They both spoke. We have a photo of them sitting together, both wearing hats. They were two of the greatest women of this century and they both ended their lives by working at the United Nations.

A Passion for the Law—and for Martin (1942–1944)

[Our first date] was a pickup. Martin was twenty-six, and I had just graduated from college. It was 1942. I had gone to an aunt in Florida, and I was bored. A friend said, "There's a concert in Miami City, Yehudi Menuhin playing the violin for Russian war relief." I used to study the violin, so I said, "Okay. Let's go." During intermission I noticed three guys looking at us, but I didn't pay much attention. Then, after the concert, one of these guys offered us a seat on the bus, and

started talking to us. He seemed to talk in free verse, and I was thinking, oh, God, poetry. I had enough of that already in college.

Then he insisted on meeting us the next day to go bicycle riding. My friend said, "Let's do it, he's handsome." I said, "You like him, so you go." She said, "No, you have to go." So we went. He insisted on taking me out to dinner. I didn't really get to know him, because he was leaving the next day. But he kept writing me, and sending me books and pictures of himself, and arranged to see me when I came back to New York. We went to another concert. In the middle of the concert, he said, "We're leaving." We went up to the West Side, and it was a farewell party at his house. He was going into the army the next day. Everybody started to eye me up and down as if I was the girlfriend—and I had barely met this guy. Whereupon he took a bottle of scotch and drank the whole thing. Just before he passed out, he said to a friend of his, "Be sure to take her home," and I thought, well, thank God that's all over.

About two days later, I got a call from a Mr. Abzug, who said, "I'm Martin's father, and we're all going to see Martin in Fort Dix. Martin would like you to come." I said to my mother, "I don't even know this guy, now I gotta go to Fort Dix with his family?" My mother said, "Well, how can you refuse a soldier?" So I wound up going to Fort Dix. "Look, what is this? Set me up here with your family, and we hardly know each other?" He said, "Will you save some room under the apple tree for me?" "Oh," I said, "I'll be around, you know."*

I must have had about six jobs in succession after college. I worked for the Board of Regents of New York State, and they fired me because I talked while I marked papers. I worked for the Psychological Corporation, and they said I was too intense, asking questions beyond the ones that appeared on their questionnaires. One day I got this call from

*The Andrews Sisters performed their classic hit "Don't Sit Under the Apple Tree (With Anyone Else But Me)" in the 1942 wartime movie *Private Buckeroo*.

Hunter College. They had an inquiry for a graduate who not only was scholastically capable but had been a leader. What do you suppose that job was? It was at Macy's department store and I was to demonstrate the different ways you could shape and wear a Chanel turban. I got about fifty dollars a week, which was a fortune in those days. I didn't get much more three years later on my first job as a lawyer. But I couldn't put my arms down without a sharp pain at the end of the day. It was like a Charlie Chaplin movie. I stayed for about three days.

Martin was in the army, determined to fight fascism. He wrote to me about how important it was to be involved in the nation's defense. So I go downtown and get a job at Gibbs & Cox, which was providing all the naval engineer designs of the ships. I was put in charge of procurement for the hull of the ship (about which I always said I was a "procurer"). I was in charge of all the confidential communication, okay? A bunch of high school kids would stamp my mail and give it to me—and they would throw paperclips at each other. I thought I was going to go crazy on that job. I lived in the North Bronx and I have to come down to the bottom of Manhattan and be there at eight. And of course there were no unions or anything like that, so they treated you like a piece of crap. Fifteen or twenty minutes for lunch because we were in Defense, right? Until finally I said, "This is not for me, I cannot do this. I've got to go to law school. It's what I've always wanted to do."

Rosalyn Levitt Bella applied to Cornell, to Harvard, and to Columbia. Harvard would not accept women at the time, so she was rejected there. After her acceptance to Columbia she came home one day and found a letter in the mailbox accepting her to Cornell. She got real excited and ran upstairs to her mother, and said, "Mama, I'm going to Cornell." And Mama said, "Where's Cornell?" Bella said, "Ithaca." "And where is Ithaca?" Bella told her where it was. Her mother said to her, "For a nickel on the subway you could go to Columbia and they'll probably give you a scholarship, too," and they did. As Bella said later, "We listened to our mothers in those days." We knew our financial limitations. We were smart, and we may have rebelled at certain things in society, but not family.

The law school faculty did not treat us well. They were condescending. They were querulous and scornful. Dean [Young] Berryman Smith was a boor and a pig, in that he was always picking on the women and trying to make us look foolish. But Jerry Michael was a cute little guy. He taught criminal law. I was a little rebellious at their attitude, you know, so he loved it. He loved to spar with me. I always feel that there is a sign of believing someone is equal when they're willing to take you on—beat you up, instead of just making you feel like a fool.

Constance Baker Motley I remember being at Bella's house one night years later when she had a cocktail party. She was talking to a guy, and he said, "Okay, okay, okay," and she got angry with him because he wouldn't argue back. She was pounding this guy, she was so angry that he would back off because she was a woman. That's the way she was.

When we were in law school, Bella would yell and scream and so forth, but her friend from Hunter, Gloria Agrin, she was as quiet as a mouse. Bella was always so brash and outlandish. Both of them were brilliant. They came from the same working-class background. I was two years behind them, and when I got there both of them were on the *Law Review*.

There were many men and women like myself—young and first out of college. There was the Oyster Bay crowd, the hicks from the sticks. There was a collection of famous foreign lawyers, victims of Nazism who were required to go to law school here and take the bar examination before they could practice. There were seven or eight women. There were even a few minorities. There was a crowd that played cards in the lounge every day. After they taunted me to come play for a year and a half, I finally succumbed and they taught me how to play poker.

Lyonel Zunz For the first time women in substantial numbers were admitted, largely, unfortunately, because many of the men were now in service. Bella was an exceptional student. *Law Review* was an achievement that very few obtained. She also gave lessons to the professors. They had no idea of what it was going to be like to deal with a Bella. They didn't have any idea of what it would be like to deal with women, because they had very little experience from the past.

Constance Baker Motley There were so few women generally, we just kind of hung out together in the alcoves of the library. We were supposed to be studying together, but we were really debating some issue of the day. And, of course, as Bella would dominate the conversation, nobody else could speak. That's just the way it was. Nobody thought anything of it. That's what we would do.

While I was in law school, Martin came out of the army. He had eczema—which he did not tell them—and when he was in officer's training, he broke out. All of his mates went to Camp Edwards and they were later wiped out. Martin was saved by being medically discharged. He would come around and mope, unhappy about not being able to fight fascism, and he was in love with me. I was dating other people, but I still saw Martin. He used to type all my papers for me. He had this rare sense of dignity about women. I was always an activist, even as a student. I would have a date and I'd sometimes send a telegram and say, sorry, I'm going to a conference. I can't show up. Martin wasn't threatened. Well, I fell in love with him.

We had a stormy courtship. We got along so well in forty-two years of marriage because we fought out all our differences for two years before we got married. And we got married when I was twenty-

four, in the middle of law school. He was just four years older, but extremely mature. I was in the middle of writing a "note" for the Law Review *when we went to Mexico on our honeymoon, so I didn't complete the note. They decided I didn't earn my credit for the third-year essay that everyone had to write unless you were on* Law Review. *So I had to write this third-year essay in two weeks. Some people spent a year writing it.*

Lyonel Zunz Bella would never let us revise an article that she wrote for the *Law Review*, which was a procedure that had to be followed. As a result, she was told, "If you don't let us revise it, you won't be permitted to get the points necessary to graduate at this time." That didn't make any difference to her. The principle was what counted. So she had to write a thesis, and finished five months later. As we spoke about it from year to year, I said, "Why didn't you just let us review it, Bella? It wasn't that important." She said, "Every principle is important, and if you compromise one, you'll compromise many."

Because of the war's housing shortage, Martin and I lived in the St. Moritz Hotel for several months. I would arrive sometimes as late as one or two in the morning, wearing a dirndl, sandals, no stockings, with books under my arms. In the lobby the ladies of the evening would look at me with shock and suspicion.

Marlo Thomas I asked her one time, I said, "You know, Bella, I've always been so scared about getting married. I don't know how you do it, how you put it all together. How do you stay who you are as a woman, and how do you become a good wife to a man, and how do you balance that out?" And she said, "Great sex."*

*Bella borrowed this quip from her husband. When they appeared together on the Mike Douglas show, along with Phyllis Schlafly and her husband, they were asked the secret to a good marriage and Martin famously replied, "Great sex."

People kept being drafted, or were coming back to law school. People were distracted—they had lots of things to do and worry about. But it was an entry point for women. I, of course, had more advanced views than most of the people, male or female. But I really didn't get a chance to do very much activity. I was working day and night, either going to school or making money slinging hash for the Navy training program—I stood behind these big steam tables and dished out the stuff to these guys in the Navy—and I was working on the Law Review, *which is a form of torture.*

Championing the Rights of Working People (1944–1950)

Ralph Shapiro It was a very exciting time for a young lawyer to be involved in labor law, because it was the end of the war, during which wage and price controls were supposed to be in effect. The wage controls took effect, but as for price controls, the major industries needed for the war effort just blackmailed the government—particularly before Pearl Harbor was attacked. If Roosevelt wanted more arms and more tanks, they'd say, "All right, we're the guys that can do it, now what are you gonna do for us?" Much to the disagreement of many of the labor leaders, no-strike became the policy of the labor movement. And the workers by and large did not strike, but there was pent-up resentment. So the years right after the war ended showed massive strikes in every major industry—automobile, coal, steel. They said, "Hey, now we wanna get ours!"

And there was the usual reaction to the strikes. The cops did not have the policy they now have of alleged neutrality. Nightsticks were in great use. So people went to jail for preventing scabs from entering, for holding picket lines, for violating injunctions, and all that kind of thing. I met Bella when I went to work for the law firm of Whitt and Cammer—we did labor law work and the firm had a major roster of clients. We would go to magistrates' court and get the people out. Frequently at night, that's where you would spend your time. As the low people on the totem pole, that was our job.

I always felt I was going to represent working people. But I had tremendous problems getting a job as a labor lawyer. First of all they would ask me if I could type. When I was going to school, we never could afford typewriters, so I couldn't type. But I would simply say, "Well, I'm not applying for a job as a typist. I'm from Columbia, I was on the Law Review *and I expect to be treated as a lawyer." Then they would offer me money which was lower than the minimum wage paid the workers they were representing!*

Amy Swerdlow Once Bella and I were writing a flyer for Women Strike for Peace. I was typing; she was talking. Then I said, "Look, I've got to go. It's two o'clock and my kids are coming home from school." That was my life in the early sixties. I'd get hysterical and run back to Great Neck. I said, "You take over and finish typing it." She said, "I don't know how to type." "What do you mean you don't know how to type?" Any idiot knows how to type. I taught myself how to type when I was in high school. She said, "I purposely didn't learn how to type, because if I knew how, the lawyers would've always asked me to type things, and I just decided I was not gonna learn how to type." I got so angry at her. It seemed so exploitative. "Like everybody's gotta type for you?"

Constance Baker Motley I guess Bella could have gotten a job in a law office, but they weren't hiring women. She couldn't have gotten a job on Wall Street. Not only did they discriminate against women, but they discriminated against Jews. Herb Feiler, who was first in the class at Columbia Law School, could not get a job on Wall Street. I started working as a law clerk for Thurgood Marshall at the NAACP* my last year of law school, and I just stayed on.

Ralph Shapiro Bella and I shared an office. We were pretty low down on the totem pole so we weren't entitled to much more than a desk and telephone space. Our relations were cordial. Indeed, my first wife and I and Martin and Bella occasionally went out together socially, but nothing unusual. She did her work and I did mine. But it was clear that she was kind of restive. She wasn't the type that could work for somebody.

I had a lot of trouble with some of the unions because of tremendous male chauvinism. I argued a big case before the National Labor Relations Board for the Mine & Smelters Workers Union. Boy, they were tough guys. The corporation had ten lawyers, and when I was sent instead of the people they knew, the two union bosses wired them and said, "You're sending us some fucking secretary? To handle this?" Later they apologized to me and told me how great I was. So at least they learned a little. At the furriers' union, a bunch of old-timers, they used to try to blame everything on me. Some of those people used to say, "We lost the strike because of the maidel *[girl]."*

Wherever I went representing my firm, I would say, "How do you do. My name is Bella Abzug and I'm here from the law firm of so-and-so." They would always say, "Yes, please sit down." After waiting awhile and seeing nothing happen, I would clear my throat and say it again. They would reply, "Yes, yes, we know, but we're waiting." I would say, "What are you waiting for?" They would say, "The

*Later a Supreme Court associate justice, Thurgood Marshall began work at the NAACP in 1936. According to his biographer, Juan Williams, he represented clients in the South and during one trip to Columbia, Tennessee, defending two men accused of shooting a policeman during a race riot, was nearly lynched (www.thurgoodmarshall.com/interviews/early_naacp.htm).

lawyer." They thought I was the secretary or the clerk, but not the lawyer. I went home and discussed it with Martin. In those days professional women wore hats and gloves. I put on a hat and gloves and whenever I appeared for my firm, they knew I was there for business. In the meantime I got to like wearing hats and continued to wear them to this day. I've since taken off the gloves—as I suppose most people have noticed.

Faye Wattleton On a delegation in Central America, around 1980, we were in the middle of Honduras, speaking to women who had lost their loved ones in the wars of Central America, and a peasant woman walked up to Bella and said, quite simply, "I like that hat." It was a beautiful straw hat surrounded with very expensive pheasant feathers. Bella simply took it off and gave it to the woman. I said, "Bella, that's an expensive hat. Why did you give her that hat?" She said, "Because she wanted it."

Ralph Shapiro At Whitt and Cammer, partners were addressed by "Mr." and the staff was addressed by a first name. The office staff started to call her "Bella" when she first got there. So she said, "When you start calling Mr. Cammer, 'Harold,' and you start calling Mr. Whitt, 'Nat,' you can call me 'Bella,' otherwise, I'm 'Mrs. Abzug.' " That is typical of her. Another woman lawyer, I won't mention her name, did work for a small labor law firm, and she was frequently assigned to get coffee and run errands and type things. She just did not have whatever it took to fight the system. She was a very bitter lady, more bitter because she was working for a progressive lawyer whose progressivism didn't extend beyond certain sexual boundaries. Bella was very aware of that whole sexist thing, and she fought it.

If I had to work eighteen hours a day as a young labor lawyer, Martin would keep me company, reading a book or typing in the room next to my office. On weekends, he would always say, "You rest. I'll go do the shopping."

Ralph Shapiro When Lee Pressman came, the firm became Pressman, Whitt & Cammer. He had been counsel for the CIO and for the Progressive Party, so he and Nat Whitt had been very close friends in Washington. Pressman was the great lord, but he didn't stay that long.

So Pressman came in and he was as arrogant as hell. He would have me go to court with him and carry his briefcase. I wasn't a clerk. I was representing whole unions by myself. They said, "Look, we want you to get along with him." I said, "Well, I'm going to get along with him. He has to get along with me." They said, "Pressman's going to make a great contribution to civil rights, civil liberties." I said, "Why will he make a great contribution, more than anybody else? Even more than me, for example?" At that time I was a young, fiery lawyer and I was chairing the civil rights committee for the New York City Lawyer's Guild. They said, "Oh, you have no respect."

I never liked the guy. I thought he was arrogant. I thought he was self-centered. Brilliant, absolutely. Give the man his due. Great talker.

Ralph Shapiro I think she was treated that way because she was young, and second because she was a woman, and third because she didn't recognize his eminence, so to speak. We represented a major client, Ben Gold's furriers' union, and Pressman did a lot of work for them. But also he was busy running for office at that time on the Progressive Party line. He ran for Congress and soon became an ardent supporter of Israel. I don't think he had thought for thirty-five seconds about Israel before then. He committed the worst act of betrayal, because when he was called before the McCarthy committee, he named Nat Whitt, his longtime friend, as a member of the Communist Party. And that was an ultimate act of betrayal.

He was a traitor. People never talked to him after that, and they stopped bragging about him. Lee Pressman had been horrible to me. I had not gotten along with him, and things were uncomfortable after that. They began to find fault with me as they had with other employees. So I left.

When I was finished with them, I went to Europe and when I came back, in 1949, the thing that made the most sense for me was to go into my own practice—a room in the Nelson Towers on Thirty-fourth Street and Seventh Avenue.

I wanted to be a lawyer. I was serious about it. I was in love, and I decided to get married. I was serious about that. I thought I would like to have children. I was serious about that. So I never felt I couldn't have it all. I do not feel guilty. I did my best. Maybe it wasn't the *best.*

On the trip to Europe, I felt that I might have become pregnant on those misty nights traveling on the Atlantic Ocean on the Queen Mary, First Class—which was Martin's idea of a treat he felt we had earned. In Warsaw I was recommended to a Dr. Shibovsky, who said he thought I was pregnant and that I should go home, not *to be easily arranged in early postwar pandemonium. In Paris one of the French lawyers I knew arranged an appointment for me with the great Lamaze* himself. He was a friendly gentleman, bearded and stocky but nice looking, jovial, and warm. He examined me and without a rabbit test or further ado, he said, "Madame, vous êtes certainement enceinte." He, too, advised me to go home.*

*Dr. Ferdinand Lamaze, a French obstetrician, developed his system of "painless" childbirth in the early 1950s.

2

Civil Rights and Civil Liberties—and Raising a Family

Chronology

1947 The Taft-Hartley Act is passed to restrict the power of labor unions.

1947 The House Un-American Activities Committee (HUAC) conducts nine days of hearings into Communist influence in film (the Hollywood Ten). These and later hearings by HUAC, in March 1951, and by the Senate Subcommittee on Internal Security, in 1952, usher in the McCarthy witch hunts, with individuals, under the threat of contempt charges, pressured to name colleagues as subversives—leading to the blacklisting of hundreds in the motion picture industry and elsewhere.

1949 Anticommunist riots seriously injure thirteen people in Peekskill, N.Y., as crowds gather to hear a Paul Robeson concert. After the rescheduled event, hostile locals and agitators throw stones at departing concertgoers, Bella among them.

1949 Bella's daughter Eve is born.

1950 While eight months pregnant, Bella goes to Jackson, Mississippi, as part of a defense team representing a black man accused of raping a white woman with whom he had a long-term consensual relationship. Willie McGee is ultimately executed. Bella loses her baby in a difficult miscarriage.

1950 An animated turtle named Bert begins to teach schoolchildren to "duck and cover" so they might survive a nuclear attack.

Early 1950s Bella serves as defense counsel for several actors brought before HUAC.

1951 A one-kiloton nuclear device (code name ABLE) is dropped from an Air Force plane over Frenchman Flat at the Nevada Proving Grounds in the first nuclear test in the continental United States since the Trinity test in Alamogordo, New Mexico, in 1945; 1957 marks the biggest atmospheric test ever conducted at the Nevada site.

1951–1953 Ethel and Julius Rosenberg, accused of passing nuclear weapons secrets to Soviet agents, are tried, convicted, and executed for conspiracy to commit espionage.

1952 Bella's daughter Liz is born.

1952, 1956 The Republican Dwight D. Eisenhower twice defeats the liberal favorite, Adlai E. Stevenson, for the U.S. presidency.

1954 The Supreme Court bans "separate but equal" public schools for black and white children, in *Brown v. Board of Education.*

1954 On June 9—during the Army-McCarthy hearings—the special counsel for the Army, Joseph N. Welch, asks the Senate subcommittee chairman, Joseph R. McCarthy, "Have you no sense of decency, sir, at long last?" The hearings, televised live by ABC, help bring about the fall of McCarthy.

1957 Committee for a Sane Nuclear Policy (SANE) is founded, the first mass organization in opposition to the nuclear arms race.

1963 President John F. Kennedy is assassinated.
1963 Martin Luther King leads a civil rights march from Selma to Montgomery, Alabama.
1964 Three civil rights workers, Michael Schwerner, James Chaney, and Andrew Goodman, are murdered near Philadelphia, Mississippi.
1965 The civil rights leader Malcolm X is murdered while speaking in Manhattan's Audubon Ballroom. The Abzugs sell their Westchester house to his widow, Betty Shabazz, and move back to New York City.

In 1951 I moved to Mount Vernon. My father-in-law had died and my mother-in-law was trying to get rid of the house, so she got rid of it on us. It was kind of nice—in the beginning—an integrated neighborhood; I thought that might be a good place to raise the kids since it was simple, not the usual hoi polloi suburban bullshit.

Eve Abzug We lived on the wrong side of the tracks, so to speak, the south side, and my parents were really involved in school integration, so there were all kinds of political left-wing people coming over all the time. People used to make fun of us in the neighborhood, that we had a "black mother," because our housekeeper, Alice Williams, was with us all the time. She used to say she all but had us, which is more or less true. Though my mother—I don't want to be misleading—my mother was emotionally supportive to me and to Liz. Alice stayed with us until I was in my twenties and going to college.

Liz Abzug Alice was very smart, very soulful. She would stick her two cents in. And my mother would sometimes say, "Alice, I don't want to hear it!" and sometimes she would engage with her.

Amy Swerdlow Once I ran into Bella in Wellfleet. We were on vacation and so was she. And we were on the lake or something, rowing, and there she was with her housekeeper, screaming at her and the housekeeper saying, "Mrs. A—shut up." She had a very close relationship with this housekeeper.

I used to take a month off every summer and go with my husband on vacation. I had planned this trip across country with Martin, and I was about to take my vacation when the Taft-Hartley Act passed [in 1947]. Howard Cammer said to me, "It'll still be here when you come back." So I learned that lesson. Was it Rockefeller or Ford who said, "I can get twelve months' work done in eleven months, but not in twelve months." That was me. I had to have that month with my kids and my husband. The funny part of it is that once I became a member of Congress, I haven't had a vacation for a month, or three weeks, or two weeks since.*

Eve Abzug When we went on vacation, my father stayed to work in the city; Alice and my mother would do everything together, they would do the cookouts together. My mother would come up with the recipe from somewhere and Alice would make it, so they were a team, especially in the summertime, because my mother was freer in the summertime. She took time off, thank God, at one point in her life, anyway.

Liz Abzug I was embarrassed at first, by my mother being different, my name being really hard for people to get, and Alice, who was this presence who I loved. They kept calling her "Aunt Jemima on the pancake box." We'd get into fights all the time with the

*An act to restrict the power of labor unions, passed over President Harry S. Truman's veto. It amended the 1935 National Labor Relations Act by provisions to empower the government to get an eighty-day injunction against a strike, to prohibit secondary boycotts, to outlaw the closed shop, and to take other measures.

neighborhood kids, because they'd say, "Who's that colored lady calling you in for lunch?" Even though it was integrated, there were a lot of Italian working-class kids there, and they would think it's terrible.

Eve Abzug When I first went to kindergarten, I don't remember what the teacher said, but it flipped me out; it was about my parents' political activities. It had to do with integration in some way, and something my mother was doing, standing out in some way. Alice had to take me there every day until I got more comfortable, because I had stomachaches, and I didn't want to go.

Liz Abzug I have memories of the tension that existed between the black girls and white girls at school. I was a very big jock, and the gym class was very important to me. This particular gym teacher would only let the white girls play the best sports and enter the competitive meets. And I took it upon myself—growing up around my mother and my father—to confront her on it. I was like in sixth grade. I asked her, "Why do you let only the white girls play?" And she brought me to the principal's office and tried to bawl me out, but when I told them what it was about, I got this lady in a lot of trouble.

Eve Abzug Mom started teaching us labor union songs, Spanish Civil War songs, really young, and both Liz and I played the guitar as well as other instruments. When I was eleven, twelve, thirteen I learned how to play these songs on the guitar, and a little later on, I was into Joan Baez and Bob Dylan. Music was a very big deal in our house; Liz has perfect pitch and she later went to the High School of Music and Art, and my mother loved to sing and play all kinds of instruments—mandolin, violin, bugle—to amuse us . . . And sometimes she did it in the nude.

My father spent a lot of time with us; he was the provider, not only financially,* but he did all the shopping, and he brought the food and Alice would make the food. He was really involved in all of that, even though my mother always said—this is true in a way—that he didn't deal with our emotional things like she did; he was like the lox-and-bagel man.

Shirley Margolin Martin was the mother—Martin was there for her. Martin cooked! Martin cleaned! Martin got the girls' first brassieres. Martin did everything! Martin was the guy who danced with all the frizzy wives of all the crappy Congress people. That was a *love affair. A love affair.* I just see him standing there and he's saying, "Don't you think she's beautiful?" And I said, "Yes, she is really beautiful, Martin. Aren't you lucky?" What am I gonna say to this man?

Liz Abzug I was perplexed and embarrassed at first, but then I figured out on my own, "Well, mine is a different situation from all my friends from summer camp and the people here in Mount Vernon." My mother's different, and my father's different, and it wasn't just the fact that we had a black housekeeper, which indicated to some people that we had a little more money at that time. It was that they were involved in New York City in very intensive professional ways, and that's who they were. However, they were there for the most important things—when I was in talent shows, and grade school plays. They managed to get there for the PTA, important meetings, parent days. Although my mother was an incredibly awful driver; she would jerk, and drive and screech, and go ninety, and if our friends were—God forbid—with us it was like taking your health in your hands. She was completely distracted, and it was not her thing. She drove like she lived—fast, passionate, wild.

*Martin Abzug had a successful career as a stockbroker, and he also wrote two novels: *Spearhead* (1946) and *Seventh Avenue Story* (1947).

June Zeitlin I was a counselor at Camp Cayuga in the Adirondacks, where I had been a camper, and I had Liz Abzug as a camper, in my bunk. So I met Bella as a parent, on parents' weekend, before she was in Congress. I was like a freshman in college. She came, she and Martin, and she was striking. The main thing I remember is her strong personality, and she gave me the biggest tip of any of the parents in the bunk.

Liz Abzug I saw my mother as someone who was so much larger than life. I used to sit next to her, in amazement at her vanity table, watching her apply her mascara, her eyeliner, her makeup, and say I couldn't believe how gorgeous she was and how beautiful she made herself look. I once took her to a Madonna concert with Rory Kennedy. We were so excited and it was so amazing. She said, "Liz, I just want you to know something," as we were walking back to the car. "I wore a black bra under a see-through white blouse way before Madonna did."

Amy Swerdlow You know, Liz was intimidated by Bella. I had this very nice house in East Hampton, with a big pool, and Liz and my son, Ezra, were playing basketball—throwing a ball into a hoop in the pool—and Liz was fantastic. Bella arrived. Liz could not get another ball in the basket. I'd observed that many times. She's more articulate now than when Bella was alive.

Maggi Peyton She used to go gambling, and in one of those Catskills places she wanted Liz to wear a crinoline to dinner and Liz wouldn't wear it. She made her stay in her room.

Liz Abzug I was sometimes completely embarrassed at the fights that she would get into with people who sat behind our family in movie theaters and playhouses; invariably, before the movie began, some guy would lean over and say, "Hey, lady, aren't you going to take off that hat?" And sure enough, waiting till the very last minute before the movie or play would start, Bella would finally take off that goddam hat.

Judy Lerner After Hunter we lost each other. I got married, had kids; she had kids. We wound up in '58, I think, at a fund-raiser for the Committee for a Sane Nuclear Policy in Harrison, where I lived. And then, right after that, Women Strike for Peace came along, and Bella became one of the founding members in Westchester, and so I had every opportunity to work with her. She had a profound effect on me. She said that the most important thing for you to do is to become politically active. And I did. I was a Democratic district leader in Harrison for forty years.

Bella didn't drive; I did, so we'd go to meetings in New York for Women Strike, and she would run a meeting. She would be standing up there, and she'd say, "Is Judy Lerner here?" I said, "Yes, I'm here." She said, "Don't go home until this is over. I want you to take me back." And then we would go back and I'd stop in front of her house and we would talk for hours. I'd say, "Bella, I'm tired. I gotta go home." But she would go over everything. That was a connection with her that I valued, and I learned so much about what to do in a community.

Eve Abzug There was definitely a lot of anger in the house. I mean there was screaming about causes. Some of my earliest memories have to do with the steam that came out of the radiator in the living room, and my mother screaming.

Liz Abzug Mom came home one day and said, "Oh, we're not drinking any milk, only powdered milk." And she told Alice, "Only powdered milk, that's it," and we were dying because powdered milk sucked! And I'd say, "Why?" And she'd show me these pictures, and she'd talk about Hiroshima, and she'd talk about the testing in the desert and how strontium 90 would get into the farmland, affecting grass that the cows would eat for nourishment and they would be infected.

Another time they had a bomb drill where you're supposed to duck under the desk—and I was so propagandized by all this with my mother; she said, "If that bomb ever falls, forget about it. You're not leaning up against the wall. You're not going under the desk. It's just ridiculous." So I refused to do it. The teacher said, "Why are you doing this?" And I said, "Well, I understand that it's not gonna make any difference," and she said, "Well, what do you mean?" I said, "Well, my mother told me . . ." She said, "You're coming to the principal's office." I was always getting into trouble, just like my mother, I was always a rebel. When I got to the principal's office and I explained it, they said, "We're sending you home for the day. We're gonna suspend you for this day. And we're gonna talk to your parents." When my mother came home from work later that night from the city, I told her. She was laughing hysterically. "Oh, isn't that funny," she said. "They thought I was gonna reprimand you?"

I wrote a letter to the school saying, "I do not give permission for my children to duck under the desk. It is psychologically maiming; it's totally political; and I think it's insane to do it." My kids used to say, "But nobody else thinks that way, Mom." And I'd say, "They will. Don't worry. They will." I was hard on my kids.

Eve Abzug My mother used to say, "We didn't push you hard enough." I wasn't really pushed, and they didn't make us do anything. My father used to say, "Well, just do the best, do the best you can," but I got from my mother, unfortunately, a great self-criticism.

Liz Abzug During the McCarthy period, there was a little paranoia—a tension in the air—but I didn't know until later the depths of what she was involved with [as a lawyer defending people called to testify before anti-Communist congressional hearings]. Throughout our life till she died, she was always telling me, "Don't talk on the phone with me about certain things." She believed that the CIA was tapping her phone—and later we got her FBI files and found they had been following her around since law school.

My father's brother—Malcolm Abzug—was called upon by those crazy McCarthyites to talk to them about my father and mother's activities, and he went. He never actually testified but he went. From then on, there was this underlying tension about him.

Amy Swerdlow There was a loyalty in that family. I had been in that house when the girls would talk back, "Fuck you!" And all that sort of thing. She never answered back. She'd yell at us, but she did not yell at the girls—not that I ever saw. And they really were most unkind, even though they were very loyal. At the end they took care of her.

Liz Abzug One of our big embarrassing moments was in the Caribbean, all four of us were there on vacation—and my mother got blasted. It was two or three in the morning. She took her clothes off and went into the pool, and was standing there, screaming, yelling, "Oh, I'm having a grand old time." My father is standing out there, "Shh, get up, come in here, come on! You're gonna get drowned, you're drunk!" And Egee* and I were looking out the window, and I'm going, "Are you seeing what I'm seeing?" to my sister, and she's going, "Yeah," and I'm going, "Holy fucking shit!" And my father's saying, "Bella, get out of there! I'm telling you, you can't . . ." And he threw in the life

*Family nickname for Eve Abzug.

ring because he didn't want to go in and get her, 'cause it was night, late at night! And finally he pulls her out, and she's singing and having a grand old time.

We fought hard to keep blacks and whites in the neighborhood and we succeeded for many years. People began moving, but it was still integrated. Then my kids were growing older and they wanted to be in New York all the time, and it was getting to be a pain to commute myself, so I finally sold the house to [Malcolm X's widow] Betty Shabazz. After Malcolm's assassination, a committee was formed—including Sidney Poitier and his wife, who lived in Mount Vernon, and Ruby Dee and Ossie Davis, who lived nearby in New Rochelle—to find a house for Betty. They came to our house. We had a big, two-family house—eight rooms on each floor—and a big backyard. She had her heart set on it, and I sold it to her. Then an interesting thing happened. Up until then [the whites in the community] were making noises if you sold to a black, right? Here the blacks objected to my selling to Betty because they envisioned riots and all kinds of crazy activities. And I say to my black neighbors, "Are you nuts? This woman is pregnant with her fifth child; she's going to school in order to be able to improve herself to support these kids. She isn't going to have any meetings. She's just going to live here, because it's a nice place for kids to grow." Anyhow, that was the end of this little saga.

Liz Abzug I think the thing that made my mom so different was not only the level of the passion and intelligence but the commitment to persevere, no matter what, in all things that she believed in, whether it's music, whether it was politics, whether it was her family, whether it was working hard, and not retreating in any of those departments. All these things were almost equally important; if she was in Congress on a very big vote, the most important thing in addition to that was to get back to the holiday Passover dinner. No matter what. When she was in Congress, she missed a lot of stuff, for me, for my sister, for my father, but yet there were certain nonnegotiables, in terms of combining her love of family, her love of culture, her love of arts, her love of her husband, her love of her children, and her love of life. That had to be there, otherwise she would not survive. Now I'm saying we, many of us in my generation, we retreat sometimes, we retreat a lot more than we should.

"February 1984. For my daughter—dearest Isobel. Who I love with all my might. Mom"—Inscription in Liz Abzug's copy of her mother's book Gender Gap: Bella Abzug's Guide to Political Power for American Women.

Civil Liberties/Civil Rights: McCarthyism to Willie McGee (1950s)

My practice was wills, deeds, property, contracts of all kinds. This guy was always sending me clients, until he sent me a client one day who was obviously some kind of a hood in Jersey—one of these rich ones. His daughter had married this guy who he suspected to be a hood, and he was trying to use me to get a divorce for her. He came to my office one day brandishing a gun. He said, "If you don't make this agreement." I said, "This isn't going to influence me so you may as well put it away." People would say I was a "Marcantonio in a girdle." When I think about him and about me in Congress, I think about the fact that he was not as good as I was—in terms of producing.*

Robert F. Wagner Marcantonio was a congressman. He adopted the tactics of Tammany Hall thirty years before his time or more. He would give people free services. I could never understand,

*Vito Marcantonio, a radical lawyer and congressman.

for instance . . . why Marcantonio would do far better than I thought he should do in the Irish Catholic areas . . . I checked into it a little bit. I found out the people would say, "Marc was pretty good to us. When the people in the Democratic club wouldn't help us at all or try to charge exorbitant fees to represent us in a fight with the landlord, Marcantonio would give us a lawyer for nothing. Maybe he's sort of a screwball . . . but I'm going to give him my vote." . . . Another one who does it—she's dressed up a little—is Bella Abzug. She operates the way the old Tammany did. She often says to me, "Bob, you and I are the only ones who really understand politics."

I also represented a lot of people who were victims of the McCarthy witch hunts. In some cases I was able to clear up some evidence. In other cases there wasn't too much I could do. People just got fired or they quit. Then I represented people before the House Un-American Activities Committee and the Senate Subcommittee on Internal Security. I represented Pete Seeger. A lot of them were actors. There had been the Hollywood Ten, who had been convicted for being in contempt when they didn't answer the questions on the grounds of the First Amendment. But I often tried to get these guys to fight it out on principle—to invoke the First Amendment [rather than the Fifth]. I believed that that was correct, and that there had to be a challenge to this outrageous attack on people's rights to think and to believe, freedom to associate and act on their beliefs. However, not many people wanted to do that. One of my clients, a famous character actor, Elliott Sullivan, did invoke the First Amendment, and he was held in contempt. He never forgave me. Those actors always thought they were entitled to get it for nothing. Like Jay Gorney—who wrote the song "Brother, Can You Spare a Dime?"—used to say, "I can get you into pictures." I'd say, "I'm not interested in pictures. I'm interested in the law."

Transcript of the HUAC Subcommittee Investigation of Communist Activities in the New York Area—Part VI, August 16, 1955

[Frank S.] Tavenner, Jr. [counsel to the subcommittee]: What was the idea in having the skit [one of ten performed at a resort on a Fourth of July program] represent the sale of the Bill of Rights for $2, and then settling for half price? Isn't that a form of ridicule of the Bill of Rights, and if so, what was the purpose of it?
[Elliott] Sullivan: You are taking a couple of words or lines out of the context of the sketch, and attempting to make it appear that I had the purpose of subverting the Bill of Rights. I insist that I believe that I am a stancher [*sic*] defender of the Bill of Rights than you are in our relationship at this moment. And the very asking of the question to me indicates as I said before, very clearly that there is an attempt here at censorship of some sort, all through—
[Representative Gordon H.] Scherer: We are trying to find out how far the Communist conspiracy has succeeded in its infiltration.
Mr. Sullivan: All through the Berkshires, and through the forests around Wingdale Lodge, and all over the place.

There is nothing wrong with taking the Fifth Amendment. It's a perfectly legitimate position, but it's not the most principled position to take. Women Strike for Peace finally put the nail in the coffin of this stupid committee. When HUAC subpoenaed those women, they made them crazy. Every time somebody was called, they would applaud and hand bouquets of flowers to the members. It was just a marvelous performance. I tried to advise them to invoke the First Amendment. The committee just got a bunch of names. They even got one woman's name wrong. It was a different Ruth Myers. She was one of my dear friends, and I said to her, "You were never involved in the Communist Party. Just get up there and say it, for God's sake." She didn't. She took the Fifth Amendment.

Ralph Shapiro When the National Lawyers Guild was founded in 1937, every lawyer of any repute joined it. So it was very much a "mainstream" organization in those days, and the New York chapter had thousands of members. I joined after the war at a time when the McCarthy forces and the Cold War were having their effect on all progressive organizations, and causing a split in The National Lawyers Guild as well. Bella was a member of the Guild, involved in some programs. I remember executive committee meetings when she used to come. But after a while, her interests became more diverse, particularly in 1948–49. That was when Willie McGee starts to surface.

During the 1950s witch hunts—the McCarthy period—if I represented anybody who got publicity, I'd lose a lot of other clients. Martin never balked. When I went to the South when our first child was still quite young, he never said, "You can't go, that's ridiculous, you can get killed down there." It was during the early fifties, during the days when there were still lynchings, and in fact my life was threatened when I handled the Willie McGee case, a black man in the South who was sentenced to death for having a consensual relationship with a white woman.

Constance Baker Motley I think she went to Mississippi because we [the NAACP] weren't going to Mississippi then. Thurgood Marshall considered it too dangerous. He didn't think he could survive, and it was true. That's why later he sent me on the Meredith case [1962]. Medgar Evers wrote Thurgood a letter and said, "I have a student who wants to go to the University of Mississippi." So Thurgood came into my office, threw the letter on my desk, and said, "This guy's gotta be crazy." And we all agreed, even James Meredith agreed, but he had spent nine years in the service. He and his brother went into the service because it was the only opportunity that blacks—males particularly—had to get an education. He took every course they ever had, and then he came out and applied to the University of Mississippi. Well he knew full well there was hell to pay but he was ready to pay it. Thurgood sent me to represent him. He said, "You know all these white men had black mammies." That was his joke. "I'm sending you, not one of the boys. They won't bother a black woman." Well he was southern, you know. Marshall was born and reared in Maryland, which was as southern as you could get in those days. He grew up in a segregated community and understood what it was all about. I was born and reared in New Haven, Connecticut. I never encountered any white people who hated blacks until I went to the South.

After a year or two in court, Meredith finally went in. He had to have marshals sleep in his room and take him everywhere on the campus. They never left his side. All the time I represented him, he walked around with a cane. I said, "Meredith, why are you using that cane?" He said, "If I have the cane I'd be able to protect myself walking around the black community." What he understood was they were going to pay a black man to kill him. That was his way of defending himself, because he wasn't a big strong guy.

Women lawyers were unheard of in Mississippi. It was so backward it was unbelievable. But Bella went down there and represented this guy, Willie McGee. Those are cases she took that nobody else would take, and she gained a lot of prominence because she was successful.

Susan Brownmiller When I was researching my book on rape, around 1973, I got tremendously involved in the history of the southern interracial rape cases where the defendant was black and was sentenced to death. Willie McGee is a very poignant case where the woman who said she was raped never identified McGee, but others, the law enforcement people, for some reason arrested him, and the woman never, never said, "That's the person who raped me," but they convicted him and sentenced him to death. So I wanted to ask Bella what she knew about it, and had she had any new thoughts about it now, because what their entire appeal was based on was that the whole town knew that Willie McGee and this woman were having an affair. The Communist Party was always spearheading the defenses in these interracial rape cases and always said, "Everyone knew they were really having an affair." There's a whole history in the left, they always wrote "rape" with quotation marks around it, if it was a black-on-white case. There was that effort to shift the blame in these cases to the white woman, either she was hysterical and having a fantasy, or she'd been having a long affair with the person.

So I wanted to know from Bella, "How do you know? How did you know that Willie McGee was having an affair with this woman, especially since she never identified it was Willie McGee?" And she got very angry with me and escorted me out of her office. I thought she could be helpful, but instead she felt very threatened. That was the first time I personally saw her temper.

The Willie McGee Case

Willie McGee was arrested on November 3, 1945, and tried and convicted of raping a white woman, Willette Hawkins. McGee, who was married, contended that it was a consensual relationship, and Mrs. Hawkins was never called to testify. The evidence consisted of an alleged confession he made during a thirty-day incarceration, while he was held incommunicado. The jury deliberated for two and a half minutes.

I was working in a law firm with a lot of progressive lawyers and I worked on an appeal to reverse his conviction, because in those days blacks or Negroes got the death penalty if they were convicted of rape. Period. So I argued that there was systematic exclusion of blacks from the jury, and we won it [June 10, 1946]. When the appeal was concluded, they—a whole bunch of guys involved in this case—said to me, "He has no lawyer because Dixon Pyle [his original lawyer] won't go on with it . . . so you'll have to go down there and get him a lawyer." I said, "What? Are you crazy? I don't know the first thing about Mississippi. I've never been there, I don't know much about the law affecting capital punishment." I was a labor lawyer, and a constitutional lawyer. "I'm going to get down there and get killed?" They were lynching people down there in those days . . . I resisted for a while and then finally I said, "Well, the poor man is going to get re-indicted and not have a lawyer. I'll see what I can do."

The state of justice there can perhaps be best understood by the statement of Harvey McGeehee, chief justice of the Supreme Court of Mississippi, in answer to the suggestion that a relationship existed between McGee and Mrs. Hawkins. "If you believe or are implying that any white woman in the South who was not completely down and out, degenerate, degraded, and corrupted, could have anything to do with a Negro man, you not only do not know what you are talking about, but you are insulting us, the whole South. You do not know the South and do not realize that we could not entertain such a proposition; that we could not even consider it in court."

So there I was, this young lawyer in Mississippi. The first thing I did was to go see Dixon Pyle. He was a decent guy, a labor lawyer, and he said to me, "You must be crazy. This whole town, in Jackson, is talking about the fact that some white, young woman lawyer has arrived to help Willie McGee. I don't think it will be safe for you to be here." I said, "What can I do? I'm here. How can you help me?" He said, "I'll tell you how you can get to Laurel, Mississippi. That's where the district attorney is."

I got in to see the D.A. He said, "Mrs. Abzug, are you crazy? Do you really think anybody here is going to pay any attention to you?" I said, "Well, I'm a lawyer, and the man is entitled to representation. And I'm trying to get associate lawyers here in Mississippi." He was sitting in this chair, I was sitting sort of here, and there was this spittoon behind me. In between each sentence he would spit over my lap into the spittoon. (Years later, when I made a women's congressional delegation to China, we had an interview with Deng Xiaoping, and every few sentences Deng Xiaoping would spit into a spittoon—and I'm saying, "God, another one!")

I came back to Dixon Pyle's office and told him I was not able to accomplish anything. He said, "Well, I just want you to know that we've got calls all day long that there's this white woman lawyer traveling to Laurel and coming back. It's a wonder you're back safe." I said, "Can you help me get a lawyer?" "No," he said. "I don't know anybody who would take this one." So I literally went from building to building where lawyers were housed and looked at the boards and tried to pick a lawyer. I finally got this contact through this brother-in-law who knew somebody who had worked at the Jewish Welfare Board. His name was Lunden. He said, "Well I have some guy I think would do it . . . I could work with him." His name was Poole and he was a hard-drinking, swearing young man who had lost a leg—I guess it was in World War II. He was a very big drinker and southern kind of personality . . . and I got these two guys involved in the case.

They didn't know much about anything, to be truthful. So I retained them and went back to New York.

A little later on, I got a guy called John Coe from Pensacola, Florida, who was a fabulous thinker and a fire-and-brimstone southern-type lawyer, who was a very progressive guy, who was marvelous. They were supposed to handle the pretrials, and I was going to do the appeals, in the district court, the circuit court of appeals, and the Supreme Court.

I spent two years on this case in which I wrote most of the material and went to Jackson very often. I had fascinating discussions with Attorney General [James P.] Coleman, who then became the governor.

He said, "You really think there's going to be integration in the country?" I said, "Of course. The next time you see me you'll probably be having little white and colored boys and girls going to school together." He said, "I heard you were pretty extreme, but I cannot believe that you would believe such a thing." It was like being in a whole other world from the one I had been raised in. I was totally unprepared for this. Nobody gave me any background. But that's the way I am. I decide, "Well, there's the objective. I've got to get a lawyer, I'll get a lawyer. I got to help these guys put the case together; I'll have to find the ways to do it even if I don't know how."

When I was in the Congress, I said I can't believe there's no procedure whereby you can force the government to answer questions. Because we come out of the common-law system . . . there must be something that's left . . . and that's how I found the Resolution of Inquiry. I got the Pentagon Papers to the floor of the House that way.

I saw Willie McGee in jail. He was a plain, ordinary guy, a simple working man. I came to see him and they didn't want to let me in. I said, "I'm his lawyer; you have to let me in. You want me to call the attorney general of the United States?"

The case was getting hotter and hotter; once, I got there and went to my hotel and they said they had no reservation. So I started going from hotel to hotel; the word was out that I was not to be given a hotel reservation. Then one guy who was driving me finally said, "I know a place but it's far from town." I said to myself, "This is serious. I'd better not go anywhere near this." So I said, "Just take me to the bus station." I went to the bus station and sat down, and figured I'd spend the night in the bus station. They paged me, so then I knew I was right. Of course I didn't answer the page. They had a public bath, I went and had a bath and arrived in court fresh as a daisy.

One day I had to go to New Orleans to argue in the circuit court. It was during the Mardi Gras and it was snowing and I had no place to sleep there. I finally got a room over a whorehouse. I went through a lot of indignities for this case. It was not exactly a fun case . . . I had a miscarriage during this period.

The Jackson Daily News *editorialized that "they should burn Willie McGee's white woman lawyer along with him in the electric chair." I had friends who were born and lived in the South who would call me every day and say, "Bella, get out of it. You'll never come out of that place alive. You just don't understand the violence, the terror, and the horror that goes on there. They'll do something to you." Well, they tried but they did not succeed!*

You can't go through something like that and not have hope. I was motivated by hope. I still am. Everything that goes down I take seriously. I'm pained by it, but I still have the optimism that it can be changed. That's essentially another guideline of my life.

In the end everything failed. There were at least ten separate maneuvers in six years as well as five stays of execution. I went up to the Supreme Court for a stay of execution; I didn't get that. The clemency hearing didn't produce anything. And he was executed. I couldn't be there, but an assistant held a phone: I could hear the bloodcurdling screams of delight from the crowd when he was executed.

When it was clear that all had failed, I visited him in jail on May 7, 1951. He wrote the following note to his wife. He was sad, but he was prepared.

> Dear Rosalie,
>
> They are planning here to kill me and I don't know if you and the people will be able to save me if I have to die I want you to say good by to my mother and the children and all the people who know it is wrong to kill a man because of his Color.
>
> You know I am innocent tell the people again and again that I never did commit this crime tell them that the real reason that they are going to take my life is to

keep the Negro down in the south they cant do this if you and the children keep on fighting Never forget to tell them who killed their Daddy I know you wont fail me, tell the people to keep on fighting,

Your truly Willie McGee

Every custom, every usage, every teaching surrounding the relations between Negro and white persons in the state of Mississippi for a hundred years not only made McGee a victim, but brutalized the judges in the state courts, the district courts, and, yes, in the Supreme Court. It deprived them of that freedom of conscience and judicial calm which prevails among them generally, except when the crucial issue of equal rights for fifteen million Negro Americans is involved . . . Willie McGee was prosecuted for a crime he did not commit, because what he really did, the southern bigots would not tolerate.

Ralph Shapiro The Communist Party, of course, was one of the major supporters of the effort to free Willie McGee, and my second wife, Barbara, was a member. Some Party brains conceived of the idea that since white womanhood was being protected in the trial and execution of Willie McGee, it might be good if half a dozen or so white women came down from the North and petitioned the governor to commute his sentence. Barbara and four, maybe five other women volunteered, or were designated, whatever. Each of them went down separately to separate hotels in Jackson, Mississippi. They had agreed before they left that they would meet at a certain time in a designated spot and present their petition. They all came out dressed in these flowered dresses and the hats and gloves, and little pocketbooks dangling from the wrists, like the Queen. They'd finally gotten together, but after they had taken no more than ten steps, the police were on them. Apparently they knew all about it. The police said, "Ladies, you can't do this," and took them into jail.

Well, they're in jail, they need a lawyer, Bella appeared after a while. She looked at them as if they're absolutely out of their minds, and said, "Alright, I'll see what I can do." They're charged with vagrancy, loitering, who knows what. But, as white women, they're being treated with a certain restraint. Bella came back and said, "Look, I've worked out this. If you leave on the next train, and promise not to come back to Mississippi again this way, all charges will be dismissed and you can go home." Well some of them said, "We don't want to do it. We want to fight." Bella said, "If you want to fight, you go fight. First place I won't be your lawyer, and no one else in Mississippi is going to be your lawyer. Secondly, and more important, you're giving me a hard time as far as the Willie McGee case is concerned." So they all agreed to go home.

Constance Baker Motley When I came on the [federal] court in 1966, if I saw one woman in a year—but now, I go down there and you wonder where the men are. That was one thing Bella did. She was a role model in the sense that women could succeed in the law. So in the seventies, women just began going to law school in droves.

When I went to court, especially when I was pregnant in 1948 and 1949 and again in 1951 and 1953, lawyers would make remarks about "menstruating lawyers." Judges would not know where to look. Even my own clients were afraid I might lose their case.

Geraldine Ferraro Now let's be honest about it. She didn't knock lightly on the door. She didn't even push it open or batter it down. She took it off the hinges forever! So that those of us who came after could walk through.

I challenge the system—as a lawyer and as a member of Congress and as an activist in the movement of change. I've challenged all systems—the family, I never obeyed my father properly. I always did what I wanted to do. In school I challenged. In the streets, I challenged the monopoly of what the boys thought that girls couldn't participate in. I've spent a lifetime in challenge. There's no way in which you can create any meaningful change unless you do that.

Joe Bologna When she gets to heaven, Bella would greet Martin warmly, maybe share a couple of dances, maybe a little sex. But having done that, I'm convinced that she immediately began petitioning God for better living conditions for the people in hell.

Originally I felt that law was the instrument for social change. But then I discovered that it was very much dominated by the status quo, that there were bigger issues than my winning a case for a particular individual. That's when I was engaged in the civil rights movement. I headed the civil rights committee of the National Lawyers Guild, and I drafted legislation that ultimately became part of the civil rights law before I was anywhere near Congress or even thinking about it. My big break with the Lawyers Guild was when they didn't want to act on the peace issue. They said, "We're too busy with civil rights." I said, "Well that's too bad, because the United States and the Soviet Union are testing nuclear weapons in the atmosphere, and we've got to have some action. So I'm going to put my energy there."

3

Building a Peace Movement

Chronology

1957 The Village Vanguard, founded in 1935 by Max Gordon, switches from a variety venue to an all-jazz club; it is later run by Lorraine Gordon, a Women Strike for Peace activist who links Bella to many celebrities.

1959 Alaska and Hawaii attain statehood.

1960 John F. Kennedy is elected president, defeating Richard M. Nixon.

1961 The border between East and West Berlin is closed and barriers are built; the Soviet Union tests a fifty-eight–megaton nuclear device, the largest nuclear weapon the world has seen.

1961 Bella helps organize Women Strike for Peace (WSP) to campaign for a nuclear test ban.

1962 The Soviet Union ships nuclear missiles to Cuba, initiating a two-week crisis that ends when Moscow agrees to remove them.

1963 Betty Friedan's *The Feminine Mystique* is published.

1963 The United States, Britain, and the Soviet Union sign the Limited Test Ban Treaty.

1963 Martin Luther King, Jr., delivers his "I Have a Dream"

address to a massive crowd of marchers at the Lincoln Memorial in Washington, D.C.

1963 Lyndon B. Johnson is sworn in as president following the Kennedy assassination.

1964 After two alleged attacks by North Vietnamese gunboats on American destroyers in the Gulf of Tonkin (the USS *Maddox* sustained very minor damage from one machine-gun bullet; the second attack was found later not to have occurred), Congress passes a joint resolution, with only two dissenting votes in the Senate, that authorizes the use of armed force in Vietnam; by the next year, the number of U.S. troops deployed reaches 200,000, peaking at 542,000 during 1968.

1964 With considerable arm-twisting by President Johnson, Congress passes the Civil Rights Act of 1964.

1967 Following clashes on the Israeli-Syrian border, an Israeli call-up of troops, and a blockade by Egypt's president Gamal Abdel Nasser of Israeli shipping in the Gulf of Aqaba, Israel launches an attack against the Arab states (the Six-Day War) and occupies the Golan Heights, Gaza, and the West Bank.

1967, 1968 WSP marches on the Pentagon and, in a Mother's Day protest on Capitol Hill, calls for a halt to the Vietnam War.

1968 Women protest the Miss America pageant in Atlantic City by throwing away (not burning) their bras, in the first national feminist action since suffrage.

1968 The United States, Britain, and the Soviet Union sign the Nuclear Non-Proliferation Treaty, agreeing not to transfer nuclear weapons to other countries.

Amy Swerdlow By the time she got to Women Strike for Peace, Bella was looking for something more political or significant than these little law cases she had. In fact, she was a little neglectful of the law cases, because it didn't interest her. She wanted to write legislation. She wanted to make a dent. She wanted to change society.

Claire Reed I had just moved from the suburbs—Harrison, New York, to Manhattan—and I had been active, but in a League of Women Voters kind of way, a middle-of-the-road, politically conscious person. When I was running the Stevenson office up in Harrison, I met a political activist who lived in Harrison, too. So I began to move toward activism, and more radical, progressive politics.

I didn't like Adlai Stevenson. He was half-baked. I think he was very limited in his ideals.

Claire Reed I don't think I was in New York City more than twelve minutes when the phone rang and it was Judy Lerner, from Harrison. "Listen," she said. "The Soviet Union has resumed nuclear testing, so we're all going down to the mission and we're protesting." I like to protest, so I didn't ask any questions. "Okay, I'll meet you there."

When I get there, at the Soviet mission right near the UN, I'm amazed. There are several hundred women. Judy had said, "Call anybody you know," and it wasn't only Judy. Women were just calling each other. Hundreds of women are circling around, and I don't see Judy, so I just step in next to a kind of heavy-set woman with a big hat. I don't even remember if we introduced ourselves. She's mumbling and grumbling under her breath, and so I say to her, "What are you so unhappy about?" She says, "Well this is all very well and good, but there's other things that have to be done." And little dumb me, because I always worked through political clubs and the League of Women Voters and rang doorbells and stuff like that, I say, "Oh, yeah, absolutely. What we have to do is get into the community and talk to people." I didn't even finish my sentence when she grabs my arm and she says, "You come with me."

We get up to her office and she says hello to the receptionist and waves me into her room toward a small couch. "You sit there." She gets behind a desk and listens while the secretary tells her what calls came in. Then she says, "Okay, now you come over here; we gotta talk." And that was my introduction to Bella. She never let me go, until she died.

This was the fall of 1961. It was just a group of women coming together. Then there was a series of meetings of women who were at the mission demonstration. We heard about Dagmar Wilson* in Washington and talked to her. That was the nucleus for Women Strike for Peace.

Amy Swerdlow There were two factions. A lot of women came to Women Strike for Peace out of moralistic persuasions, like Dag-

*Wilson, the mother of three daughters and a successful illustrator of children's books, was alarmed by talk of a possible confrontation between the nuclear superpowers during the Berlin Wall crisis. She read the British philosopher and pacifist Bertrand Russell's statement upon his arrest for an act of civil disobedience and called the SANE (Committee for a Sane Nuclear Policy) office only to learn that SANE planned no active response. Days later, she met with a group of women from SANE and began planning a massive women's peace demonstration in Washington.

On September 22, 1961, the Washington women issued a national call—using personal phone books, Christmas-card lists, and contacts in PTAs, church and temple groups, women's clubs, and traditional peace organizations—urging women to suspend their daily routines on November 1, to "Appeal to All Governments to End the Arms Race—Not the Human Race." The resulting network was able to reach thousands of women who participated in sixty-eight local protests in Washington, D.C.; Los Angeles; New York; Cambridge, Mass.; Philadelphia; Cleveland; Cincinnati; St. Louis; Baltimore; Denver; San Francisco; and Newark. See Amy Swerdlow, *Women Strike for Peace: Traditional Motherhood and Radical Politics in the 1960s* (Chicago: The University of Chicago Press, 1993) 18, 54–57.

mar Wilson. Bella was a political person from the beginning. The first time I had met her since Hunter—except one time in Wellfleet—we were meeting to plan a January 15 [1962] demonstration in Washington. She came in and said, "So what are you gonna ask for? What are you gonna do?" We were going to demonstrate. It never occurred to anybody that we would lobby, that we would have any demands except "Stop Nuclear Testing."

I can't really recall my first contact with Women Strike for Peace. I have this recollection of a crazy meeting. I said, "Well, it's okay to scream about nuclear testing, but you've got to know what you're talking about. You have to learn what it is. You have to go to Congress." They said that was too political. "It's not political," I said. "It's fundamental. These guys make policy on whether or not the United States is going to have a treaty or not have a treaty. It's okay to show your emotion and come in as a mother and as a woman to say this is going to hurt my children, but it's not good enough."

Judy Lerner We all came in our fancy fur coats and we said, "We're mothers, and we want you to stop nuclear testing. Our kids are dying of cancer." I said someplace of Bella that "She taught me how to lobby, and she taught me how to put on eye makeup." She was always very conscious of the way she looked. One day when I'm trying to put on makeup, she says, "Listen stupid! That's not the way you do it." And she showed me.

They thought their cry would be heard if they were naïve. Don't forget, we were coming out of the witch hunts, and organizations that appeared to have progressive policies were being persecuted for just having ideas.

All I wanted to do was to say that in addition to showing outrage, despair, and other emotions, it was important to have a process in *which we tried to influence change through existing procedures and by changing procedures. I said to them, "I'll tell you what. Let's make a deal. When we go to Washington,* have whatever demonstrative action you want, but then we have to go visit members of Congress and the White House."*

Amy Swerdlow Bella knew how to write legislation because of her work with the National Lawyers Guild. In one second, she was head of the WSP political action and legislative committee.

I tried to get Women Strike for Peace to do two things. One, to lobby Congress to end the nuclear testing (and later to withdraw from Vietnam). The other thing, I tried to get them involved politically, to support candidates who were strong peace candidates.

Amy Swerdlow I was more in the moralist group: Politics are dirty and we don't want to be part of it, that sort of thing. Bella would come to meetings and say, "Listen, you people are all people of leisure. I'm giving up my practice. I'm giving up my time." She was always yelling at us, and no one paid attention. They couldn't stand her. There was a lot of, "Okay, Bella, enough already." And she was amazingly articulate, you know. Anybody who worked with her knew that. Later, when she was a congresswoman, she was speaking on the steps of the Forty-second Street Library, and one of the women said, "You know, she used to say the same thing and nobody listened." But the Women Strike people were very loyal and worked for her when she ran for office.

*On January 15, 1962, six weeks after the first strike, WSP chapters on the East Coast picketed the White House in drenching rain and conducted a massive lobby in Congress. It was described in the media as the largest protest rally since the beginning of the cold war. Bella convinced the New York chapter to adopt the demonstrate/lobby format, which became "a WSP hallmark throughout the 1960s and early 1970s." See Swerdlow, *Women Strike*, 84, 144.

They often said, "Don't let her speak, because she represents something different than what we're trying to portray." I was not reflective of the typical Women-Strike-for-Peacer, who was a mother and took care of her kids. I was a lawyer. A lot of those women said, "She doesn't have that innocent image of just being an angry and concerned mother of children." I didn't speak out of the mother culture. I did speak about our children. I cared about that, but I also spoke about the rights that women had—that women had a right to peace, not only for the sake of their children. It was in some ways a little humiliating to me. A little insulting.

Gloria Steinem She wasn't all that well treated by the Women Strike for Peace women, because they were organizing as mothers. Remember "Another Mother for Peace"? They told her at some crucial juncture that she couldn't represent them because she wasn't motherly enough. And I think that encouraged her feminism, because they were biological determinists at that moment in time. They've all become something else since.

Amy Swerdlow I learned a lot from Bella. I don't think Bella would ever think she ever learned anything from anybody, but we discussed everything. And we didn't always agree. There was a period when we weren't speaking to each other, but that was short-lived. I had gone into the Jeannette Rankin Brigade* and was on the executive board, and Bella felt that was competition with Women Strike for Peace.

*In the fall of 1967, a number of WSP members joined other women leaders from church, labor, civil rights, and women's liberation groups to form the Jeannette Rankin Brigade, inspired initially by a speech by Rankin, the first woman elected to the U.S. Congress and, at that time, an eighty-seven-year-old Gandhian pacifist. She had voted against both world wars and advocated that women organize mass civil disobedience demonstrations to protest the Vietnam War. The organizers tried to reach across class lines by linking the issues of war and poverty, and Rankin's radicalism attracted younger women's liberation movement feminists. Some five thousand women participated in a

You had to be totally in her camp. I remember her screaming, "You're absolutely wrong. Wrong. Wrong!" I couldn't stand the screaming. When she was in Congress, I would hang up on her. Twelve o'clock at night she would call me up to talk. My husband's got to go to work the next day, and you couldn't get off the phone. So I would hang up and then the next day I would get a call, "The congresswoman wants to talk to you and she doesn't want you to hang up." So I said, "Tell the congresswoman I won't hang up if she doesn't yell." People ran away when they felt their ego was being bruised, but I didn't feel that way. I'd say, "Jesus Christ, give me a break."

Cora Weiss I was not in the first ring of friends around her. We were colleagues, both leaders of the WSP, both public speakers. She was much more interested in electoral politics and in legislation than I was.

She was opposed to the Jeannette Rankin Brigade, because Rankin voted against World War II, for which Bella never forgave her, and Bella didn't speak to a few of her close friends who worked on the JRB during those years. I think she was probably, like all politicians, and all Democrats certainly, careful not to get entangled with or too close to anything that might be cause for red-baiting later on.

Claire Reed I was her puppet. Because I had no affiliation with any red party—communist, socialist, anything—because I was pure and naïve in a sense and came from a very upper-middle-class

march on Washington on January 15, 1968, but, in a concession to women from the church groups, the steering committee had rejected the idea of violating a seldomly applied law by marching onto the Capitol grounds. The group convened a Congress of Women after the protest, which was cochaired by Coretta Scott King, and featured a welcome by Jeannette Rankin and a variety of speakers, including civil rights leader Ella Baker, WSP founder Dagmar Wilson, and Charlotte Bunch, representing the radical young women's faction. See Swerdlow, *Women Strike*, 135–39.

bourgeois family, Bella saw that she could use me. She would say, "Now you go to the meeting and you tell them that this is the way it should be done." So I'd go, and I'd listen very quietly, and I'd say, "But on the other hand, don't you think this would be a good idea?" Bella would have come on strong with, "That's not enough. You gotta do this and this!" They would listen to me. Consequently, she would send me to meetings in Great Neck, in Westchester, in Queens.

One time my husband said to me, "Can't we have our dinner without forty calls from Bella?" It was like extrasensory perception. The minute I opened the door, the phone was ringing and it was Bella. One weekend I said to Lorraine Gordon—from the Village Vanguard, Max Gordon's wife; she was a PR person for the Upper East Side Women's Strike—I said, "Lorraine, come out this weekend, and when Bella calls, you tell her I'm at the beach, that I haven't come out yet, tell her anything." So we walk in the house and within five minutes the phone rings. Lorraine picks it up and says, "Oh, I'm so sorry, Bella, but she hasn't come. Well, yes, we expect her." But do you think Bella fell for that? She told Lorraine, "Okay, tell her to call me when she comes in." Then she waited ten minutes and called again. I thought it wasn't Bella and picked it up. She started right in: "Okay, now listen to me. This is what you have to do."

Shirley Margolin Bella worked all day and worked all night. So it was not unusual somewhere around three o'clock in the morning, sometimes one o'clock, sometimes eleven if we were lucky, the telephone would ring. Leo would hand me the phone and say, "It's her." I would take it and she would say, "Well, I've been thinking about this. What should we do?" But she had already decided what she wanted me to do. I would scribble notes and say, "Okay." The next morning I would get up and say, "Wait a minute. What did she say?"

But it was alright, because Bella worked twenty-four hours a day and was devoted to the things she believed in. The only thing that bothered me is I wish she'd call me at one o'clock at least. Not at three o'clock. Leo was always saying, "It's her again. Can't you just let me sleep tonight?" I would say, "She does her best work at night. Go back to sleep. I'll talk soft. Bella, don't yell. Leo is sleeping." Finally I would hang up and this poor man would say, "Did she go away?"

Barbara Bick I'd just moved from California with my family, and I saw a little item in *The Washington Post* that some people were meeting at a church. That was the first couple of meetings held by Dagmar Wilson, Eleanor Garst, Folly Fodor, and others. Most of them had been in SANE but left over an issue having to do with a loyalty oath.* I immediately got in touch with them, so I was part of the whole beginning. And Bella was with her group in New York. I didn't know any of them. Amazing, because now I feel like I've known them all my life. The center of Women Strike was not New York. In fact, there wasn't a center. There was a center in L.A., a center in San Francisco, and somewhere in the South, and in Seattle. Washington had the national office, which I ran. But I have to say the New York women are smart. They're savvy and sophisticated and they know how to get things done.

Amy Swerdlow [W]hat is most unexpected and quite shocking is to discover that the liberal Daniel Patrick Moynihan dismissed the group at a White House meeting in October 1969 with the comment, "They are only Jewish ladies from New York."

*Under pressure from McCarthyism, the SANE board voted to issue guidelines calling for chapters to exclude past or present Communist associates from membership. The WSP founders viewed the board's action as a "capitulation to Cold War thinking." See Swerdlow, *Women Strike*, 46.

Barbara Bick Bella was not running for office in the early sixties, but she really wanted to go where the power was, to the decision makers. I edited the national newsletter, so Bella and I had a lot to do with each other. I have to say, she intimidated me a great deal. She could shout and demand that you do things. She always did more than that herself. So I wouldn't say we were intimate friends at the beginning. Not like Mim and Amy and Judy—people who had gone to college with her.

I remember once I was in the office with Kay Johnson, who was a full-time volunteer, as we mostly all were. Her husband, Byron Johnson, was a peace congressman from Colorado. Kay was tall and Norwegian-looking—a very Christian kind of person, Fellowship for Reconciliation. One of the great things about Women Strike for Peace is that we really did come from such different backgrounds and we became so close. Kay and I were alone in the office when Bella called up from New York furious about something. We got so scared we ran out of the office. We were standing there shivering and giggling and wondering, "How could Bella intimidate us from New York?"

But the thing about Bella is that she just sort of demands friendship, too. She's a very loyal friend. So it was a couple of years before we became intimate friends. She would talk to me about a lot of things. But I didn't tell her too many personal things, because I didn't want to waste her time. I didn't want to bore her.

Robin Morgan She has that unusual presence in that you think you've always known her. She was one of a small group of lawyers you could always call on in the sixties. They would show up at protests. There were two or three women—Kris Glenn, Emily Jane Goodman—and the rest were all guys; she may have already gotten me out of jail on some civil rights matter with a group of other people. But the first time I clearly remember we met was after a demonstration in '66 or '67, something like that. We were with a group of people who went for coffee afterward around Columbus Circle. We were talking about the cusp between peaceful demonstrations and going for armed resistance. I was in the latter group, saying, "It's time enough already. We've marched. We've done everything." I was in a heated argument with somebody over this. And she became involved, saying, "That doesn't do any good." She was so forceful that at first I glowered and backed down. And then she said to me, "What's wrong with you? You've forgotten how to argue? Do you believe in what you believe in?" And I said, "Yeah. Damn right I do." "Well then argue with me." So I argued with her. Nobody won. If anyone did it would be Bella, of course, but that established a decibel of dialogue between us.

This Mother's Day will commence a mighty women's movement, a movement in every state of this country, in which the women of this country will organize their political power . . . to build a society for our sons, and everybody else's sons, and for people here and across this country.

Ethel Taylor We were sidetracked by the war in Vietnam. Even though we knew that while the war was going on the nuclear arms race would continue, we had to make a choice on what issue we would deal with immediately. There was no question it would be Vietnam because this was so urgent.

Gloria Steinem I remember meeting Bella in 1967, during a women's antiwar demonstration in which we all went to Washington on a train—hundreds and thousands of us. There are wonderful photos of her, barreling through Union Station with hordes of women behind her. She was not yet a member of Congress.

It was a very important movement—the conscience of this country in the question of nuclear testing and later on the war in Vietnam. Even among peace groups, we were much more free. You don't have to go to a board meeting because we make decisions through a telephone tree. So we were able to act on the spot. I have always enjoyed working with women because there are fewer boundaries and impediments and areas of potential conflict. It is always easier to come to a confluence of opinion.

Amy Swerdlow WSP was the first peace group to carry a mass protest to the steps of the Pentagon in the winter of 1967, when twenty-five hundred women, carrying enlarged photos of napalmed Vietnamese children under the slogan "Children Are Not for Burning," demanded to see the Pentagon generals who were responsible for the killings . . . WSP women literally stormed the military citadel, having removed their shoes to bang against the Pentagon doors that were hastily locked in their faces.

Gloria Steinem We all demonstrated outside the Pentagon. What I remember most was then some of us, as many as could get in, went to an auditorium in the Capitol or some official building where we were going to present our complaints and demands about Vietnam to members of Congress. Of course, the only members who would come were people who agreed with us already. So [the New York Republican senator Jacob] Javits was there. This delegation was presenting, among other things, proof of the use by the United States of an illegal weapon in Vietnam—something we said we weren't using—and Bella was leading this presentation. And she scared the shit out of me. She was just so aggressive—assertive doesn't do it—aggressive and carrying on. She also annoyed the shit out of Jacob Javits, because he ended up saying, "I will oppose the war *in spite* of you."

I had never seen a woman being that out there. I was very, very put off by it. It was not a good experience. And then, perhaps a few weeks later, I met her in Ellie Guggenheimer's* living room. There was a women's meeting, and we were plotting something to do with city politics and the war. Bella and I ended up walking down Lexington together afterwards, talking. Gradually I began to realize that my response to her was my problem, not hers. If I was afraid to see Bella being a whole person, anger and all, that was because I was still afraid to be a whole person myself.

Once we had raised the public consciousness through demonstrative action, then you'd take that consciousness and turn it into political action. That's my view. The building of a constituency was done very effectively. This organization struck at the hearts of the nation, and many people feel that, were it not for the energy it unleashed, President Kennedy might not have been able to sign the partial nuclear test ban treaty.

Amy Swerdlow Bella was very clever, very strategic. We never, never endorsed anybody until very late—and you couldn't run for anything in New York that Bella's political committee didn't approve.

Well before anyone thought up the gender gap, we used my slogan, "The women's vote is a peace vote." Women were trained to speak softly . . . and carry a lipstick. Now we demanded a bigger stick. We want to be everywhere, at every table, not just the kitchen table. Because women were outside, because they had nothing to do with mak-

*Active in the formation of the National Women's Political Caucus, Elinor Guggenheimer is a New York Democratic Party fund-raiser and founder of the Child Care Action Campaign and the New York Women's Agenda, among other organizations.

ing policy and did not get trained to solve problems violently, I always thought they could make a big difference in peace. Not every woman is for peace. Golda Meir took us to war, and Indira Gandhi and Margaret Thatcher. But these women did not come out of the women's culture and women's agenda. They happened to be women who came out of male power structures.

One of the big things that happened [years later] in Beijing is that there was finally recognition in that UN document, which talked about the major role that women had to play in the development of the culture of peace, as well as the importance of women being at all negotiating tables and all mediations at all places of conflicts. Now if that is implemented in any meaningful way, that's a big step for the United Nations, because you've never seen women at the negotiating tables.*

When I look at what I have done over the years, there's a strong trend of being against violence in many forms, including the way the establishment and institutions do great violence to people. I attended the Jewish Theological Seminary and got involved in studying the Bible somewhat intensely. All I was interested in were the prophets who spoke for peace.

*The UN Fourth World Conference on Women, 1995.

4

Transforming Local Politics

Chronology

1964 Patsy Mink, a Democrat from Hawaii, who became Bella's closest pal in Congress, is elected to the House.

1966 Bella organizes the Seventeenth Congressional District Peace Action Committee to question potential candidates in New York City on their position on the Vietnam War.

1966 The National Organization for Women is founded in Washington, D.C., by Betty Friedan and members of Kennedy's Presidential Commission on the Status of Women, who were radicalized by the experience of serving on the commission and on the panel that replaced it.

1966 Indira Gandhi is elected prime minister of India and serves from 1966 to 1977 and again from 1980 to 1984.

1967 Launching the Dump Johnson movement, Allard Lowenstein meets with Senator Robert Kennedy and, later, Senator Eugene McCarthy to encourage an antiwar Democratic presidential candidacy.

1968 Within a few weeks of the mounting of the Tet offensive by North Vietnam, eleven hundred American troops die. Following Eugene McCarthy's strong showing in the New Hampshire Democratic primary, Robert Kennedy enters the race, and Bella endorses him. President Lyndon B. Johnson announces he will not seek reelection.

1968 On April 4, Martin Luther King, Jr., is assassinated, and riots break out in more than a hundred cities, though not in New York, where Mayor John Lindsay, who had been supported by Bella, goes to Harlem and speaks of shared sorrow, as does Robert Kennedy. Chicago's mayor, Richard J. Daley, criticizing his police superintendent's handling of rioters, says he would give police specific instructions "to shoot to kill any arsonist and to shoot to maim or cripple anyone looting."

1968 Columbia University students occupy several campus buildings; city police rout the protesters a week later.

1968 On June 5, Robert Kennedy is assassinated in Los Angeles, minutes after proclaiming victory in the California primary.

1968 Vice President Hubert Humphrey wins the Democratic presidential nomination while thousands rally and protest in the parks and streets outside the convention in Chicago. A national commission later calls the reaction of Mayor Daley's force a "police riot." Humphrey loses to Richard Nixon in November, with the third-party candidate, George Wallace, winning about 13 percent of the vote and five southern states.

1968 Shirley Chisholm, a Democrat from New York, who became Bella's collaborator on the Hill and off, is elected to Congress.

1969 U.S. astronauts walk on the moon.

1969 With an agenda to make New York City the fifty-first state, the author Norman Mailer and the journalist Jimmy Breslin run a symbolic campaign for mayor and city council president against the Republican mayor, John Lindsay. Bella campaigns for Lindsay, who wins reelection on the Liberal and Independent Party lines.

1969 Five hundred thousand people participate in the four-day Woodstock rock festival in upstate New York.

1969 New York police raid and shut down the Stonewall Inn, a popular gay bar in Greenwich Village. The ensuing riots come to symbolize the beginning of the gay liberation movement in the United States. In 1970, the first gay liberation march, in New York, commemorates Stonewall.

1969 The women's collective that will produce *Our Bodies, Ourselves* first meets in Boston.

Ronnie Eldridge Bella organized in a very basic way, which was organizing what she used to call the grass roots, and trying to make people respond. We were a great act together, because in the sixties I was always inside and responding to the pressures outside. She was building the pressures, and I would move the inside toward her goals. It's a very good, basic tenet of organizing and politics. We were just a great combination.

Doug Ireland I met Bella in 1963, when I was a teenager. She was in the process of organizing something that eventually became the Metropolitan Council on Peace Politics. It was pretty much a paper organization but its goal was to take activists from the antiwar movement and the peace movement and put them into the Democratic clubs all over New York City to turn those clubs against the war in Vietnam. This was primarily Bella's idea. Her goal throughout the sixties was to use the electoral process to fight against the Vietnam War. I was on the staff of the Students for a Democratic Society, working out of the New York office as the assistant national secretary. As opposed to the leadership of SDS, my faction was very interested in electoral politics—and the trade union movement.

I went to some meetings and right away I was quite impressed, both with her political strategy and with her pragmatic radicalism. I always believed that American radicalism had to speak with an American idiom—that the left had to anchor itself deeply in the American experience. That was instinctive on Bella's part. Although she came out of left-wing labor Zionism, she had deep roots in the trade union movement, having represented a goodly number of trade unions from the beginning of her legal career. And she was a product of the popular front culture of the thirties and forties—at a time when the popular front was much influenced by the propaganda posture that the American Communist Party adopted during World War II, wrapped in American images and American rhetoric. Bella was never in the Party, though Martin was in the Young Communist League at City College. She was a "fellow traveler."

As a teenager, when I found someone who was older and smarter, I had a habit of attaching myself to them, to suck in everything I could learn out of them. It's a form of self-education. And I said to myself, "Well this is a very smart cookie, this Bella Abzug." A notion of what was called then "political realignment," was in the air. You had to get the arteriosclerotic Dixiecrats evicted from positions of power and renew the Democratic Party with an infusion of activism from the various social movements that were burgeoning at the time.

Ronnie Eldridge Bella and I first worked together when Allard Lowenstein was running for Congress in 1966—a race he lost. He had called me from England and said, "I'm thinking about running on the East Side. I'd like you to do this and this and this." Allard was very much like Bella in being so driven. They're all very manipulative with the people who are helping them. He said, "Call Bella Abzug. She has the Seventeenth Congressional [District] Peace Action Committee and they're interviewing candidates. I want to meet her." Later he called about a dinner. His family owned this restaurant on Lexington Avenue and Fiftieth Street that was a meeting place for everybody. "Come down to Granson's and meet Bella Abzug." I got down there, and there was this beautiful woman—and Martin. We just hit it off right away.

Shirley MacLaine She was really beautiful—those high cheekbones and those slanted tartar eyes. She looked like Merle Oberon. And rather thin.

Harold Holzer You know who she looked like? Look at Shirley MacLaine in *The Apartment*. I'll tell you a story: One day in 1954 Bella's walking through the street. Somebody says, "Miss, we must have you." She said, "What are you talking about?" "We must have you, we're shooting a movie here, and we need you as a double." She said, "A double?" "Yes, for Shirley MacLaine. We need you to fill in for some scenes. You're a dead ringer for Shirley MacLaine." Think of Shirley in 1954 in *The Apartment*, with those sloe eyes and wide Slavic face; and Bella said, "Honey, I'm a lawyer, I don't have time for this crap." But later she became Shirley's friend and she told me this story. She said, "Never tell Shirley this story, because Shirley would be offended because I'm so fat." I said, "Yeah, but she's seen pictures of you." She said, "Just don't tell her the story." Anyway, we never told her the story.

Ronnie Eldridge After Allard lost the primary, he started the Dump Johnson movement, and Bella and I were both involved. We formed this committee that Sarah Kovner* and I cochaired—the

*A New York City Democratic Party activist and later special assistant to Donna Shalala, the secretary of health and human services in the Clinton administration.

Coalition for a Democratic Alternative. Democrats in California were taking out ads in the paper with pages of names of people opposed to the Vietnam War. It sort of rolled east, and we did the same thing here. Then Bella and I devised a system where we would get delegates to run who pledged to support antiwar candidates—that had not been done before.

Larry Eldridge used to complain that Bella called all the time. I would say, "I have to get off the phone. My husband wants in," and she would say, "I'm an independent woman. I don't have those problems."

I worked to organize support for the district seat that I ultimately ran in myself, because Ted Weiss was a strong peace candidate. Ultimately I created a caucus in every Democratic club in the district to change their position on Vietnam. It was a prelude to the Dump Johnson movement. When I supported a candidate, I would supply people to go to the subway stops, to go to the supermarkets. But if he didn't maintain his position, the next day there would be no people to go to the supermarkets or the subway stops.

Ronnie Eldridge We would work together. I'd be a poll watcher, and because she was an attorney, she'd be able to get accredited by the state as an inspector. We would go out to Brooklyn, and before we got there, we stopped in the car. She put her lipstick on, she did her mascara a little bit, and then, separately, we go into the polling place. I go in with my poll-watcher certificate. I stand at a place where they're having trouble and I say, "What is this?" I say, "Well, we need a lawyer." So I call over, and Bella comes. We would do that all the time. We had a good time with that.

Liz Abzug She got really more into politics when we moved back into the city. She would do a lot of her talking in the kitchen, on the phone—on a director's chair—and she would hit the counter tops like this [bangs on table] as she talked about the politics—always. And particularly when we lived on Bank Street, I lived right under the kitchen, so you would hear her in the mornings. We moved in there about '69, and so she lived in that duplex, all through her congressional years and all through her races. It was a brownstone with four exposures, okay? Windows on four sides—and she would often go nude and get on that director's chair and start in about various issues and—"They're whores" and so on. Saturday mornings were like a nightmare because she would get into calling, making and returning phone calls, or reaching out to people in the party, or talking campaign issues. There were continual campaigns during that period, too. She would be screaming her frustration out in the morning, and at night. And I would sometimes come upstairs and say, "Cut that shit, will you stop it?" Because it would keep us all up!

Doug Ireland Bella and I had both become very active in the Dump Johnson movement, which led directly to the antiwar candidacy of Senator Eugene McCarthy. Bobby Kennedy had been asked to run and refused at that point. The question of whether or not to form a third party was a key issue at the New Politics conference,* and I was of the opinion that the defeat of Lyndon Johnson and the possible ending of the Vietnam War was so crucial that the moment was not ripe for a third party. Running a third-party candidate would endanger the unity of the antiwar movement and insure the election of Richard Nixon. Bella at that time supported a third-party candidacy and it was over that issue that we had our first really serious run-in. When Bella's side went down in defeat, the volume went up

*The National Conference for a New Politics convened a five-day convention of new-left groups, with some three thousand delegates, in Chicago in 1967.

considerably. But by this time, we were working together closely for so long that I was used to these volcanic eruptions of Abzugian temper.

Liz Carpenter Over the years, after Lyndon came back to Texas, I kept telling Bella that I would like them to meet. I told her that he was really charming and that he liked strong women and that she would like him. She always replied, "Not a fucking chance!"

Shirley MacLaine I didn't really understand her until I went to Israel and sat in the Knesset for a week, where a bunch of Jews are screaming at each other, and I thought, "Oh, it's not only me she's mad at. They are all mad at each other all the time." In this way, that if one little thing is off, you've destroyed the planet.

Ronnie Eldridge When Bobby Kennedy was senator, I would talk to him about Bella and the Women Strike for Peace position on Vietnam. Finally I got Kennedy to meet with them in his office—which was then in the Post Office at Forty-sixth Street and Lexington Avenue. It was hysterical, because people's image of Bella was so different from her personal, one-to-one connection. Most people were surprised to see that she was so attractive—that she was dressed up and could be very refined. When they came to the office, Kennedy was very worried. He made some joke—did he need a helmet? Were they coming on their motorcycles, and did he need protection? In walk all these women, most of them with mink coats on. Everybody stood around waiting for this tirade, and there were all these nice ladies. He and Bella hit it off, and it was a very interesting meeting.

When he first announced he was running for president, I was up in the suite with him at the Hilton Hotel. We were making up lists of people to call. Steve Smith was running the campaign and he called Bella. She became very important in the campaign, and I helped her by always involving her. I knew she was an excellent politician. She had great political skills.

I was very upset about the [Robert] Kennedy assassination, because I had just gotten to influence him about the war in Vietnam. I had brought a whole group of women in.

Ronnie Eldridge In '69, I found myself helping John Lindsay. He was running as an independent for the mayoralty after losing in the Republican primary. I formed the Democrats for Lindsay, and we had a big headquarters at the old De Pina's department store. Bella, by this time, was doing peace and urban priorities, and I talked Lindsay into bringing her and her people into the campaign. So she ran this thing, the Agenda for Urban Priorities or something, with an office in De Pina's. She did a very good job. All the Women Strike for Peace women were there.

When Ronnie called about Lindsay, I told her I'm tired of supporting men who don't do what they're supposed to do. I'm really disillusioned. But she said the campaign would be about the issues, so I developed a major campaign called "New York Spends More on War than on New York." I had the budget department develop all the monies we send to the federal government that goes to war and how much more money we would have to fill the potholes, pick up the snow, et cetera, if they didn't use our tax dollars the way they did.

Then I organized a hundred and eighty community groups. It was a very crucial part of Lindsay's campaign—we developed the only real issues. And when it was all over, he won.

Ronnie Eldridge During the Lindsay campaign, Bella wanted to put a full-page ad in the *Times*. Dick Aurelio and Sid Davidoff and everybody said they didn't have the money. She got so angry that she punched me—on Fifth Avenue in front of De Pina's. That was the only time she ever really hit me. But Davidoff, who was this Republican tough guy—he used to go out into the ghettos and buy people off and do that kind of stuff—he was so taken with Bella, he went and borrowed the money from the Republican county leader, Vincent Albano, to pay for her full-page ad.

When Lindsay asked me what role I wanted in his administration, I said I'd like to continue this activist group, as Washington liaison, whatever. "You should have an activist arm of government. You should have a big constituency that can organize support behind you." He said, "Are you serious, Bella? You don't know what you're talking about. Don't you want to be housing commissioner? Wouldn't you want to be a judge?" I said, "I only want this one thing." It was too shocking even for Lindsay to have an activist arm of government.

Ronnie Eldridge She was very angry that she didn't get a job in the Lindsay administration. I could not think of a job for her. I went as special assistant to the mayor. She could never have been a special assistant to the mayor. Everybody thought she was a very successful lawyer, and nobody knocked themselves out to get her a job. She was so angry about that, she decided to run for Congress—which was a very good thing.

I was pretty upset. Right after that Martin and I went to Martinique and he said, "Why don't you run yourself?" I remember this like yesterday: I was doing deep-sea diving. There's no experience like it. It is a sound and a world different from anything you've ever experienced. There's no interference, there's no conflict—you're just down there with yourself, intensely. You have complete openness and clarity. Some people say that's how you feel right before you die. There's a clarity and bright opening up. It was down there that I said to myself, "Well, God damn it, I think it's overdue. I will run!"

Shirley MacLaine There were times out in Malibu—she would swim way out and she would find walruses and seals, and look into their eyes and swim and float; she described how they would circle around her and she would just look in their eyes. And she would go to the bottom of people's pools, and decide whether to run for something. She found real solace at the bottom of water.

Liz Abzug She used to tell me all the time, "You fight for change from without and from within." She understood that she had done plenty of it from without the system. By the time she was fifty and people were saying, "Well, why don't you run for office?" it started to make sense to her. There's a position of power, and there's an advantage to being inside—to breaking that open on the inside. She said to herself, "I've done it on the outside. So let me see what it looks like on the inside. Let me try it that way." But the way she managed that first campaign—the fact that she won her first race against all the odds—was so novel at the time.

When I decided to run for office myself, they figured I'd be another one of those schnook peace candidates. But they forgot who I was—that I was a different personality and that I was a woman. I was not just a person who was going to get up there and make an ideological speech. I was also running on women's rights and on urban priorities. A big emphasis in my campaign was really that this woman's place was in the House.

5

Running and Winning: Building a New Coalition

Chronology

1970 Campus protests grow following a U.S./South Vietnamese ground attack in Cambodia. At the Kent State campus in Ohio on May 4, Ohio National Guard troops fire on protesters; nine are wounded and four killed. Ten days later, in Mississippi, a Jackson State student and a high school student are killed and fifteen students are wounded by police in the wake of campus unrest.

1970 At age fifty Bella makes her first run for elective office, to represent Manhattan's West Side in the U.S. House of Representatives. Her slogan: "This woman's place is in the House, the House of Representatives."

1970 *Sisterhood is Powerful*, edited by Robin Morgan, is published, one of the first anthologies of the politics of women's liberation.

1970 Stars stage "Broadway for Bella" at Madison Square Garden; the Jewish Defense League pickets outside.

1970 Barbra Streisand hosts a fund-raiser and campaigns on a flatbed truck.

1970 Fifty thousand women march down Fifth Avenue, New York City, on August 26 in celebration of the fiftieth anniversary of suffrage.

1970 Bella is elected after defeating a fourteen-year incumbent, becoming the first Jewish woman ever elected to the House; at the time, there are only nine women serving.

1971 As Bella takes office, her reelection campaign begins almost immediately because her district is merged with another when the city loses a seat following the 1970 census.

1971 The National Women's Political Caucus is founded by Bella, Patsy Mink, Shirley Chisholm, Betty Friedan, and Gloria Steinem, among others.

1971 Ms. magazine's preview issue appears within a special end-of-the-year issue of *New York* magazine.

1972 Bella loses the primary to Representative Bill Ryan, who is sick with cancer and dies before the general election. She is named the Democratic candidate, and she wins back her seat in November.

I hadn't been a club person. That's not my constituency. I come from the movements of change, the labor movement, the peace movement, the human rights movement, the civil rights movement, the women's movement. Those are the people I bring into campaigns all the time. And they want their own candidate.

When I ran for Congress, there was a real division among people who were for it and people who were against it. If I lost, it's like a defeat for the peace issue. Dagmar Wilson was always a little leery of my trying to make Women Strike for Peace more political. It was all very moralistic. The high ground. I never opposed the high moralistic ground. It's a significant part of leadership of any kind. Lacking that, you don't have leaders. You have phonies.

So many people asked me, "Are you really running?" that I had the button made—orange with purple letters—which said, "Abzuglutely." We were clever.

Claire Reed Most of the people thought, "That's great—a woman running for Congress, somebody representing our point of view." Also they kind of liked the idea she's getting out of Women Strike. We don't have to handle her anymore. But she really had tremendous support from Women Strike for Peace.

Amy Swerdlow I was scared stiff when she ran for Congress. I didn't see how she could win. We had worked against [Leonard] Farbstein* before, and I was a poll watcher. He had a political machine and he'd bring people out from the old-age homes and that sort of thing. I was just a coward. When she was elected, and we were standing outside the headquarters, she said to me, "You see! You see!"

Gloria [Steinem] was always afraid that they were going to hurt me, that people are mean and cruel, particularly in politics. She always had that to say about every campaign, even though she was one of my biggest supporters.

Doug Ireland In New York you don't have to live in the district you run in. There was some consideration of various congressional districts—discussion of her running on the East Side, but it was awfully clear to those of us who were politically savvy that the Farbstein district was the logical one for her because of its political composition. It included at that time the entire West Side of Manhattan, which was the most progressive piece of land anywhere in the country. It also included the Lower East Side, with its aging Jewish population still much imbued with the spirit of the old socialists and communists. The *Forward* was still printed in Yiddish at that time, and so was the *Morgen Freiheit*, which was the communist newspaper.

*Leonard Farbstein was a seven-term Democratic congressman whom Bella defeated in the primary in 1970.

Jerrold Nadler There was a civil war going on in the West Side reform movement from 1968 to about 1972. This consisted of the "West Side kids"—me, Dick Godfrey, Dick Morris, a few others. We were a bunch of kids who, when we were in college, organized the "Clean for Gene" [McCarthy] campaign in New Hampshire and elsewhere. When we turned twenty-one, in 1969, seven of us ran for district leader against seven incumbents and beat all seven. We attacked the reform movement from the left. Farbstein had this "J" shaped district, running from Fourteenth Street on the Lower East Side, down around the West Village, and up the West Side to Eighty-sixth Street. Every two years the reformers ran against Farbstein in the Democratic primary. In 1962, Assemblyman Bentley Kassal lost by 4,500 votes. In 1964 Bill Haddad lost by 2,200. In 1966 Ted Weiss lost by 140 votes.

Harold Holzer Farbstein called Haddad "an Arab in Jew's clothing," or something, and that was the end of him. Then Ted Weiss lost by a few votes—imagine how close we came to not having Bella. If any of these men had won they would have been there forever.

Jerrold Nadler But then in 1968 reapportionment took some of the West Side away from the district, so in 1970, the question was who was going to run against Farbstein. Not too many people thought he could be beaten, because he always got huge margins on the Lower East Side, and most of the Village was no longer in the district. Some really good people had run in the primaries over the years and wanted to run again. There was a procedure in which the members of the various reform clubs in the district voted separately, and then the votes were amalgamated. The candidates always said they would abide by the outcome and support whoever ran, because if you split the reform vote, you couldn't beat Farbstein. Okay, in 1970, along comes Bella, who was not widely known. She did Women Strike for Peace, and she was, along with Ronnie Eldridge, one of the heads of Democrats for Lindsay, and we had also supported Lindsay the previous year for mayor. We were preparing to go through the reform club procedure and all of a sudden, Bella said she was going to run. She was not going into the procedure. "I'm running, period. If you want to split the vote and put up another candidate, you're welcome to do it." She was saying, "Pick me, or else," which is not, perhaps, the "reform" thing to do. Members of the establishment reform group said, "Really? And who's gonna circulate your petitions?" And up popped the seven new district leaders, saying, "We will." That gave her a lot of credibility, because it meant she could get on the ballot. The Women Strike members would be collecting petition signatures, but you never really knew if volunteers could do the job the way political clubs are trained to.

Eventually, after a lot of hemming and hawing, Bella became the reform nominee. And she astonished people, winning by about thirty-five hundred votes. She carried one of Farbstein's strongholds on the Lower East Side. She went to the Grand Street Houses, the heart of Farbstein territory, as a Jewish mother with her gefilte fish recipe.

I was there in the streets, day and night, talking to people in the buildings with a megaphone, going to those big housing projects down there, standing on the corner until twelve o'clock at night and starting early in the morning, getting that personal contact with the people in that district. And that's what won it for me.

Marilyn Marcosson It may have been in the second campaign that Ronnie Eldridge was managing, but I remember once saying, "You've got to give Bella some time off. We're just not gonna do a morning subway stop." I canceled the driver. I canceled the people who were meeting her at the subway. I canceled myself. But I forgot to tell her. So Bella gets up and dressed. It's 7:30 a.m. and there's nobody there. She apparently tries to find the car, and she calls Ronnie all hysterical. Finally she takes a bag of literature and goes to the subway herself.

Harold Holzer At the end of 1969, my soon-to-be wife and I were running a newspaper called *The Manhattan Tribune*, and there was going to be an early debate scheduled, with Bella Abzug, Leonard Farbstein—who didn't show up—and the radio talk show host who was running, Barry Farber. We'd never seen Bella before. She strode in and really just took over the room. She raked Farbstein over the coals for not being present and dismissed Barry Farber, who actually wound up running a very tough race on the Republican and Liberal tickets in the fall. Bella told Farber, "Honey, you're gonna have to give up your radio show if you run against me. No radio show." She was just something we'd never seen before—a frank, strong, funny, earthy, brilliant woman, sort of the "*über* Jewish Mother" in a way. We were completely mesmerized, and we went up to talk to her afterwards, and said, "We've got to do more stories about you."

Doug Ireland Bella was a very hands-on candidate, though I used to tell her that the old saw about the lawyer representing himself having a fool for a client was certainly applicable to electoral politics. But Bella was such a great organizer herself, she obviously thought she knew better than anybody else what had to be done. She was an extraordinarily dynamic candidate who had a charismatic physical presence on the streets when she campaigned. I knew a lot of journalists, so we were able to get an enormous amount of very positive publicity for Bella.

Susan Brownmiller Pete Hamill and Jimmy Breslin wrote columns about her. Breslin made her into a Damon Runyonesque character. They loved her because to them she was like a big mother figure.

Pete Hamill The one final thing I admire about Bella is that she is a real New Yorker. New York is in her voice, which has a raw, street hoarseness; it is in the way she walks, with a bold swagger all of us picked up from Warner Brothers movies and watching guys who ran numbers in the late 1940s. When she talks she throws punches; she never whines, she never backs off.

Eric Hirschhorn I had graduated from Columbia Law in 1968 and got a fellowship to work as a legal services lawyer. I was working on the Lower East Side and was often up against this guy who prosecuted juvenile defendants. He had a friend running for Congress from that district who wanted to know more about a situation involving a crowded shelter for delinquent adolescent girls. "Her name is Bella Abzug." I said, "I never heard of her, but if she's a friend of yours, of course I'll help her out." So I went down to her headquarters, which was the old *Village Voice* office on Sheridan Square.

The first person I met was Marilyn Marcosson, who had her long black hair caught in the mimeograph machine, all caught up in the ink. I had to wait awhile because Bella is on the phone, and I hear this woman screaming through a very thin door. I'm not sure I ever heard her scream like that again in the thirty years I knew her. I whispered to somebody, "Who's she yelling at?" "Albert Shanker." And I said, "You know what? Count me in."

Jerrold Nadler Shanker and the United Federation of Teachers hated Bella—probably for her position in the 1968 strike.* That's another reason I would like Bella. I thought the UFT was badly organized at the time.

*In 1968, the UFT, with Shanker as its president, went on strike in a bitter fight to resist decentralized control of the schools, a cause that was heavily supported by the African American community and by Bella and other progressives as well.

Marilyn Marcosson I'm sure Eric told you about my hair in the printing press. The other part of it is that in my attempt to get my hair out, I got my finger caught. So he wanted to take me over to St. Vincent's to make sure nothing was broken, but I said I wasn't going to the hospital until I washed my hair. This was in the spring of 1970, and it was a June primary. I must have had some ability to handle people, so I started getting a little bit more responsibility. Then it became pretty clear that I could also deal with Bella. So I became what is known colloquially as the "body person." I would be in the car with Bella for most of the day—on the streets with her and at meetings. Her ability to talk in Yiddish, to work that community, her amazing memory for names and faces—that was really an important element.

Eric Hirschhorn During the campaign, I did whatever was asked. I wrote press releases. Peter Riegert and I took turns driving her around. He was the pickle man in *Crossing Delancey*, and he's been a character actor in a bunch of other movies.

Marilyn Marcosson There was a guy, Gerry Roe, a very senior executive at NBC, who designed and wrote a lot of Bella's stuff. He did the shopping bags that said, "Carry Bella Abzug to Congress," and the posters that said, "This Woman's Place Is in the House."

They said I won by forty thousand shopping bags.

Doug Ireland We also had a capacity to produce instant leaflets that were usually written by me and designed and printed in-house. They were tailored for campaigning in specific neighborhoods or at specific events. For example, because Little Italy was in our district, and because we were seeking the support of the Italian American Civil Rights League headed by Joe Colombo—

yes, the gangster—I wrote a special leaflet centered around Bella's opposition to Nixon's Omnibus Crime Bill. The headline was, "It's Not a Crime to Have an Italian Name."

Amy Swerdlow Bella knew my kids, but she didn't know them that well—we didn't socialize as a family. But once, when she's running for Congress the first time, she's in her headquarters and in walked Robbie, my soon-to-be son-in-law, and my daughter Joan—they had been gone for about a year on a kibbutz in Israel. Bella walks right up to them and starts talking to them in Hebrew. I don't even know how she could recognize them. She'd walk in the street and she would remember people. It was just amazing.

Susan Brownmiller At one point, she was doing something for us feminists, but before that she was doing something for another group, and to get her to our thing on time she said, "Come to my apartment," and she was asking me, "What's the issue?" while she was undressing. The amazing thing was that she was so girdled. I thought, "My God, look at how she's trying to stuff it like a sausage into this long brassiere-and-girdle combo."

One thing she never did accept about the new movement was that you should not be girdling yourself like that, and it was not good for her health. In fact when her health really did begin to fail, people did say, "Maybe what she did to her body was a contributing factor." She was forcing herself to wear shoes she shouldn't have worn, and she certainly was severely corseted. But she couldn't stop eating, and it was part of her oral enjoyment, the talking in front of a microphone and the eating, she loved that.

She was utterly unself-conscious, and probably just a bit of an exhibitionist. They all do that; it's like Lyndon Johnson, or the Kennedy brothers, they thought it was a great honor for you when they invited you in to see them change out of their outer garments and you got to see their inner garments.

Claire Reed I primarily did fund-raising for her, and when it became more widely known that she was running, celebrities started calling the office. They were always referred to me because we could use them for raising money.

Harold Holzer Bella has always had just tremendous contacts in the theatrical community. She's a hero to the community because of her work during the House on Un-American Activities Committee blacklisting, purges, trials. She represented people—Zero Mostel, Lee Grant, Tony Randall—who then stayed with her and campaigned with her. All these guys knew that she was there, representing them, their fighter and their advocate, and they never forgot her. There was this buzz in the theatrical community that went on to a new generation, so Renée Taylor and Joe Bologna, the young progressives, knew of that great history. They had it handed down from older actors.

Marilyn Marcosson There was a whole bunch of things. There was an art auction, where I actually bought a piece. There was the Barbra Streisand concert on the Upper West Side and "Broadway for Bella," which was one of the most astounding events in theatrical history as far as we were concerned—a Sunday night event at Madison Square Garden that would've made the Tony Awards look like nothing! The outpouring of support was just phenomenal.

Lesley Gore A speech is not unlike a performance. I used to watch Bella stand up, and they'd introduce her, and she'd thank the people that she had to thank, and you almost get the sense that she was kind of tired; you'd kind of think from her personality that she'd start out with a funny story—"a funny thing happened to me on my way to my hotel this morning," or something like that—and she didn't, she would start quite easily and begin to draw people in, and not very loud at first, either, very quietly. And at some point—maybe five or six minutes, ten minutes into her talk—something would happen. It was almost as if the switch went on, and you could almost see her fatigue melt away, you could see the years disappear from her face, and she became so involved with what she was saying, and communicating these thoughts, that suddenly the speech became alive as though she was actually singing a song that everyone knew and loved.

She was the consummate performer. There's that moment in a show, after you put it all out there, and you sort of know, "this is the time," and you still got to dig down a little deeper and really come up with the stuff.

Claire Reed The theater community was progressive and very supportive, and that's how I got Barbra Streisand's help. She had someone from her office call Bella. She had just bought a town house in the Seventies, somewhere off Madison, and I ran a fund-raiser there. And then we had her come to East Hampton in a very elegant area, so we got a lot of big names. Raising money for Bella was not that hard. We got Arthur's, which at the time was the in place. Cybil Burton, Richard Burton's wife, owned Arthur's. Burton Lane is a famous musical theater composer, and his wife, Lynn, was in Women Strike for Peace. For the Arthur's event, Burton got me every leading musical theater composer, and each played their own music and sang songs from all the shows. But along with all that fancy expensive stuff, there was also a fund-raiser at Katz's Delicatessen on the Lower East Side.

[March 28] I flew back to New York for the "Ball for Bella" fund-raiser at Katz's, which I approached with a great deal of reluctance. I

feel very self-conscious appearing at a function where money is being raised for me . . . I did begin to feel better after a little while, though, because the spirit in the place was just great. But I still can't get over the strange mixture of people who were there. Some who should have been . . . weren't, but others whom I would have least expected did come. Elliott Gould, whom I don't know very well, for instance . . . He looked strange, I thought, very scruffy, but I guess that's the acting field. I don't make judgments on it. It's just hard to relate to sometimes . . . But more than that, as Mary Perot Nichols of The Village Voice *commented, a slice of the community was there—Puerto Ricans, Jews, Chinese, Italians—even kids off the street, who wandered in and sampled the hot dogs.*

The setting was also a little bizarre. Izzy Tarowsky, who owns Katz's Delicatessen, closed the place to the public for the first time in eighty-three years, he said, so the party could be held. A sign he had made during World War II hung in glaring irony from the ceiling: "Send a Salami to Your Boys in the Army." Everybody was stuffing themselves with hot dogs, sauerkraut, pickles, french fries, and corned beef.

[April 2] I met [Barbra Streisand] in a restaurant during the campaign, when she came up to me and said she had a young son and wanted to do something for peace. She gave a fund-raising event for me in her new house in Manhattan, did a show and radio spots for me, and even came out on the streets and campaigned with me. "Ya betta win," she used to say. She was great, and I really feel indebted to her.

"How was the ball at Katz's?" she asked when I got her on the phone. "Sorry I couldn't make it."

"It was fine," I said, "but to tell you the truth, I felt a little funny about having Elliott [Gould, her husband; they're separated] as one of the hosts."

"Why?" she asked. "He's the father of my child."

"Well, I thought you'd kind of resent it."

"No, not at all. How was he?"

"Fine."

It's interesting: Elliott had also said he wanted to do something for the cause of peace and, like Barbra, said he couldn't think of a better way to do it than to help me.

Barbra Streisand I was happy to call Bella my friend and to work for her, appearing on a flatbed truck in the Manhattan district where I lived. She was outspoken and unconventional—two characteristics I deeply admire. Under that famous wide-brimmed hat was a woman of courage, charisma, and commitment to the battle for social justice.

Ronnie Eldridge Bella liked moving around in high circles. I used to make fun of her grass roots; we called them "the weeds."

Helene Savitzky Alexander At the Madison Square Garden affair, we were bombarded by that crazy Zionist group—the Jewish Defense League. We had a tremendous program and the JDL were picketing us outside the Felt Forum. Bella would say, "No arms for Israel. No planes," and they took that out of context. There was a big fight—my son fought with them. Bella never fought with them, but they were always there.

Jimmy Breslin The unfairness comes from people in the Jewish Defense League who have seized on part of a statement Bella made on radio one night, the sense of it being that she didn't see how anybody could rely on Phantom jets to settle Israel's problems when a political settlement was the only sane approach. The Jewish Defense League began to spread the story that Bella Abzug was against giving planes to Israel, and therefore she was against Israel and should be condemned.

"There she is in the purple dress, that's Bella Abzug, she's against Israel," a little guy from the Jewish Defense League began yelling at a rally on the East Side the other night.

Bella grabbed a young guy who had driven her to the meeting. "Hit that bastard in the mouth for me," she said. "I can't do it where people see me."

[T]he way people reacted you'd think I had suggested giving the country back to the Arabs or something. It was unbelievable! Fueled by the Jewish Defense League and Barry Farber, a tremendous smear campaign was launched against me. Up and down the Jewish neighborhoods, I was held responsible for, among other things, killing Jews in World War II. Boy, did they make me suffer for those words. Those lunatics from the JDL even went so far as to say that since I was a peacenik, I was anti-Israel. People got hysterical, really hysterical. No matter how much I tried to set things straight, the malice and viciousness spread until a lot of people were convinced that Bella Abzug was not only not a good pro-Israel Jew, but possibly anti-Semitic. It was terrible, and quite honestly, it hurt me so much at times that I broke down and cried.

Ed Koch I first met Bella Abzug in about 1968. I'd never heard of her before that. But in 1968 I was trying to get this nomination. She had formed something called the Seventeenth Peace Action Committee, and in that group there were basically the Women Strike for Peace group, and they were interviewing people, and I went to see them, and I remember going to her house, and she was there and Doug Ireland was there and a number of other people, and they asked my various positions, and my position on the war was a very good position from their point of view. I opposed the Vietnam War. But my positions on other things were not so good. They were for ending NATO. They were opposed to support of Israel's request for arms. At that time the big issue with respect to Israel was jets to Israel and the Communist line was opposed to it, and Bella Abzug was absolutely opposed to jets for Israel in 1968.

Doug Ireland Her candidacy for Congress the first time around came a year and a half after the riots at the Stonewall Inn in Greenwich Village, which marked the beginnings of the modern gay liberation movement, and there was a significant burgeoning activism by out-of-the-closet gay folks in New York City, who were moving into political activity. I persuaded Bella to take this seriously as a potential constituency—there wasn't any serious disagreement about that—and Bella was the first major electoral figure or candidate to actually go to the gay community and openly seek its votes. It was a rather extraordinary thing.

So we had her in Fire Island and in the gay bars. I put the Continental Baths on the schedule—at that time it was a very well-known cabaret as well as being a bathhouse. It's where Bette Midler got her start. I arranged for Bella to make a campaign appearance during the break in show time. So I was sitting in headquarters and Bella calls up and says, "You cretin. What have you done to me? I'm up here in these fucking baths—filled with guys in towels held up by Bella buttons and some are only wearing the buttons and not the towels!"

By this time we had already done a bar tour and people from the Gay Activist Alliance were active in her campaign. Bella was a veteran of the civil rights movement and had an instinctive response to the need for gay rights. Karl Marx once said, "Nothing human is alien to me." She had a radical interpretation of human rights and a respect for those who would fight for their own rights. When gay people stood up and said, "We're not gonna take it anymore," she understood that they were applying to their own human condition the lessons a lot of us had learned in the struggle for black civil rights. She didn't have much trouble grasping the concept that discrimination on the basis of one's identity, even if that identity was a sexual identity, was just as fundamental a problem of civil and human rights as being black or being female.

Ronnie Eldridge Bella had a receptionist who was this very tall African American woman with a deep voice, and one day I said to Bella, "You know, whatever-her-name-is is really a man, I'm sure." She said, "Don't be ridiculous." Anyway, it turns out that she was a man; Bella was remarkably naïve. She never, for instance, knew that Doug Ireland was gay, and Doug became her campaign manager. There was a whole big thing about it, with Doug. He got offended, I think. She had no idea about people's things around her.

Harold Holzer Bella won pretty handily—like 55 to 45 percent—so she ran a good race. And unseating a guy who has been there for fourteen years was not that easy. But the district was changing—less Lower East Side, more Village—and she made it very exciting.

Ronnie Eldridge Then in October, Larry Eldridge died, and she was incredible. She was at the house all the time. My mother became very jealous of her. She kept saying, "Isn't that woman ever going to give us a moment of peace?" She would arrive at the house while we were eating, and she'd be there the whole time. She was the one who discovered that Larry Eldridge's insurance had lapsed—the life insurance that I thought he had had all along—and my great awakening. But she went over everything, and she was a great help.

That was it. Then, of course, she wanted me to come to Washington, but I just couldn't. I had the three children, and I just couldn't do it; leaving the house and doing all of that. So she never quite got over that. She used to joke about it. But I think she really was serious.

But she was wonderful. She would take [my son] Danny to rallies down at the peace marches. She hired Danny one summer as her page, in Congress. When we got a second dog, the kids wanted to name her Bella. But Bella didn't like dogs and was very insulted at the idea, so we named the dog Bessie. It was a big white malamute. She kept saying, "Get that dog away from me." On my fortieth birthday, in January, I had a big birthday party. Somebody gave me two joints as a present, and I never really had smoked a joint. I'll never forget. She used to call me every night, to see how I was. One night she called, and she said, "You sound very mellow. Did you have a drink?" I said, "No. As a matter of fact, I'm smoking a joint." I was sitting in the middle of this double bed, smoking. She said, "Don't ever say that to me on the telephone!" and she hung up. She was always afraid people were listening in—always. When she'd come to the house, sometimes, and talk, we would have to go into the lavatory and she would run the water, so you wouldn't be able to hear. I don't know where that came from.

Doug Ireland We had just sweated bullets to get Bella elected the first time. And then, before the 1972 election, there was a redistricting based on the 1970 census and Bella was put into a congressional district with one of the leading lights of the Reform Democratic Movement, Congressman William Fitz Ryan. Even though there was more of her district in it than his, there was an effort to get her not to run because he had more seniority. Her politics were radical, whereas Bill Ryan was an old procedural liberal, although he played a very honorable role during his service in Congress, most notably in helping to abolish the House Un-American Activities Committee. But his best days were behind him—he was about to die of cancer.

Bella called me: "Now listen. These motherfuckers have put me in a district with Bill Ryan. And he is dying. But they're saying I have no right to run here, and you gotta come help me." I agreed with her that it was terribly important that she remain in Congress. The attacks on her were vicious. There was the traditional resistance of males to any strong woman. New York was still a heavily Jewish city; there were an awful lot of Jewish men who didn't like a Jewish woman representing them. But Bella was capable of great charm when she wanted to turn it on. She had a great sense of humor and an ample vocabulary of blue words and employed them with great frequency. She could laugh at a smutty story as well as a guy could.

I'm not running against Bill. I'm running to represent the people; the people desperately need representation. I have a mandate for that. In seventeen months I've become a national figure, and a national spokeswoman in and out of Congress. People need change.

Ralph Shapiro She was looked on as a carpetbagger, coming into that district. But look. If you want to do something, you do it. There's got to be a certain amount of ruthlessness.

Jerrold Nadler All the reform clubs in assembly districts with legislators in the older group supported Bill Ryan. We, the kids, supported Bella in '72. I remember thinking that I loved Bill Ryan, but if he left Congress what would we lose? Maybe a term because he was obviously ill and couldn't serve too much more. If we lost Bella we would lose a heck of a lot more, plus someone who at that point was a major national voice, which Bill Ryan wasn't. We were all supporting McGovern at this time, and the other group was futzing around with Lindsay. You'd be petitioning for the McGovern delegates, and you'd say, "Have you given any thought to Congress yet?" The smile would disappear, and the answer would be, "Bill Ryan," the tone being, "You want to make something of it?" And you'd say, "Thank you very much," and walk out of the building with thirty or forty signatures on the McGovern omnibus petition and two on the one for Bella if you were lucky. She got murdered in the primary.

Scott Stringer I first saw Bella on television, on primary night in 1970. My parents were at the local Democratic club, and I was watching election results with my grandmother. This woman comes on the screen, and my grandmother says, "You're related to her." "I am?" "Yeah, she's now gonna be in Congress." Then in 1972, the district was extended to our neighborhood, a very conservative community at the time. And I got involved in the Bella Abzug/Bill Ryan battle at the age of twelve. I went to the Dyckman Street office and we signed Impeach Nixon petitions and sold buttons and carried Bella shopping bags. It was very dicey, because Bill Ryan was such a hero, and my mother, even though she was related to Bella, had to support Ryan in the primary. Bella got so mad, she came to the local headquarters one day and said to me, "You don't have any family anymore. It's just me! You're the only good one!" So I went home and told my mother, "I hate you!"

Letty Cottin Pogrebin My husband, Bert, campaigned with Martin—in the Bronx, I think—and Martin would ring the bell and say, "Hi, we're here to talk about Bella Abzug," and Bert would say, "Tell them it's Martin Abzug." He said, "I don't want to do that because they'll think I'm biased."

Scott Stringer I spent so much time campaigning that my school told my father I wouldn't graduate sixth grade. I had to take a week off to make up all the homework assignments. That race was so defining for the West Side. *Life* magazine said it was "Left vs. Left." Then the primary results came in, and I went off to summer camp just crushed.

Claire Reed There was terrible hostility and animosity on the Upper West Side. People would not accept the fact that Ryan was dying, and he wouldn't admit to it. She might have just held back and waited, because she came on like a steamroller. People felt, "He's dying. Why are you doing this when he's denying it?"

Helene Savitzky Alexander It was one of the worst campaigns. Campaigning for her was murder. People spoke about it for a long time.

*There was a double standard applied against me. I ran not as a woman, but as a woman who challenges the establishment . . . Don't go too far away. We'll all be back together again continuing our fight.**

Ronnie Eldridge She had an episode where someone in the paper—I think it was the *Daily News*—accused her of having her mother on Medicaid, and milking the Medicaid system. Whenever she had a problem, she arrived at my house. I knew all her drivers, everybody. It didn't matter what time it was, and this happened to be very late. It was like at midnight that she arrived. She's sitting in the living room. We lived in the brownstone, it was the front window and the French doors were open. I guess it was a fall or spring evening. She's telling me about this series of things going on about her—her mother living in a kind of nursing-home situation—and the doorbell rings. It was our friend Arthur Schiff, who lived up the block. He was in charge of the Medicaid

*She is speaking to supporters after losing the primary.

program in the city at the time. He said, "I could hear on the street. I think you may need my advice."

Jerrold Nadler Ryan had throat cancer, and he could hardly talk. But about two weeks before the primary, a letter to the editor appeared in *The New York Times* signed by six doctors saying what a healthy, perfectly fit man he was. I remember going into shul on Yom Kippur and seeing the headline, "Bill Ryan Died." He died the day before Yom Kippur. So you then had a county committee meeting to select the nominee of the party for the general election.

Harold Holzer When Ryan died, you'd think that she would automatically get the Democratic nomination from the state committee, but no. Ryan's widow decided to run, and Al Blumenthal and the other West Siders decided to support her. That was a struggle.

Jerrold Nadler There were a bunch of candidates who had been reapportioned out. But it eventually came down to Bella and Priscilla Ryan. The Ryan people hated Bella. They were already saying she killed him—by putting him through this tough primary she hastened his death—and I'm sure people believe that to this day. Unlike some other political wives, Priscilla Ryan had not been terribly active politically, but there was a lot of support for her in the county committee. The district then included all of Washington Heights and Inwood and a piece of Riverdale. The district leader up there was a State Senate minority leader, Joe Zeretski. The female leader in his district was Arlene Stringer, Scott's* mother. She had gone into politics a decade before, supporting Bill Ryan against the old Tammany candi-

*As of this writing, Scott Stringer is Manhattan borough president.

dates. Arlene loyally supported Ryan and they delivered their district in the primary against Bella. But then, with the committee meeting coming up, she goes to Joe and says, "Joe, I'd like permission to get our county committee members to go for Bella." He looks at her and says, "Why would you want to do that?" She says, "Because we're first cousins." That he understood, and the entire old-line county committee block up there went for Bella against Priscilla Ryan because Arlene is Bella's cousin, and Joe Zeretski understood that and appreciated her loyalty in supporting Ryan as the incumbent in the primary. Bella gets elected in '72, and now there's no more feud on the West Side. It's sort of gone.

Claire Reed For the general election, the whole West Side got behind her. I used to walk with her, and truck drivers would yell, "Bella!" You'd think they would resent her, this big, brassy woman. But at some level, they understood that she was passionate for their interests.

Scott Stringer There would be a rally on the West Side starting at Seventy-second Street, and you'd move uptown and hit Zabar's. Bella would storm into the store. They'd stop promoting what's on sale and give her the store microphone. She'd announce, "I'm here. It's Bella!" The campaign would move on to another stop and they'd leave me on Seventy-ninth Street, which wasn't such a great neighborhood then, and I'd have to call my mother to pick me up.

I went to Susan Brownmiller, who was very progressive and who was a district leader at the time. I said, "Susan I want to talk to the radical feminists." She said, "Are you crazy?" I said, "What do you mean crazy? I'm running for office. I'm a feminist. I'm probably the only feminist that's going to run, in God knows how many years . . . I ex-

pect the feminist support." She said, "They will not support you." I said, "Why not?" "Well first of all," she said, "you wear lipstick." I said, "Well, look, I'm not changing that, for the radical feminists or anybody else. I'm fifty years old." She said, "That's the other thing. You'll have to tell them how old you are, and I'm sure you'll never tell them that." I said, "That's the craziest thing I've ever heard. I'm proud of it." . . . Then she said, "Well, you're going to tell them a key part of your campaign is the Vietnam War?" I said, "That's right." She said, "They don't give a damn about the Vietnam War, they only care about their rights; their individual rights, their abortion rights . . ." I said, "Listen, I can give them a feminist interpretation as to why they should be opposed to the war in Vietnam." This is the radical feminists.

Susan Brownmiller I knew her as head of Women Strike for Peace. She came to this incredibly volatile Second Congress to Unite Women—all the radical women's groups. She came in and spotted me and asked me, "What are the issues? I'm planning to run for Congress." She thought this was just another new constituency . . . She also said, "It's my fiftieth birthday." I told her that's what you have to tell the group. I was thirty-six. She was not happy, but she did it. She began by saying, "Today is my fiftieth birthday." She got it. She continued to get it, and so many women from the movement worked on that first campaign.

Jerrold Nadler We never conceived of her as a "feminist" candidate, we conceived of her as the Reform candidate, the Antiwar Candidate, the Left-wing Candidate, period. She was not elected because she was the feminist candidate, nor was she opposed because of that, it just wasn't there. After the election she suddenly sprouted this additional quality of her persona and everything else. Now, had she campaigned that way, whether it would have helped her for it, I don't know. It might not have helped on the Lower East Side.

Robin Morgan She came late to feminism. She used to say that she didn't really call herself a feminist until after she was in Congress. She saw herself as a champion on civil rights, and on poor people. Sure, women had it bad, too, but the big thing was peace and war. And then she was in office and visible. She began to get mail from women, saying speak out for us. So she found herself the voice of women. She was really honest about that.

Lifetime Documentary After Bella's official swearing in, inside the House of Representatives, Congresswoman Shirley Chisholm swore her in with a special oath outside, on the Capitol steps, attended by five hundred women. That very day, her first in Congress, Bella introduced a bill to end the war in Vietnam.

6

An Outsider on the Inside

Chronology

1971 On January 21, her first day in Congress, Bella introduces a motion calling for withdrawal of troops from Vietnam.

1971 With Shirley Chisholm, she introduces a comprehensive child care bill; it passes, but Nixon vetoes the eventual bill.

1971 On June 13, *The New York Times* begins to publish the Pentagon Papers, a top-secret report that revealed, among other things, that the government had deliberately enlarged the Vietnam War while President Lyndon B. Johnson had been promising not to escalate. Daniel Ellsberg, a former State Department official, was the source of the leak.

1971 Bella introduces a bill, which is enacted, to allow the use of "Ms." as a form of address in government documents so that women, like men, would not be identified according to marital status; she also introduces a clean-water bill.

1972 The Equal Rights Amendment passes through Congress and is sent to the states for ratification.

1972 Bella becomes the first member of Congress to call for President Richard M. Nixon's impeachment, introducing a resolution on May 9, following his decision to mine North Vietnamese harbors.

1972 Congress passes Title IX legislation, banning educational discrimination against girls and women; Bella then works with the Women's Equity Action League to write strong implementing regulations. Over the years, Title IX proves to have a dramatic impact on women's participation in sports.

1972 *Bella! Ms. Abzug Goes to Washington*, by Bella and Mel Ziegler, a diary of her first year in office, is published.

1973 Outraged that a U.S.-Soviet summit includes no mention of the conflict between the Arab states and Israel, Egypt and Syria attack Israel on October 6 across the Suez Canal and from the Golan Heights. The Syrians are pushed back, and, after a confrontation with Israeli tank divisions led by General Ariel Sharon, Egypt's president, Anwar Sadat, accepts the UN's October 22 call for a cease-fire.

1973 Congress passes the War Powers Resolution, which is intended to limit the president's power to wage war without congressional approval by requiring that U.S. armed forces be removed from hostilities if Congress has not authorized the use of force within sixty days.

When I first came to Congress, there was a display of surface politeness. Underneath, I believe, many members of Congress and the press regarded me as one would an alien from another planet. Yet later on, in a U.S. News and World Report *poll among my peers, I was found to be the third most influential member of the House.*

Edward M. Kennedy Bella was in the House of Representatives, and I was in the Senate. But she was bigger than just being a member of the House. Bella Abzug was a central figure in the politics of the country for twenty-five years—kind of a revolutionary.

Doug Ireland People forget how radical she was—that she had radical, left-wing, socialist politics and came out of a movement that was revolutionary. You know, one of her proudest things was the little scar that she had above her eyebrow that she got at the Peekskill riots in 1949—somebody threw a rock at her when the American Legion [and other groups] came to protest Paul Robeson's concert for the Civil Rights Congress* in Peekskill, New York.

Ronald Dellums It's one thing to be an activist. But it's another thing to be willing to take that level of activism to governance. And Bella was willing to step up to it. As progressive people, you have to get up every day and do your job with this view in mind. We've been jumping up and down for years about what ought to be. "Okay, Ron Dellums, Bella Abzug—we're gonna give you a chance; run the country. So what's your foreign policy?" You have to step up and be intellectually honest enough to put an alternative on the table. That's why I respected Bella, because she was willing to take her activism to another level. Everybody doesn't have to do that, but the people who are prepared to step up, I applaud, because that means taking on a whole other burden of responsibility.

Martha Baker When women are elected now, you're thinking, "Will they really do what they're supposed to do when they get

*A concert scheduled for August 27, 1949, in Peekskill, New York, by the legendary African American actor and singer Paul Robeson—who had been hauled before the House Un-American Activities Committee as a subversive—was cancelled when a mob including members of the KKK and the American Legion stoned the gathering. A week later Robeson returned along with some twenty-five thousand people, who heard him sing. However, people were stoned and beaten upon leaving the concert.

there?" Nobody thought for a minute that Bella wasn't going to speak out. We knew she was going to lay it out to them, and little by little she did.

My first resolution was to end the war in Vietnam. Rather than participate in the inauguration of President Nixon, I spoke at a counter-inaugural. I was the first to call for his impeachment—regularly. It took one year before the Congress and its Judiciary Committee did so, and only when President Nixon beheaded his own Justice Department and a million telegrams arrived to members of Congress did they move.

Ronald Dellums So this heavyset, very intelligent, aggressive, white woman from New York wins her election, and this tall skinny black guy from Berkeley wins his election, and we come together as the peaceniks.

Everything was going smoothly, because we embraced the same values that came out of our time. But our personal relationship got a little rocky at a certain point. Bella called a meeting in the anteroom right off the floor of the House, and for whatever reason, I was a few minutes late. So I turned this corner. There's this wonderful picture of Bella with her hat on, and she's lecturing all these males. They were almost up against the wall with their eyes kind of bugged, and you could tell immediately that they were absolutely intimidated. I'm trying to get around to where I can be part of whatever is going on, and Bella saw me. "You're late!" she said. "You'll be late to the God damned revolution!" And that so ticked me off, because punctuality is very significant to me. Going back to my childhood, it was a value instilled in me as a countermeasure to a stereotype. So when she said that, she unwittingly stepped into that history, that part of me. And I heard myself saying—I wanted to take it back immediately—"You white elitist!" I saw this look on her face that allowed me for a brief moment to see the very vulnerable part of this woman. I said to myself, "Oh, why did I say that?"

The moment passed, but later that day I got a call asking me to come to her office. So I went in to see her, and I was feeling a bit self-conscious. "Be in control, be disciplined," I was telling myself. She looked at me and she said, "There are too few of us. We have to be friends." I realized then she was hurt by what I had said. One of the things you learn growing up—in the 'hood, you know—is how to fight. I didn't think it through. If I had, I would have just allowed the moment to pass and we could have talked about it later. In one sense, I was happy that it happened. It allowed us to come together as friends. Not only were we colleagues and comrades in the struggle, as it were, but we became friends who respected each other. In conversation, she allowed me to visit the human side, the more gentle side of her.

[May 13] Mary Perot Nichols has printed some real political bullshit about me in this week's Village Voice. *She . . . says that I berated Ron Dellums "angrily" for not showing* [up], *and he told me, "Shut up! You white elite motherfucker."*

Well she wasn't there and she completely missed the point. Ron and I are very good friends, and we joke a lot. We have our disagreements—mostly in terms of approach—because he chooses to use Congress more as a platform, and I as both a platform and *a vehicle to get things done. Well, I was kidding him, see, and his comeback was purely a joke. There was nothing angry about it, Mary.*

Carmen Delgado Votaw I put an end to it the first time she acted up with me. I said, Listen, I don't take this kind of shit from anybody. So you mind your p's and q's when you address me. And I am very, very good in New York, so I can go and get you defeated. I will tell people that you called me a "spic." I told her that. She never in the rest of our relationship ever did anything.

She used to call me at one in the morning. I said are you charging this to your account, or are you charging it to me? Because if it's to me, I don't want to talk to you anymore. So I would always sort of come back at her, telling her what I disapproved of or what I didn't like.

Ed Koch Bella and I just disliked one another intensely, personally as well as politically. I think that Bella is a radical . . . I do not support radicalism, and I don't think it is good for the country, and I don't think it effectuates what we want, which is to remove the inequities without destroying the system . . . She is very smart, *very* smart. She has a lot of innovative ideas, which either come out of her own head or out of her staff or out of volunteers, and so she's had an impact there. Then there is her truck operation—I'm talking about her personally running over you . . . She bulldozes people. And then there is also a sweet side to her personality. She can be a charmer. But overall, . . . she is not as effective as the press would have you believe. Let me put it another way for you: there's always the feeling, and there's much to be said for its accuracy, that if Bella is for something, there's an automatic number who will be opposed to it . . . I would say there are at least thirty or forty people who have an intense dislike for her not in that ideologue category, who will not vote for something Bella is for.

Charles Rangel I remember Ed Koch standing at the door of the members coming in and he says, "Vote against this; it's Bella Abzug's." He would say, "She is not pro-Israel." Koch knew how to get attention, and Bella brought him a whole lot. If you pick a target which you think is unpopular, it enhances your popularity, so he did not mind at all being known as "the guy that doesn't like Bella."

Eric Hirschhorn In the beginning Bella wanted people on her staff who already knew the Hill. I wanted to go down to Washington with her, but she said, "No, that's not going to work out." So I took a job in Albany working for eight Democratic assemblymen who were completely in the dark about what their leadership was doing and needed someone to read all the bills and figure out where the dirt was hidden. I hadn't been there two weeks when I started getting calls from Bella. People say you could never quit Bella's staff—you always worked for her after you left. But you also worked for her before she hired you! "What about this? What about that? When can you come to Washington?" "Well, gee. I have this job," I said. "I'm committed until the end of the session." "This is more important." She wanted me to quit the job I took when she turned me down. At the end of the session, she said, "Can you start on Monday?" "No, I'm exhausted." "You'll come right away because the welfare bill is coming to the floor. You'll take a vacation in a while." I go down, walk in the office, put down my bags, and she said, "How should I vote on the rule?" I knew a little about welfare legislation because of my experience in Legal Services, but I didn't know what a rule was. I learned. Barney Frank, who was Mike Harrington's* AA [administrative assistant] at the time, was one of the people who showed me around the Hill.

After a few weeks I said I had made arrangements to take a vacation in September. "What is wrong with you?" Bella said. "There's a session in September." So I go back and talk to my friends and say, "Okay. I've rearranged it. I'm going to go during August." She said, "You are really something! You know we can't both be gone at the same time!" By then I had figured it out. I didn't say another word and took my vacation in August. Every

*Michael J. Harrington, representing a district north of Boston, served in Congress from 1969 through 1978. Barney Frank currently represents a congressional district south of Boston.

time she'd call for me, they'd say, "He's not here," and it worked out fine. I always tell people you should work on the Hill when you're young and stupid. Sometimes I'd go hide in another office. The neighboring congressman, Paul Sarbanes, would come in and say, "What are you doing here?" I'd say, "It's too hot down the hall."

Among Bella's colleagues were a dozen or so really serious antiwar Democrats: Shirley Chisholm and Bill Ryan of New York, Don Edwards and Ron Dellums of California, Father Robert Drinan and Mike Harrington of Massachusetts, Toby Moffett of Connecticut, Bob Eckhardt of Texas, John Conyers and Lou (Lucien) Nedzi of Michigan, and Jack (Jonathan) Bingham and Ben Rosenthal of New York. I guess it's not "PC" today, but we called them the Kamikaze Squad. "Set a date. Stop the bombing. Set a date. Stop the bombing." That's a lot of what I worked on.

Peace Protesters at the Capitol

Bella! Ms. Abzug Goes to Washington, by Bella Abzug and Mel Ziegler (New York: Saturday Review Press, 1972), is a journal of Bella's first year in office. In the segment excerpted below (from pages 136 to 148), she describes the Nixon administration's reaction to Vietnam War protesters in Washington, as Bella, members of her staff, and Parren Mitchell, a member of the Congressional Black Caucus, try to intervene.

[May 3, 1971] I went to my office, and as the morning progressed, word came that the cops were arresting everybody in sight, en masse, without any identification, without any charges, without any anything, and herding them off to a fenced-in football practice field near RFK Stadium, where they were being held without food, water, and

sanitation facilities. It was like the whole thing was finally coming apart.

I immediately decided I had to go to the stadium. Esther Newberg told me about a friend of hers by the name of Captain Dan, who does traffic reports from a helicopter for a Washington radio station. A few phone calls later, I was taking off in Captain Dan's flying machine.

I don't know what's the matter with me. I didn't think. As he started the helicopter going up, I suddenly got this very insecure feeling that I was about to fall out the door. I was terrified.

"I think I'd like to go down," I told Captain Dan. "I'm not going to lose my life over this." Then, as he was about to land the thing, I suddenly thought to myself, "Gee, what if this is the only way we can see what is happening?"

"Okay, Captain Dan," I said, dwelling on that thought, "I'll tell you what: let's try it again."

From the air, when I allowed myself to look, I saw quite a shocking scene. All these thousands of people in one large field on this raw and nasty day, wire and cops and soldiers all around them, and off in the distance, machinery and artillery. You wouldn't believe it.

When we landed near the stadium, my two LAs [legislative assistants], Judy Wolf and Nancy Stanley, met me and we walked together toward the gate, past an ominous line of cops and soldiers with bayonets. It was gruesome. When we got to the gate, I boomed, "Step aside, I'm Congresswoman Abzug, and I'm going to go inside." And, like the Red Sea parting, they stepped aside. The moment I walked in I was mobbed—literally. You know, "There's Bella . . . Bella baby . . . hey, Bella . . ."

Perhaps the most shocking thing of all is the number of people I spoke to who were doing nothing at all to warrant getting arrested. It's clear to me that anybody in the dragnet area who was not wearing a business suit was hauled in. People who just went out to move their cars. Students on their way to classes. People walking their dogs. One young man and young woman I spoke to were on their way to get *married. People who had merely brought food and thrown it over the fence for those inside were herded inside themselves. I saw old friends, Dr. Spock, Barbara Deming, Grace Paley,* members of my campaign staff—all of them arrested for no reason at all. It's very sad—like the Constitution has been suspended, and this stadium is a detention center, a concentration camp.*

When I left the stadium I went back to my office and started calling any and everybody I could think of: the Red Cross, the attorney general's office, Mayor Walter Washington's office, other congressmen. By this time more than seven thousand people had been arrested, a one-day record for the city—in fact, for the entire country—and I explained to the Red Cross that these people were being treated like cattle. You know what Mayor Washington's office told me? "We're working on it," they said. The liberals I spoke to—I can draw their replies into one composite: "Bella, cool down, at least it's not Chicago.† At least they're not breaking one head after another."

"You make me sick," I told each and every one of them.

Finally, later in the night, procedures were finally set up to formally "arrest" people after more than fifteen hours of illegal detention.

They had never been properly arrested. No charges had ever been filed. They were not informed of their legal rights. They were denied access to lawyers. They were not promptly arraigned—and as a last insult they were asked to forfeit collateral [paying ten dollars and entering a plea of guilty] in order to be released. Is there anybody who's going to tell me that the Constitution meant a damn thing to the government today?

I went over to the Coliseum with Congressman Parren Mitchell of Maryland when the demonstrators were being moved there. As Parren

*Dr. Benjamin Spock, the pediatrician and author; Barbara Deming, the feminist and nonviolent activist; and Grace Paley, the short-story writer and activist.

†A reference to the police riot at the 1968 Democratic National Convention.

and I got close to the arena we were stopped at gunpoint by a liquored-up cop who unhooked the safety catch on his gun and said to Parren, who was walking a little ahead of me, "Where do you think you're going?"

"I'm a congressman," he said.

"I don't care who the hell you are," he said.

I took Parren by the arm and said, "Look, let's forget it. We'll go around the other way."

[May 7, 1971] Did I tell you what Hugh Scott said this week? A reporter was pressing him about the conditions under which the kids were incarcerated and he said, "Nobody in the Democratic Party was down there except Bella Abzug. She's the only man in the House."*

Margot Polivy I was doing First Amendment, fairness, and equal-time cases at the FCC. But after the Nixon people came in, it wasn't someplace you wanted to be. Someone prodding me said, "What would you really want to do if you did something?" I said, "I think I'd like to work for somebody like Bella." So I sat down and wrote her a letter. It must have been a couple of months and I suddenly get a call from her office asking if I'd come in and talk to her. My appointment must have been about four in the afternoon, and my partner, Katrina, came with me and sat in the car, because there was nowhere to park. Bella's on the floor of the House, and after a while somebody says, "Why don't we walk over and meet her there." She came off the floor and we started to talk. Then she went back on. It must have been nine or so

*Hugh Scott was a Republican senator from Pennsylvania who opposed the war in Vietnam.

when we went back to her office. Finally at ten I said, "Look, I have to go downstairs." She said, "Well, if you have to go home." "No," I said, "but somebody's sitting in the car waiting for me, so I think I'd better tell her I haven't been abducted." "Oh," she said. "Should we get something to eat?" "Fine, where do you want to go?" "I don't know, anywhere," she said.

By this time everyone had gone, and I'm starving. So we go down to my car and she said, "What's that? I'm supposed to get into that?" I had the [Datsun] 240 Z, which is this little tiny car. Katrina gets out and climbs into the back, which is just a dent. Bella gets in, and I said, "You may as well come back to my house. We'll get something to eat." We got home, and Bella's sitting on the couch with my dog, Sinbad. She says, "Go away. Go away." I said, "Look, you gotta make peace with him. It's his house!" She always referred to him as the Rat Dog. We ate whatever was in the refrigerator, and she said, "Don't you have a little cookie?"

When we're finished I said, "Come on, I'll drive you home. Where do you live?" "Oh, I don't know." "Well, how am I going to get you home?" "Well," she said, "go down by the Longworth building and I'll recognize it if I see it. It's a big building." What can I tell you? God protects. We start cruising around. She said, "Well, I don't really live there, you know. I just come there occasionally." We go up M Street and down First Street. Finally she said, "That's it. Over there." She lived on G Street, in one of the big apartment houses that they had leveled South West to build. So she says, "Do you want the job?" We'd spent the entire time talking about the world, so I said, "What are you talking about?" "Do you want to be my AA?" I didn't even know what an administrative assistant did. "You just run my staff," she said. I told her I'd never worked on the Hill. "Oh, it doesn't matter." She gets out and goes into this building, and I'm hoping it's the right one. That's how I met Bella.

Shirley MacLaine Bella had a terrible fear of dogs. She was up at my place in Seattle, writing her book. I had two or three dogs and she was afraid to feed them. She was afraid to take them for walks. I'd say, "Bella, why?" "I'm a Jew," she'd say. "Jews are scared of dogs."

Margot Polivy She was great on strategy, but she didn't really have the patience to have it get from point A to point B. There was no reason that she should have. In fact, I think a lot of difficulties came from her trying to micromanage. But as far as vision was concerned, her vision was dead on. She had a very fine mind. She had a wonderful instinct. And she was a very, very talented strategist, which is why she needed all of us to run it for her and do all the detail work. Mim was the perfect Sancho Panza for her. Mim could translate this stuff for her. And it fit very well.

Mim Kelber She was a terrific legislator and she knew how to manipulate things. But all the speeches were written, mostly by me, from New York. We had some sort of thing where we could send it by wire.

Robin Morgan It's no exaggeration to say that they were the Elizabeth Cady Stanton and Susan B. Anthony of our time. Personally, I never fully realized just *how* challenging it had been for Mimmie to write speeches or statements for Bella—for years—until I tried it for the first time myself. I just about killed myself, draft after draft, revision after revision. Finally, Bella approved the text. "It's okay." She shrugged. "But it sure ain't Mimmie."

June Zeitlin Bella was well respected by the leadership, particularly the Democrats, but across the board people recognized her skills. It's hard to put your finger on it. For one, she was incredibly smart. And she did her homework in a way that I, personally, haven't seen that many public officials do their homework. She read everything. She knew everything—not only the substance but the procedure. When she first got to Congress, she had all these experts on procedure come and talk to her. Later in her life, she learned the UN procedure in the same way. She was a force that couldn't be ignored, because she had so much knowledge and she had these troops behind her.

[January 20, 1971] *As far as I can tell, there are very few experts on procedure in the House . . . I'm determined to become an expert on procedure, but unfortunately it takes time. The precedents haven't been compiled since 1936. They're all in the head of the parliamentarian, Lew Deschler. You've got to be creative, experienced, and know how to use the library to ferret out what you need.*

Koryne Horbal I spent a lot of time lobbying in Washington in the early 1970s, often with Carol Burris of the Women's Lobby. We would have lunch with Bella at the Capitol, and I remember her colleagues kept coming over to her, some of them her political opponents, asking for advice about how to get some amendment passed. And she would tell them, "First you do this," and so on. She'd help them whatever their political differences, I think as a matter of courtesy to a colleague.

[June 17, 1971] *Not only have I found ways to tie up the House, but I've just discovered a way to force it to act too. I found out how to get a resolution through committee and onto the floor, bypassing the Rules Committee, within seven days! It's called a "resolution of inquiry," and it is rarely used. In fact, it's only been used maybe a dozen times in this century, most recently in 1950 and 1965.*

Here's how it works: You write up the resolution and you can direct it to the president or a cabinet member, asking that they produce for Congress certain facts that exist with respect to a particular event or situation. The resolution is privileged—that's the amazing part about it—which means that it must be sent immediately to committee and reported out either favorably or unfavorably within seven working days. If it's passed in the House, the executive branch then has fifteen days to come up with whatever you're asking for, and even if it doesn't, it's a good way to force a debate.

It's a way of holding the government accountable, maybe the only way. In Britain the government has to come down in front of Parliament every day to explain its actions, but here the president never answers directly to Congress . . .

Now that I've discovered the resolution of inquiry I'm putting one together to demand the Pentagon Papers.

Margot Polivy Ron Dellums put the Pentagon Papers into the *Congressional Record*, which created a *huge* furor and a new rule in Congress that you couldn't put everything that you wanted to into the *Congressional Record*. Of course if it happened today he probably would have been impeached and sent to Guantánamo. But Bella was on the Government Ops Committee, and the only reason she didn't put them in was because she didn't want to irritate her committee chairman. She was pretty good about trying to maintain some civility. But I think she would have if Ron Dellums had not. At that point there was a pretty cohesive group of fairly active members of Congress who were very much involved with trying to end the war.

Every month or so, there was a major demonstration. Half the time all of downtown Washington reeked of tear gas. There were all kinds of famous people who were afraid that they weren't going to get arrested before the war was over, and they were desperate to do something. Carl Albert was the Speaker at the time, and he didn't want to arrest these liberals. He kept begging them to leave. All the Nobel Prize winners started to get arrested, and they didn't have jail space for them. They'd leave them at precincts. Of course, Bella was supposed to be their lawyer for everything. That's the way I spent my weekend evenings, bailing people out. People are funny when they get locked up. They freak out as soon as they lock the door. But some of them take it all in stride. Judy Collins came prepared. She must have had a couple of thousand bucks shoved in her bosom. She gives the desk sergeant money and says, "Why don't you go and buy pizza for everyone?"

Flo Kennedy* came to help get these people bailed out. Most of the way you got people out was simply by striking up a good relationship with the desk sergeant. Flo was a fine person, but she never met a desk sergeant that she wanted to have anything to do with. We made a deal one day. They would give us a little closet to do client interviews, and the deal was she would stay in the closet and interview people and I'd go talk to the desk sergeant. In particular, the Women Strike people expected Bella to provide for them, which she did. She gave her staff. Well, she also worked herself to the bone.

Charles Rangel It would seem to me that Cindy Sheehan† is a "Bella Abzug type"—even though she hasn't had the training that Bella had. But you don't have to lose a son to say murder is wrong, it's immoral, it's unconstitutional, it's against everything

*Florynce Rae Kennedy, who died at age eighty-four in 2000, was a New York feminist lawyer who represented civil rights leaders, such as H. Rap Brown, and fought for abortion rights. One of the first black women to graduate from Columbia Law School, she was Gloria Steinem's lecture partner in speaking tours around the country during the 1970s. She was instantly recognizable in her leather cowboy hat and was known for what Steinem called her verbal karate, one-liners such as "Freedom is like taking a bath: You got to keep doing it every day" and "It's interesting to speculate how it developed that in two of the most antifeminist institutions, the church and the law court, the men are wearing the dresses."

†The anti–Iraq War activist whose son, Casey Sheehan, was killed during his service in Iraq.

our country stands for. And one day someone will ask us, "Well, what were you doing or saying when all this was going on?"

Ronald Dellums The conventional wisdom among the Democrats who wanted to end the Vietnam War, whether they were antiwar or pro-peace, which are not necessarily the same, was embodied in the War Powers Act. The president as commander in chief could deploy troops if he perceived the United States in danger. But he would have to come to Congress within sixty days to report, and this legislation was an effort to get a handle on the president concerning the war. People were lining up in its support. So the gentleman from California, Mr. Dellums, is recognized by the chair and says, "I rise in opposition to the legislation on the grounds that the Constitution of the United States is very clear about Congress's prerogatives with respect to the declaration of war. This piece of legislation waters that down and muddies the water. If the president deploys troops on foreign soil, putting them in harm's way, how many of you would be prepared to stand up and oppose the president and demand an immediate withdrawal? What we're passing now is a permanent blow for the Tonkin resolution."* So I walk off the floor to the absolute rage of my darling Bella Abzug. It was only the second time we had a conflict, and she read me the riot act. Years later, when Bella was out of Congress, I was invited up to New York to give a speech, and Bella came. I hadn't seen her in quite a while. But I was very pleased to see her in the audience—I could find out what my former colleague, my buddy, someone that I respected intellectually and politically, thinks of what I'm saying. At the end she came up and said, "Ron! Let me tell you why I came. Remember your

*Following a 1964 attack by North Vietnamese gunboats on the destroyer USS *Maddox* in the Gulf of Tonkin, Congress passed a resolution granting the president authority to assist any Southeast Asian country whose government was in jeopardy. It provided Lyndon Johnson's justification for sending more American troops into Vietnam.

position on the War Powers Act?" "Yes, I'll never forget that, Bella." And she said, "I just came to tell you that you were right and I was wrong." And we hugged each other.

Marilyn Marcosson If she could, Bella would give the Speaker and Democratic leadership a vote when needed. The War Powers Resolution was a famous instance of that. It says in essence that the president has to go back to Congress if he's going to commit troops without a declaration of war. Bella voted against it when it first passed because she thought that committing troops without a declaration of war was not appropriate constitutionally. The resolution passes and Nixon vetoes it because he sees it as an impingement on his power. It comes back for a veto override. The chairman of the Foreign Relations Committee comes up and says, "Bella we need to override his veto. This is the first one we have a chance to override. Would you change your vote?" It was a way of getting at Nixon, and she gave the chairman her vote to override. That's unusual to see a switch like that, but she was strategic in how she did things. She had the ability to be both strategic and tactical in her relations with Congress.

If we are going to get anywhere, Congress has got to begin to reflect in its composition the great diversity of this country. Although women represent 53 percent of the electorate, there are only thirteen of us in Congress (twelve in the House; one in the Senate). The country has twenty-two million black citizens, and there are only a dozen black congressmen. There are no artists, intellectuals, scientists, mathematicians, creative writers, architects, Vietnam veterans, musicians, and not even any leaders of the labor movement on Capitol Hill. There are no young people. The average age of a congressman is 51.9 years, and a Senator, 56. Two-thirds of these people are lawyers, businessmen, or bankers. No wonder Congress is such a smug, incestuous, stagnant institution! It reeks of sameness.

Charles Rangel But you know, in the Congressional Black Caucus, we never saw the same support for blacks, as blacks commonly would always support women. I cannot think of anything kind that Shirley Chisholm had to say about the lack of support of white women when she ran for president, and she was in all of the movements: the black movement, the women's movement, and at times critical of the Congressional Black Caucus for not being more supportive of her candidacy. Yes, and I think the black community was kind of slow to get involved in the antiwar thing, too.

Ronald Dellums Here are these three incredibly strong women in Congress. Bella, brilliant, with a nonstop work ethic, a high-energy person with a lot of passion—and enough of an edge that you know you have to deal with it. And Shirley Chisholm had a number of the same characteristics. Their styles were different, but they felt very strongly about themselves. And here's [Congresswoman] Barbara Jordan, who in one moment during the Nixon impeachment catapults herself into history—almost with one speech, "The Constitution states . . ."* Those words were echoed around the world. All three of them had that very same thing, although they manifested it in different ways: "I'm here to be dealt with." Barbara Jordan once said to me, "Ron, I can walk in a room now, just do nothing but walk in a room, and get a standing ovation. You and I both know how much time it would require me to gain the power and influence that they already

*Barbara Jordan's influential opening statement at the televised House proceedings on the impeachment of President Nixon, July 25, 1974, reminded her Judiciary Committee colleagues of the constitutional basis for that action: "My faith in the Constitution is whole, it is complete, it is total. I am not going to sit here and be an idle spectator to the diminution, the subversion, the destruction of the Constitution." And later, "If the impeachment provision in the Constitution of the United States will not reach the offenses charged here, then perhaps that eighteenth-century Constitution should be abandoned to a twentieth-century paper shredder."

think I have." I was one of the people who knew that she would have greatly wanted to be appointed attorney general. And Shirley Chisholm went out there to run for president, which was such an audacious move that I just said, "Let me get on a plane and fly to New York and stand with this feisty woman." Across race and gender, she said, "Deal with me, as a human being." As Barbara Jordan did, and Bella. They got along with each other because they respected each other. Here are three incredibly strong women who could have butted heads, but they didn't. They were very different people, and they staked out different turf. But when they came together, they came supportive of each other.

Midge Costanza In 1967 I was elected a Democratic state committeewoman from Rochester, New York. And in 1972 there was a big meeting of all the women delegates from New York to the national convention. Don't ask me why we were separated, but that's where we were. And so I'm at my first meeting like a babe in the woods, and all this screaming is happening. I'm sitting next to this very attractive, stately, classy looking African American woman, and she turns to me and says, "Get up there and stop this noise." And I'm looking around and I'm looking at her, and I said, "Excuse me, are you talking to me?" (Which is I think where what's-his-name got that line for *Taxi Driver*.) So I go up there, and I said, "Oh, my God, what do I do?" And I scream into the mike, and everybody stops. I looked around, and then I looked at this woman, and it was almost like I was compelled to say something, and I said, "This really isn't getting us anywhere." And I said, "If everyone would speak one at a time, I betcha we'd even have something we could vote on." And everybody started to applaud. And I'm going back to my seat, and this big woman says to me, "Who told you to do that, kid?" I said, "That woman over there." And she said, "And who are you?" I said, "Midge

Costanza. I'm from Rochester, New York." "I'm Bella Abzug. It was a good thing you did." And I went and I sat down, and I turned to the woman next to me, and I said, "Wow! That was Bella Abzug." You know who the woman was next to me? Shirley Chisholm. So, that day I met two mountains. And there I was. Do you think I had any choice but to become an activist in human rights, in peace, in justice, and in feminism?

Nadine Hack I grew up in Brooklyn, and Shirley ran for Congress in Brooklyn. And I worked on Shirley's campaign, and I worked with Bella on Shirley's congressional campaign, which was 1968, and Bella's was 1970. I worked with a lot of civil rights activists, and I worked with a lot of women's rights activists, and there were many people in both movements who kind of sacrificed the other movement, because they always said, "Well, this is our movement, and that one comes second." But the two of them were just constant in their articulation that we cannot deal with these issues separately, they're inextricably connected, and we're going to be the stronger if we work in coalition. For me, it referenced back to the first wave, because I think that when the suffragists and the abolitionists worked together, that's when the movement was the strongest. When there was the split—and there was a real split, and a very conscious decision on the part of each of the movements to say, "No, we have to promote our movement"—those two movements lost momentum, each of them by their loss of the other. Shirley, Bella, and Gloria are the best proponents of the whole constellation of social justice issues. There are very few people who helped shape that as much as Shirley.

Shirley had the same quality of steely strength that Bella had, an unshakable, unstoppable, inner core. "I know who I am. I know what's right, and I will not be shaken. I will not be moved." She absolutely shared that trait, but it came in a different package. She was raised in the West Indies, where politeness and kindness and gentleness and respectfulness are very high qualities. So Shirley had been raised to have that kind of control, but she was no less determined. It just was, "I can push you really hard. I cannot yield, but I do not have to even raise my voice to do it. I can just stare you down."

Margot Polivy The women in Congress worked pretty well together, and we had a wonderful run of successes. We did Title IX. We did the Equal Rights Amendment, sent to the states for ratification. It was all easy because the right wing really hadn't yet mobilized. It was kind of a throwaway for the guys. In fact, they thought the ERA was a joke. "Hey, you want to have civil rights? Okay, let's give it to the women, too." NOW was very active, and then the National Women's Political Caucus people. It was like cutting butter. None of the men were feeling any pressure from home to oppose it. So, certainly, they'd go along. Patsy Mink* was Bella's best buddy. She never bailed out, which is more than can be said for some of the others. When she gave her word, she stuck with it.

Legislation to institute a universal child care program in this country is very high on my personal list of priorities. As a matter of fact, I've drawn up a bill and passed it on to Shirley Chisholm, who's now working on it and who will be its cosponsor, in which we ask for at least ten billion dollars for child care facilities by 1975.

Ten billion is a trifling amount when you consider that since the

*Patsy Mink, a Democrat from Hawaii, was a member of the House of Representatives from 1965 through 1976, when, like Bella, she made an unsuccessful bid for the Senate, and again from 1991 until her death, in 2002. A Japanese American, she was the first woman of color to serve in the U.S. Congress. She was a prime sponsor of the Title IX Amendment—for which Bella worked to write strong implementing regulations. After Mink's death, Congress renamed it The Patsy T. Mink Equal Opportunity in Education Act.

Second World War this country has spent more than one trillion dollars for military purposes alone. Ten billion is one-eighth of the annual military budget. Can you imagine that? We could have a universal child care program in this country for what it costs to maintain the military for a month and a half . . .

Shirley Chisholm and I introduced our own child care bill today, held a press conference on it, and testified before the Select Subcommittee on Education of the House Committee on Education and Labor. We've been waiting to do this for a long time, having been persuaded to wait by some other people who were trying to put together a broad coalition to get more support. But the bill these other people have come up with is short on emphasizing the needs of all women (it provides services mostly for the very poor), doesn't provide adequately for coverage in small communities, and doesn't specify how much money will be needed . . .

Our bill has some essential features: We provide for twenty-four-hour child care facilities; we give the parents a voice; we prohibit sex discrimination in the administration of the program; we clearly establish a formula for moving toward universally available child care, which is vital to make it possible for all women to function totally in society.

Ed Koch She's not well liked by the members of the [New York] delegation. Shirley Chisholm hates her, but Shirley Chisholm won't say it publicly. Shirley Chisholm will say to me, "Oh, that woman has no class . . . That woman is so vulgar."

Letty Cottin Pogrebin Bella came into a room like a lumberjack. Truly, there was just no missing her. This is not a nice thing, but I almost worried that if she lost weight, she'd lose that aura of occupying space in such an important way. The hat, the voice, the girth, and the way she walked into a room almost elbows out. It's an advantage over someone like Barbara Boxer, who is a small person. It's just a theory, but I've always felt Bella was very physically commanding. Like Gerry Ferraro isn't—but then Gerry has a swagger. It's like she's Queens, and Bella's the Bronx.

I will tell you all the diets I've been on, starting with Dr. Blakeley Donaldson, who believed that primitive humans survived on buffalo meat and wild berries and were better off than modern man. I ate meat for breakfast, meat for lunch, and meat for dinner. Then came Dr. Atkins, another carnivorous fellow. Then Weight Watchers, where I learned, "in every fat person there's a thin person seeking to come out." I even went to a guy who injected me with pregnant mare's urine—and, whatever the reason, that weight loss was the most effective.

I had total recall about when I began eating myself into a fat person—those sandwiches and candy bars during labor negotiations and nights in the night court—those tension-filled years during the McCarthy period and my two years in the South on the Willie McGee case—those great meals prepared by our housekeeper, Alice Williams—those furious days on the floor of the House of Representatives, where I ate junk food in the cloakroom to wipe out the bad taste of what was going on on the floor of the House and to seek some satisfaction for my frustrations.

Edward M. Kennedy We've seen the march for progress where we knocked down the walls of discrimination on race. We knocked them down on religious discrimination, and then we knocked down many on gender. And Bella Abzug carried that kind of emotion and feeling to knock down walls of discrimination and prejudice against women. She took this whole momentum—from the March on Washington and Dr. King, the work my brother Bob was involved in at the Justice Department with desegregating a lot of the universities—and she headed it in terms of women. That was very revolutionary. It doesn't appear so today. It seems almost self-evident. But it wasn't. She did it basically by force of personality. If you look at why things are achieved, it is leadership, and that really is personality. She understood very well the character of herself and played to that. She was unique. She was boisterous. She was stylish, flashy with her hats—all of which reinforced her personality, her presence. And she used her presence and enormous ability to move a cause—whether it was women's rights or ending the war.

7

Building a Political Women's Movement

Chronology

1971 Bella cofounds and serves as a cochair of the multipartisan National Women's Political Caucus, dedicated to increasing the number of women in elective office at all levels of government.

1972 The first issue of *Ms.* magazine appears.

1972 On the night of June 17, five burglars are arrested for breaking into Democratic National Committee headquarters at the Watergate complex in Washington.

1972 Shirley Chisholm runs for president; at the Democratic National Convention, which nominates George McGovern, women are 40 percent of the delegates. Frances (Sissy) Farenthold is second in the balloting for vice president. A *Ms.* cover features them—a black woman and a white woman together—as "The ticket that might have been." Some Southern newsstand owners refuse to display it.

1973 Senator Sam Ervin, a Democrat from North Carolina, opens Watergate hearings.

1973 The Supreme Court legalizes abortion, with *Roe v. Wade*.

1973 The tennis star Billie Jean King beats Bobby Riggs in the "Battle of the Sexes."

1973 U.S. troops withdraw from Vietnam; the war ends two years later, when South Vietnam capitulates.

1974 After some litigation, the Little League accepts girls as players.

Liz Carpenter My personal journey into the women's movement began on a July weekend in 1971, when the National Women's Political Caucus (NWPC) was born in the Statler Hotel in Washington, D.C. Life would have been easier if I had not gotten so deeply involved. But I would have missed out on so much.

I got a phone call from the writer Shana Alexander, an old friend from *Life* magazine, saying, "Betty Friedan thinks the feminist movement has gone as far as it can go until it gets some political clout behind it. You know more about politics than anyone I know. Will you talk to her if she calls?"

"Sure," I said. "I'll talk to her, though I haven't even read her book. Tell her to call."

She did, about ten minutes later, spouting forth in the rapid staccato that is Betty's native tongue, about the need to elect more women, the need to pass legislation that would help women work, the desperate need to make Congress aware of all of the inequities the working woman faces. I was impressed with Betty's sharp mind and intense focus. Finally she said, "There's going to be a meeting next weekend with a core group on the Hill. All the women's organizations will be represented there. Three congresswomen, Bella Abzug of New York, Shirley Chisholm of New York, and Patsy Mink of Hawaii, and, of course, Gloria Steinem. I hope you'll be there, too."

"Can I bring my daughter, Christy?" I asked.

"Sure," she said . . .

We were a mixed group, with our different backgrounds

sometimes putting us at cross purposes. The Business and Professional Women's Club wanted an Equal Rights Amendment out of Congress and ratified after forty-seven years of foot-dragging. The peace seekers, the Women's League for Peace and Freedom, wanted to be represented at the peace tables; there were lots of "Make Love Not War" buttons around. The NOW group was already pushing abortion, and the League of Women Voters and AAUW [American Association of University Women] were more genteel in their approaches, but not moving fast enough. It was an exciting kaleidoscope of the sounds and fury of women. Bella was the hostess, making sure everyone had coffee and sweet rolls.

We all introduced ourselves. I said I had covered the Hill for sixteen years and worked in the White House for Lyndon and Lady Bird Johnson for the past five. I could feel—maybe it was my imagination—a cold resentment when I talked about LBJ, and as time went on, I felt it even more, except from the black women, who let me know they were his friends.

At the end of that day we set the date for another meeting a few months later. People were on the phone all the time, and a small group of us kept meeting in grimy offices, wherever we could find space. There was a growing tension between Betty on the one side, and Bella and Gloria on the other.

Betty, having energized the women's movement with her book, was understandably possessive. Bella, whose clout as congresswoman from New York gave us all greater entrée and a podium, was unyielding in her own strong beliefs. Gloria, softer-spoken and conscious of her large following among young women throughout the country, was equally unrelenting in her position that the women's movement had to embrace every female issue.

It was a period of all chiefs and no Indians—except, perhaps, for Shana, who needlepointed her way through it all like

Madame Defarge, and me, who knew that each woman there was needed for different constituencies and different public appeals. All of them brought something, but Betty felt that Bella and Gloria were "separatists" and "anti-men," narrowing the movement with the radical chic clichés of the time. She saw the movement more as part of the general drive for equality and civil rights.

"They talk so . . . well, strong," I said once to Shana, dismayed at the shouting and dissension.

She calmly continued on her pillow cover and said quite matter-of-factly, "These are strong times."*

Eleanor Smeal Liz Carpenter was a miracle woman. I asked her, how are you getting this press? Because the caucus meeting was front page all over the country, and there was so much press there. Liz said, "Press releases don't do anything. I'm using every chit I ever had in the White House, that's how we're getting it." She told me that press was really personal relationships. There were a lot of the characters there that you got to know of afterwards—like Ann Richards—but Bella was key in that meeting.

Eileen Shanahan There was a famous story about that . . . They summoned this meeting . . . The most visible leaders were Bella Abzug and Betty Friedan and Gloria Steinem and Shirley Chisholm. They sat in a row up front . . . And I covered it . . . I wrote the story for the Sunday [*New York Times*] saying two hundred women had assembled in Washington determined to start a movement that would find half of the public offices in the country filled by women. This is one of these "God, she is on our side" things. There wasn't another item of significant news in the

*Liz Carpenter tells much the same story at greater length in her book *Getting Better All the Time* (New York: Simon and Schuster, 1986).

world for that Sunday paper. It was just about the slowest news day anybody ever saw. And the consequence was that my story not only ran at the top of the front page, there was . . . a picture taking up close to half of the top part of the page—of those four I have just named. If there had been any other news to put on the front page, I might have gotten a lower left-hand corner, if that.

Alice Cohan It's the spring of '71. I was a student at American University at the time. And got involved in helping to plan this convention that was going to take place in the summer here to form the National Women's Political Caucus. At that convention this friend of mine and I ran for the steering committee, and we formed the Youth Caucus. Then there was an Older Women's Caucus and the Prime of Life Caucus. They were like in their thirties and forties, and they came and negotiated with us, the Youth Caucus, saying if we supported them, they'd support us.

Then two women came into our caucus. And I'll never forget it. This woman dressed in a blue polyester pantsuit was Ellie [Smeal]. And they started telling us that we were going to get screwed by the Prime of Life Caucus, and that they really weren't dealing with us fairly. We listened a little bit, and then we kicked them out because they were over thirty, clearly. They were right. We got screwed.

Eleanor Smeal It was the first national conference that I went to in the women's movement. There was a fight between Bella, Shirley Chisholm, and Betty Friedan. And Gloria was the peacemaker, of course. I was just a kid, and I didn't know very many people. I would sit back and watch this fight going on, and I couldn't figure out what the hell to do about it. Because it was like beyond those of us who were sort of newcomers and young;

we could see it going on but we didn't know what to do. I kept thinking they all wanted to run for Senate. A lot of us thought that. We said, my God, why do they all have to be in New York? And clearly Bella was far more in control. Betty didn't stand a chance.

I remember Gloria didn't want dues. And those of us who had been in NOW wanted dues, because we kept saying, how do you measure if you're a member or not. And they put through dues very low, the compromise was like five dollars or something like that. But then the real donnybrook also occurs on whether men could join or not. And they make it so that men cannot join but they can be supported as candidates. I was on the other side. I mean it was the dumbest thing, we won't take your money but you can give them support. It made no sense to me. I wanted it to be that they couldn't support men candidates but they could take their money.

The other major fight was, was it going to be bipartisan, Republican and Democratic chairs. And I was opposed to that, too, because I wanted it to be just feminists. I didn't care whether they were Democrats or Republicans, but they had to be feminists first. But anyway, that loses too. And they become Democratic and Republican chairs.

It was a wonderful convention, and I was so excited. I had spent my whole whatever years interested in politics. And there was going to be a women's political movement.

Joanne Edgar The older women dominating the meeting—they weren't that old, of course, but over thirty-five and older than me—seemed to pay more attention to the structure of the organization, who was going to sit on the policy council, than the issues. Betty Friedan, in particular, was afraid that emphasizing strong feminist issues would turn away the more conservative Republican women. I wrote an article at the time for the *Man-*

hattan Tribune, the West Side paper Harold Holzer edited, and I complained that the meeting's final statement concluded only that "NWPC-backed candidates must oppose 'sexism, racism, violence and poverty.' " Actually, today that sounds pretty progressive. Right after the meeting, UPI quoted William P. Rogers, Richard Nixon's secretary of state, commenting on a photo of Bella, Betty, Gloria Steinem, and Patsy Mink as "a burlesque." Nixon replied, "What's wrong with that?"

Fannie Lou Hamer If you think about hooking up with all these women of all different colors and all the minority hooking on with the majority of women of voting strength in this country, we would become one hell of a majority.*

Shirley Chisholm Fannie and I attempted in a very assertive manner to tell the ladies that they had to pay attention to the concerns of women of color . . . Many of the ladies were quite surprised at what we had to say . . . They were stuck on the word 'sisters,' and they thought we were all sisters. What we were saying is that sisters had different agendas. It was a revelation to some of those women . . . But they knew, or someone behind the scenes told them, that if they expected to start a women's organization, they should have Fannie Lou Hamer and Shirley Chisholm there. We were both known to be fearless.

Margot Polivy With the founding of the caucus, there was a new avenue for everybody to express themselves. And of course there was the question of bipartisanship—how to find acceptable Republicans, or willing ones. But all in all, at least for a couple of years, it worked well. Afterward it started to get institutionalized. There were a lot of people who, like Bella, would have liked to

*She is addressing the founding meeting of the NWPC.

use it as a platform. There was nothing wrong with that. It was just that a lot of people wanted to be on the same platform. But I think Bella would look at that as one of her more significant achievements.

Bella and Betty—that relationship was intense. They disliked each other very much. It predated the Women's Movement. They punched each other's buttons pretty well. Betty had a bad temper, and one night at Liz Carpenter's house she was on me about something Bella had done, I can't even remember what it was. She picked up a lamp to throw it at me. I said, "I'm out of here. I'm not part of this fight." Liz couldn't believe it, and Liz always wanted everything to be nice. There were a lot of egos in the same place. It wasn't just Betty and Bella. And Gloria always wanted things to be nice.

Letty Cottin Pogrebin I got included in the caucus because of Betty Friedan, which was the weirdest moment of my little trajectory into feminism. I had published *How to Make It in a Man's World* and got involved in Bella's campaign. I got recruited to do the Working Woman column for the *Ladies' Home Journal.* That spring of '71, the column appeared. I get a call from Betty Friedan, out of the blue, saying—she was very gruff—"I like how you write. I need you to come to a meeting." I went up to her apartment, on Ninety-fifth Street, I think. She had a garden apartment. We were all given assignments, and told that we were going to Washington for a meeting in July. Now, I never leave Fire Island in the summer. But it was Betty Friedan summoning me. I had always admired Gloria from afar but I had never met her. So I go down there and I'm like Betty's person. And then it was time to write the statement of purpose, and for some reason I'm in there with Gloria. We pulled an all-nighter, and we worked together on the statement. Once that happened I just kind of moved into Gloria's realm, and Bella and Gloria were always together. I don't remember what the conflicts were about, but I would assume it had to do with a lesbian plank, but it might have been about supporting any woman for office, or was it choice? I mostly remember at some point signing onto whatever was Gloria and Bella's version. Betty was very angry. It was a betrayal, but I can't say things I don't believe. And her strategy was to universalize in a way that flattened out differences about important issues.

What a time it was! Growing up I always envied people who'd lived through the thirties. Now I think people today should envy any of us who lived through the early seventies. It was such a time of hope and possibility, and ferment, and progress, and change, and media attention, and brilliant activist women everywhere you turned.

Betty Friedan We were lucky. We lived at a critical point in history, and so what we did hit the wave of history just right. If it made changes far more than we'd ever dreamed of, it was because there had been no precedent for it—a revolution without a single shot being fired. I miss Bella. We might have gone in slightly different directions, but she was a vital force. When we were on the same side, which we usually were, she was a very good partner, very alive. It was sort of a love/hate relationship. God, you'd think there wasn't room for two of us, but it turned out there was.

Gloria Steinem Between July, when the caucus was founded, and August, when the Democratic National Convention opened in Miami, there was no time to organize women delegates and alternates state by state. But they responded to what they had heard about the NWPC and came to our meetings each morning. We did not know them and they did not know us. Thanks to Bella, all these women who had not strategized together before and were doing it on the spot became a force to be dealt with. It was really a Cecil B. DeMille moment on Bella's part.

Midge Costanza Bella ran everything behind the scenes at the convention—for women. And it was nothing to be up all night for two and three days in a row, because we had to mimeograph everything. I was the one who had to run around delivering all the papers to everyone who was going to vote the next day. We had to get these things out, and Bella was the captain. She was telling us all what to do. And she was the most brilliant strategist I have ever met. She would plan how we would get microphone time the next day. She would plan who would speak. And she would plan how and when we would vote on the floor, and whether or not we would disrupt it.

Marlo Thomas I had just finished *That Girl* in 1971, and found the freedom of having time to give after so many years of doing the television show. I had found my political voice through feminism and through candidates. I had campaigned for Bobby Kennedy. I ran on the McGovern slate in California and got to the '72 convention. I knew Gloria already, and Bella. I was part of the group screaming at Gary Hart when he wanted to dump abortion. We were trying to get him to change his mind. Bella was organizing things.

Shirley MacLaine I was a movie person, and I wasn't supposed to have a brain in my head. But George McGovern appointed Bella and me the two heads of the women's part of his 1972 presidential campaign. I was running a lot of stuff out of my apartment, and the dirty tricksters from Nixon would come in and enter the drawers and trash. They never stole anything. I think Bella wondered what was I doing heading up anything. That was how she felt about me. And that hurt my feelings a little bit because I was on a consciousness-raising learning curve. Then at the convention in Miami, the right to abortion was not included in the platform so it had to be voted on as a minority plank. And George McGovern and Frank Mankiewicz and the rest of them didn't want to do anything to enrage anybody. So I got up and said vote your conscience. Bella was furious.

Marlo Thomas When McGovern dropped abortion off of the platform, and I saw Bella that night take after someone involved in that decision, she was so angry and so eloquent. It was breathtaking. And it was the first time I ever saw Gloria cry. She lost it. But Bella stayed in there and really tried to get them to change their minds.

Alice Cohan By the Democratic National Convention in New York in 1976, when Jimmy Carter was nominated, there was a women's caucus with an agenda, and there really was discussion of issues—not just a show like conventions today. We brought forward a plank to change the rules of the conventions to have equal representation of women and men. My recollection is that Bella didn't think we could get it. She was more into trying to negotiate with the Democratic leadership.

Eleanor Smeal There was a committee trying to reform the bylaws of the Democratic Party to move gradually toward equal representation, and National Women's Political Caucus leaders—Millie Jeffrey* and others—were involved. They were making a report, and a handful of us thought, "Gee. This is a great women's plank. Why don't we move on it now." At the begin-

*A UAW activist and president of the NWPC from 1977 to 1979; as director of the union's Women's Bureau in 1944, she was the first woman to head a UAW department. Awarded the Presidential Medal of Freedom in 2000, she died in 2004.

ning, it was a small caucus, maybe about sixty people; and we began to get momentum. Bella thought we were pushing too far but that with this kind of pressure, we could negotiate something. She could at least get in the door. The rest of us didn't even know there was a door. We were just rabble-rousing, keeping it up at every caucus meeting. People on the floor are trying to make motions, but now others are screaming, "Point of order."

At one point a women-of-color crowd that had planned to make a motion got so mad they charged the podium. They were convinced it was racist that they weren't being called on. In the midst of all this, Bella realizes it is total bedlam. She stands up at the mike, and with a booming voice says she will negotiate a settlement that feminists and all Democrats will vote for. She chooses the door farthest away from the mike where she's standing and makes this dramatic exit, followed by Millie Jeffrey and others on the committee. And now—because they don't know what else to do—everybody is cheering. I think the Carter people were totally traumatized. Bella exits, and they get an agreement that there will be fifty-fifty in the 1980 convention. Carter gives his word. Bella helped engineer that, obviously, and we were the rabble that had caused the showdown. We win equal representation for women, and minorities get a huge role in the Democratic Party.

Eileen Shanahan When I look back on it, there's a verse of poetry that comes to me—Wordsworth. He was talking about the early days of the French Revolution, before it became a bloodbath. "Bliss was it in that dawn to be alive. But to be young was very heaven." Well I wasn't young. In 1971 I would have been forty-seven. And it was bliss for me, too . . . To see those possibilities and to be involved in covering it, in many respects it was the happiest experience I ever had as a reporter, not primarily, though partly, because I saw something happening that I believed was good—good for individuals and good for the nation and maybe even good for the world if it spread that far. It was the people I was coming to know . . . I always kept a certain distance, which you must do as a reporter—but coming to know people like Betty Friedan and Bella Abzug and Gloria Steinem and Shirley Chisholm and . . . Jill Ruckelshaus, who was the great Republican leader in that group, and the younger ones as well. It was just such a pleasure. They were so smart and so full of vitality. But they were also for the most part very human people, even Bella in her bulldozer way, who could get angry and yell at you for very little reason.

8

Becoming a Legislative Force in Congress

Chronology

1973 As a member of the Public Works Committee, Bella pulls in multimillions to serve her New York district, including financing the curb cut for wheelchair (and baby carriage) access (Interstate Transfer Amendment; 1973 Federal Aid Highway Act).

1974 The House Judiciary Committee, including Representatives Elizabeth Holtzman, a Democrat from New York, and Barbara Jordan, a Democrat from Texas, adopts three articles of impeachment against President Nixon; he resigns on August 9, and Vice President Gerald Ford is sworn in as president. Over Bella's objection, President Ford pardons Nixon.

1974 Bella coauthors the Privacy Act and the Freedom of Information Amendments to require government agencies to open their operations and records to public scrutiny.

1974 Golda Meir finishes her five-year term as prime minister of Israel.

1974 Bella writes the first law banning discrimination against women in obtaining credit, loans, and mortgages—the Equal Credit Opportunity Act.

1975 Bella introduces the first national gay rights bill, to have the 1964 Civil Rights Act extended to gays and lesbians.

1975 Bella introduces legislation to authorize and fund International Women's Year meetings in all fifty states, leading up to the National Women's Conference in Houston.

Eileen Shanahan I am horrified at the degree to which today younger women, feminist women, do not know what an effective member of the House of Representatives [Bella] was. The male view . . . that she just stood up and screamed and antagonized everybody and accomplished nothing is just absolutely false. She did stand up and yell a bit and she could in fact be harsh on her staff and had a lot of high staff turnover. Ed Koch . . . was in the House at the same time she was and had an equally high staff turnover and nobody ever wrote word one about it. Bella did yell at people a lot. But she also was effective and, within the House leadership, known to be effective.

There's a long hallway that runs the whole very considerable length of the House of Representatives chamber. It's called the Speaker's Lobby. A friend of mine was walking along with [then majority leader] Tip O'Neill. And Bella was walking a few paces in front of them. And he said to my friend, "You know, I kind of like that woman."

Edward M. Kennedy She had a rather interesting relationship with Tip O'Neill, because I think Tip couldn't understand her, couldn't read her, couldn't figure her out, but he admired the fact that she could get things done, and she was feisty, and she was a power, she understood power. Both of us invited her to come up and speak at our Democratic dinner up at the Crane Estate, which is north of Boston; it's a lovely, lovely old estate up there.

We flew up and it was *hot*, like you couldn't believe it, and this plane's slow; it must have taken us three hours to fly up, and she just started telling stories about her youth, and it was the one time that you saw this enormously sensitive, kind of a loving, feeling, young girl, young woman. And Tip started to talk, telling about how he mowed lawns to get into Boston College, and about the problems that they had at the time of the Depression. I'll always remember that trip up there as one of the important memories in my political life, and remember the two of them really sort of giant personalities, giant political leaders, different traditions but having the exchanges, the conversation, and the humor. I never looked at Bella Abzug again the same; this was a gentle, thoughtful, considerate person with wonderful feelings and emotions.

Eileen Shanahan Bella was one of the people behind the equality-in-credit legislation. But there was something more than legislation. There were things that she believed—and she was right—could be done by the Federal Reserve as a matter of bank regulation. They didn't really need a law to tell banks that they had to cut out this unequal treatment of women and just look at the economics of a given loan applicant, an economic decision. Bella called the chairman of the Federal Reserve at that time, Arthur Burns, a brilliant man, but one of the most high-handed, arrogant people I've ever known, who would just brush aside anyone—pretty much regardless of gender—who disagreed with him on anything . . . Anyway, she requested that he come up to meet with her and some other people on this issue of credit for women. I will say I had a very good source inside the Fed at that time, a young woman economist who was telling me what was happening behind the scenes, which is how I know about this.

Burns went up there expecting to meet with Bella and "some screamers from NOW" was the way my source put it. Instead, she had—I forget how many women there were in the House at that time. If there were sixteen, she had fourteen of them there. And he walks into this room and she took him around the room saying "I would like you to meet Congresswoman So-and-So and Congresswoman So-and-So," until he realized that she had virtually all the women members of Congress there. I guess there weren't any in the Senate at that time. And they were all saying to him, "You get those regulations fixed." And it worked.

Ed Koch Bella, [Ben] Rosenthal, and I went to Israel on a special trip in November of 1973 . . . On this trip she did something that both Rosenthal and I thought was an outrage. What was it? All of us visited Golda Meir in Jerusalem; [she] was complaining that the Syrians had committed more atrocities and took out pictures showing Israeli [soldiers] killed after they'd been taken prisoner with their hands tied behind their backs . . . It was a tragedy, a tremendous tragedy . . . It's considered protocol that whatever a delegation learns on a trip, [they announce it together] when it comes back, especially if the people are of the same philosophical bent. Well, when we leave Golda Meir, Bella lingers and doesn't come out for another ten minutes. I store that in my head. I wasn't sure what she was doing, but I was sure that it wasn't for any good that would come out of it. When we get back to Washington, Bella . . . calls up Rosenthal and she says, "Let's have a press conference tomorrow on the atrocities . . ." And he says, "Fine." But then he reads in the paper [the next morning that] she's already had her press conference in which she takes out the pictures . . . that she had gone back to get from Golda Meir . . . Rosenthal was so angry . . . he was yelling, "That beast of Buchenwald!" That's how he referred to her . . . A little while later—and this happened throughout our careers . . . she came over and said, "Listen, I don't know why we are constantly fighting with one another. There are only three people in this whole delegation who work—me, Rosenthal, and you." That's of the thirty-nine members of the delegation, she's talking about.

Stanley Pottinger When I was director of the Office for Civil Rights [OCR] at the Department of Health, Education, and Welfare [1970–1973] my office, along with the rest of the world, discovered affirmative action.

When Ann Scott and AAUW [American Association of University Women] and others discovered what was happening with minorities in unions, they figured there was no reason not to turn Executive Order 11246* into an engine on behalf of women in colleges and universities as well. (In those days, to be accepted by male faculties you had to put your gray hair in a bun—leaving many wisps uncaptured—wear large flowered dresses, and wipe your nose on the back of your hand. And, of course, you had to be so brilliant in your field that you couldn't be denied.)

Because OCR was the enforcement agency at HEW, it fell to my office to enforce the executive order. Soon after we started talking to university administrators, the program became a bitter pill for higher-ed institutions everywhere, including in the heart of American liberalism, New York City. The New York congressional delegation got so many complaints from Columbia, NYU, CUNY, and others that Manny Cellar, the dean of the delegation, called a special hearing to investigate the "excesses" of the Office for Civil Rights.

As director, I was the guy in the hot seat. Cellar chaired the session, which went pretty much as expected, with the congressmen making speeches for the record against affirmative action

*Executive Order 11246, for equal employment opportunity, originally signed by Lyndon Johnson in 1965 and later amended, prohibited government contractors from discriminating and required that they implement affirmative-action plans.

(well, not quite—they were for it in principle, but against it if it was effective) and the "harassment" of their higher-ed constituents by our office.

I was getting beat up pretty badly, as I recall. After explaining that women were covered by the executive order (a given with the delegation), and after trying to explain why the federal government of the United States had a point of view on the value of women on higher-education faculties (not a given), I was slugging it out with someone on the dais when a colleague leaned over to me and whispered, "I think your ship just came in."

I turned around and saw Bella striding toward her seat on the dais. After listening to one of her colleagues—but not long—she launched her attack. Part of it was against the federal government for not having an adequate point of view on the value of women on higher-education faculties, but a lot of it was reserved for her colleagues on the New York delegation.

All I remember is that once she got there, the whole game changed. She must have had three, maybe four colleagues that day whining, complaining, and bickering about how affirmative action was ruining higher education as we knew it (which was not an incorrect observation, considering that, to some extent, that was the objective). But, as she did in all situations, she not only held her own but gave it back big and ended up on the winning side. It was fun to watch and be a part of, actually.

Marilyn Marcosson Bella was like the congresswoman for every woman in the world. And she also had this incredible ability to work. The joke of the office was that she would pick up *The New York Times*, see a story that was of interest to her, see another Congress member's name on it, and say in her street voice to me or Eric or Margot, whoever was there, "Why didn't you think of this?" Which is the perfect unanswerable question. And each of us had a different way of reacting to that and handling her. I brought a kind of equanimity to the job of AA. Margot was more of a yeller than I was. Bella would get equally as angry over some atrocity in Vietnam as the fact that she got a white-meat turkey sandwich when she asked for dark. But her anger wasn't at the person who was getting the brunt of it, so it didn't bother me. And what she wanted were reasonable things, in my opinion. It wasn't outrageous. I could learn to anticipate them.

Our general work pattern was that she'd come in Monday afternoon, and she'd leave on Thursday for New York. And because she was staying at a motel for most of the time, her idea of working late was to work until ten to eleven. One night we're getting ready to leave—it's ten-thirty, quarter to eleven—and I'm going to drop her off at her motel. I pick up the phone and she overhears me arranging a date that's going to start at eleven. So she goes into her Jewish mother mode. "What are you doing?" "I'm having a date." "At this hour?" I said, "Bella, when else can I go out?" "Who is he? What does he do? Where did you meet him?" "Well, he works for AP and he's working the night desk, so he's off work now, too." I have to find people who work nights. She gets all this, and then she laughs as we get into the car and says, "You don't have to come in too early tomorrow."

The work was just extraordinarily important. I always say, "I worked for Bella for two and a half years and got five years experience." The Skyline Motel was on South Capitol Street; she always had a room that had a view of the Capitol. She'd wake up in the morning, open the curtains, and she'd say, "What are those bastards gonna try to do to me today." So she had that fighting spirit all the time.

Ed Koch [Once when] Congress stayed [in session] on a Saturday, a lot of people went home on Friday, and Bella was one of them. I stayed over and [Saturday morning] at nine o'clock there's a telephone call. You have to understand, Bella doesn't talk to me.

But it's Bella at the other end. She knew I'd be there because I'm always in the office early. With her very distinctive voice: "Hello, Ed." "Hi, Bella." "Ed, I forgot my hat. Could you bring up my hat?" I said, "Of course, Bella." And the staff roared, because who else would she trust to bring up her hat? I brought up her hat, carried it on the goddamn plane in a box, very careful, brought it to my house and Martin picked it up.

Outside of Martin and the kids, I don't feel very related to most people at this point. On the surface I appear to be very involved in a lot of social relationships. But that's just not the case, because inside I'm not relating to anybody. I find it all a strain and an interference. I feel detached in social situations. I'm always thinking about other things, about Congress, about the issues, about the political coalition I'm trying to organize. It never leaves me. I even have trouble relating to some of my closest friends, though God knows I still love them, even if they don't know it.

Pat Schroeder When I was elected to Congress in 1972, it was big national news, and because my kids were so young, all my friends started saying, "How are you going to do this?" It was a transitional time. Progressives were saying that women could choose to have a career or choose to raise a family, but they weren't yet saying you could have both at the same time. So I got a call from Bella, and I thought, "Oh, she is going to be a good support." And she was wonderful. She said, "This is really great." But then she said, "I hear you got young kids. I don't think you can do the job!" And I'm like, "Oh no! That's not what I need from you!"

Geraldine Ferraro Bella did things differently from the way I did. She was a highly intelligent, highly effective person. But she was thwarted every inch of the way by a lot of the members of Congress. With Bella, you either loved her or you hated her. She was up-front and honest: "Here's who I am." There were these stories about how she wanted to swim, and there were these men like Mario Biaggi, who used the pool a lot and they all used to swim naked. She got there and said, "I want to swim." They said, "We swim naked." And she said, "I'm still gonna swim!" So rather than have Bella observe them, they put on bathing suits. They all got elected the same way. Every single member of Congress represents the same number of people no matter how long you've been there. His job was no more important than hers. When I got there, the same thing happened to me. They said, "You know, we swim nude." And I said, "That's alright. I swim with one hand over my eyes." Barbara Boxer, all of the women swim now, a practice that started early, thanks to Bella. It sounds like a silly little thing, but it's not. It's a matter of respect within that very small community of members of Congress. "Don't tell me that I'm a lesser person than you and I can't use the facility." She made it very obvious that she was not going to be treated like a lesser member.

Margot Polivy One of the funniest conversations we ever had was when Jim Crawford—he did all the veterans affairs stuff—decided to resign from the staff. He was also a major purveyor of recreational drugs for everyone in the surrounding area. Bella didn't know anything about it. She would be horrified. She was the biggest prig the world's ever seen. Jim announced that he was leaving. And she said, "What do you mean you're leaving? What are you gonna do?" He said he was going to farm. "What? You're gonna farm!" Jim had beautiful blue eyes, which Bella was a complete sucker for. She really just liked having him around to look at, aside from the fact that he was very good. Jim said that's what he wanted to do. She said, "Farm! You mean with dirt? Why would anyone want to do that?" We must have sat there for two hours while she tried to bully him. She really couldn't conceive that you wouldn't want to keep doing what you were doing. But Jim Crawford actually did farm. He started a truck farm and brought produce into Washington every week. His kids still run it, and I see him occasionally. He still has blue eyes.

Amy Swerdlow Bella was very accepting of lesbianism—but she's also a prude. She'd say, "I don't want to hear what they do."

New York Post Rep. Bella Abzug insists that she has no objection to poking fun at a political figure—so long as the satirist saves his jokes for the policies and not the figure.

Along with others who attended the Inner Circle's annual dinner at the New York Hilton over the weekend, Mrs. Abzug was still upset today over a skit that lampooned the women's liberation movement while taking some heavy-handed swipes at her physical proportions.

The Manhattan Democrat was reportedly so shaken by the mockery that she began to cry and had to be restrained by her husband, Martin, from leaving her table.

"It was absolutely one of the most offensive, vicious characterizations I've ever seen," said Saul Rudes, a lawyer who had invited the Abzugs to the $100-a-plate affair, which gives city political reporters a chance to spoof local officials.

The Abzug skit surprised many in the audience, especially since it was the first time the Inner Circle, present and former City Hall reporters, had allowed women officials to sit as guests on the main floor. Wives and other women had to watch the show from the balcony seats assigned to them by long tradition.

The congresswoman's tears were brought on by a skit in which *Daily News* reporter Tom Poster, by no means a small or slender man, padded his front and posterior and wore a large, floppy hat, a yellow satin blouse, and a vivid floral-patterned skirt. The get-up was for Poster's song, "When I Just Wear My Hat," sung to the tune of "When I Just Wear My Smile."

Just before the number there was some imaginary dialogue between Mayor Lindsay and Mrs. Abzug that went like this:

Lindsay: "I stole two elections but how the hell did you win?"

Bella: "I have broad-based support and something else."

Then came the song, which went, in part:

> I guess I've never been the high-fashioned kind.
> Mother Nature gave me a big behind.
> Whenever I go, I know I won't fall flat.
> When I just wear my hat . . .
> Oh, I'm filled with jubilation.
> For Women's Liberation—
> We rang our liberty bell.
> We'll burn a bra and girdle,
> But dammit there's one hurdle:
> When we take them off
> We all look like hell.

I worked late again . . . and then rushed uptown to have my hair done for a dinner given by the Inner Circle Press Club in New York . . . I wasn't particularly excited about going. Ronnie Eldridge had heard that I was going to be lampooned and Saul Rudes . . . insisted that it was only proper for me to attend. Little did I know . . . the Inner Circle has a long tradition of being a sexist organization and there were only a few women like myself who were allowed to sit on the main floor . . . I really hate to go into the details of what happened once the skits began, because I was subjected to a great deal of humiliation by a group of men engaging in megalomania or male-omania, if there is such a word. What they did and said was vicious and repulsive and disgusting and vulgar, a product of their Playboy *mentalities.*

After the song somebody came out in a white apron with frills and he was depicted as "Mrs." Martin Abzug, which was probably the most vicious thing they did all night.

Whereas I'm perfectly willing to receive political *criticism, satire, jousting, spoofing, lampooning, and whatever, and I get it all the time, what these guys did was very crude and in poor taste. To make an attack on a woman's figure or physical appearance is to make an attack on all women . . . None of the men were lampooned for the way* they *look. Everybody else was satirized in terms of what they stand for and what they believe in. But I as a woman was considered fair game to be ridiculed for what I* look *like.*

Gloria Steinem In 1973 Al Goldstein, a pornographer who published a tabloid called *Screw*, was harassing the staff of the then-new Ms. magazine. He did this in all kinds of ways; for example, advertising an oral sex service with our phone number. What we heard when we picked up the phone was pretty depressing.

One day, just before my birthday, I left the office to discover a special birthday present from Al Goldstein. On the newsstand outside our building was a display of *Screw* hung open to show its centerfold, a graphic nude drawing of a woman with my face, sunglasses, and long hair. Down the side of the page were drawings of diverse penises and testicles, and at the top was the headline "Pin the Cock on the Feminist." I knew this issue of *Screw* couldn't last forever, so I decided to wait it out. But Goldstein made sure I learned that he was planning a glossy color poster of the centerfold, something that could stay around for years. When I asked Nancy Wechsler, Ms.'s publishing lawyer, what to do, she suggested sending him a lawyer's letter. After all, the poster was for profit, nothing that could be protected as editorial comment, so the notice of a lawsuit might make Goldstein think twice.

Soon, his answer arrived at my desk. It was a box of chocolates with a note that said, "Eat It."

(*left*) Bella Savitsky, circa 1930, growing up in the Bronx; (*above*) with her father, Emanuel, and mother, Esther, her greatest supporter; (*below*) her grandfather, Wolf Tanklefksy, teaches her Hebrew and takes her to synagogue. (Courtesy of Eve and Liz Abzug)

A lifelong athlete, Bella is featured on the cover of her Zionist camp brochure and (*below*) with sister campers.
(Courtesy of Eve and Liz Abzug)

lla, student council president, wears a hat; so es Eleanor Roosevelt. The first lady would ake two appearances at Hunter College during e 1941–42 school year. (Courtesy of Eve and Liz zug)

Vacationing in Florida, 1942, where she meets Martin: "Our first date was a pickup." (Courtesy of Eve and Liz Abzug)

Bella and Martin marry in 1944. (Courtesy of Eve and Liz Abzug)

(*above*) Women Strike for Peace rabble-rouser in the 1960s; (*right*) by 1975, Bella is a member of Congress but still pickets for peace outside the White House (with aide Lee Novick). (© Dorothy Marder)

August 26, 1970, Women's Strike for Equality: on the fiftieth anniversary of women's suffrage, Bella addresses a rally in Bryant Park in New York after fifty thousand marchers take over Fifth Avenue. (© Bettye Lane)

With congressional colleagues. Left to right: Barbara Jordan, Bella, Martha Griffiths, Yvonne Brathwaite Burke, Margaret Heckler, Lindy Boggs, and Patsy Mink. Griffiths, Heckler, and Mink are among the women already serving when Bella takes her seat in 1971; Jordan, Burke, Boggs, and others join them in 1973. (Courtesy of Eve and Liz Abzug)

The Women's Seder, using a feminist Haggadah written by Esther Broner, begins in 1976 and becomes an important tradition. Left to right: Lily Rivlin, Phyllis Chesler, Bella, and Letty Cottin Pogrebin hold the "sacred schmata." (© Joan Roth)

Bella at play: pitching ace for the “Mad Hatter’s Batters,” her staff’s softball team (© Ed Starr); carrying on her family’s musical heritage, 1976 (© New York Daily News); celebrating her birthday, 1977—a dance with Shirley MacLaine (© Joan Roth); skating at Rockefeller Center, 1982 (© New York Daily News)

(*top*) House majority leader Tip O'Neill (later House speaker) makes Bella a deputy whip (Courtesy of Eve and Liz Abzug); (*bottom*) in 1976 he supports her bid for the Senate (© New York Daily News)

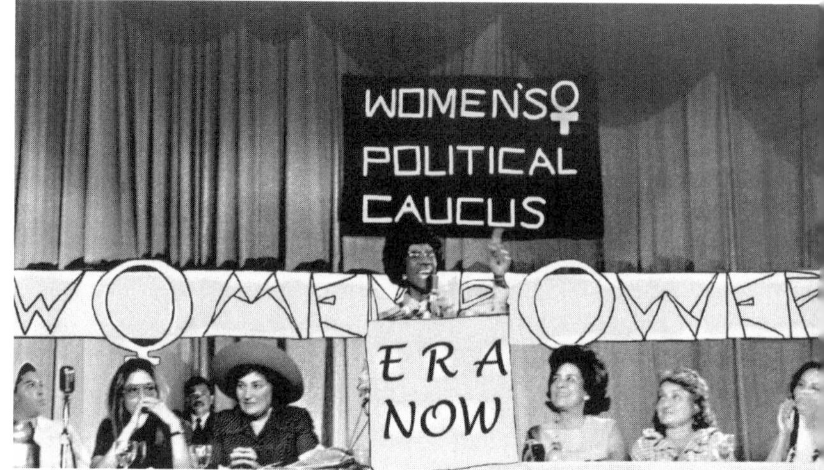

1972: early meeting of the National Women's Political Caucus. Left to right: C. DeLo
Tucker, Gloria Steinem, Bella, Shirley Chisholm (speaking), Gracia Molina de Pi
Betty Friedan, and LaDonna Harris (© Bettye Lane)

Fact-finding mission in Cambodia, 1975 (Columbia University Rare Book and Manuscript Library)

77: Bella tosses her hat in the ring for mayor of New York City (© Bettye Lane)

n the campaign trail in the streets of New York, 1977 mayoral primary (© Joan Roth)

Campaign buttons: mayoral race (with Bellamy running for city council president and Eldridge running for Manhattan borough president); Senate race, 1976; Houston National Women's Conference, 1977

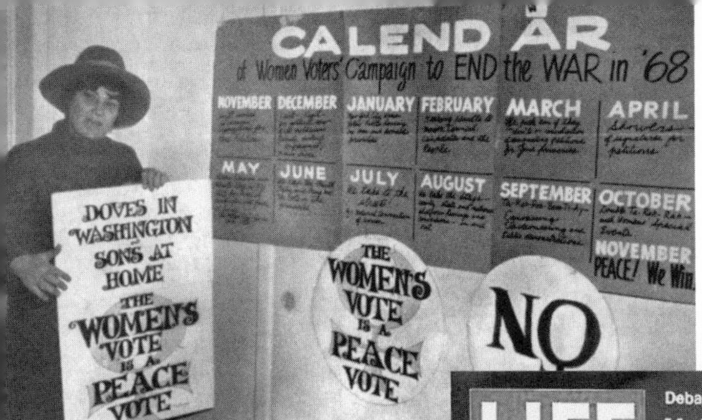

ɔmen Strike for Peace, *Memo*, Novem-
ɾ 1967; cover treatment: *Life*, June 8, 72; Ms., February 1973; *Rolling Stone*, :tober 6, 1977. *Rolling Stone* commis- ned this Warhol silk screen for an issue ırking its move to New York City. ımped by a cover on Elvis's death, it ap- ars on the day Bella loses the primary for ıyor of New York.

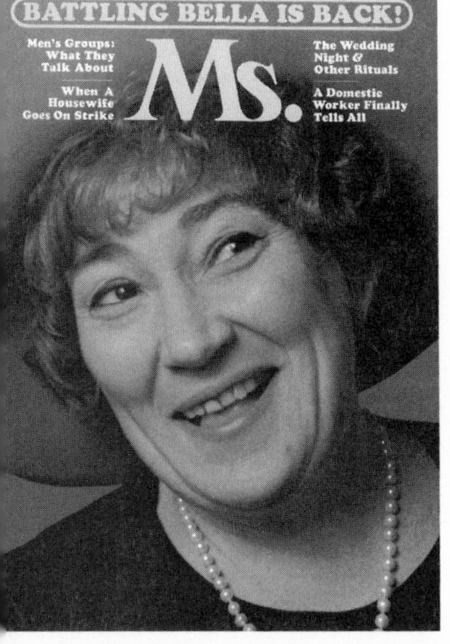

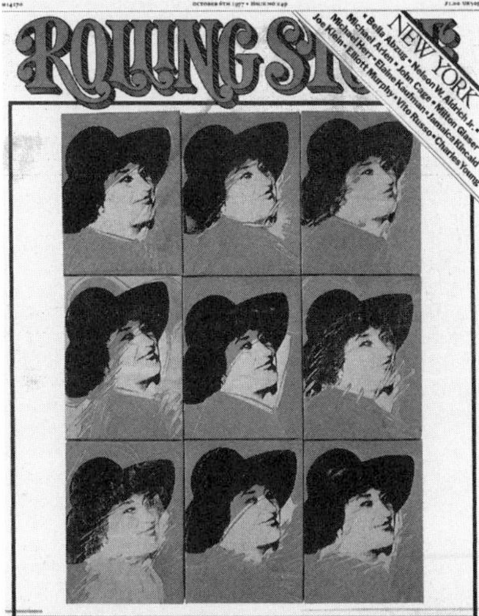

The torch arrives in Houston, 1977. Left to right: Billie Jean King, Susan B. Anthony (grandniece of the suffragist), Bella; torch carriers Sylvia Ortiz, Peggy Kokernot, and Michele Cearcy; and Betty Friedan (© Bettye Lane)

First Ladies, present and past, at the Houston First Plenary Session, November 19, 1977. Left to right: Lady Bird Johnson, Rosalynn Carter, and Betty Ford, with conference presiding officer Bella Abzug (© Joan Roth)

"Friday Night Massacre" press conference, January 1979: President Carter fires Bella as cochair of the National Advisory Committee for Women, and her cochair and other members resign in protest. Behind Bella (left to right): Carolyn Reed, Jean O'Leary, Mim Kelber, Brownie Ledbetter, and Koryne Horbal (© Ann Chwatsky)

August 1979, with Gloria Steinem in a rowboat in Central Park, launching Women USA's anti-inflation campaign (© Bettmann/CORBIS)

The astronaut Sally Ride, with Bella and Martin, celebrates Gloria Steinem's fiftieth birthday at the Waldorf-Astoria in 1984; Joanne Edgar in background (© Robin Platzer)

In the years following Martin's death in 1986, daughters Eve (left) and Liz lend support (© New York Daily News)

With her older sister, Helene Alexander, pianist, teacher, and occasional campaign caterer, 1990 (Courtesy of Eve and Liz Abzug)

With friend and fellow traveler Faye Wattleton, 1990s (Courtesy of Faye Wattleton)

Uncharacteristically hatless, 1990s (© Joan Roth)

UN conference in Beijing, 1995. From left: Wangari Maathai, Devaki Jain, and Susan Davis with a wheelchair-bound Bella (© Joan Roth)

Labor Day, 1997: Bella goes public with her legendary Marlene Dietrich impersonation, under Lesley Gore's direction. (Courtesy of Lesley Gore)

Somehow, this was the last straw. It left me feeling hopeless and vulnerable. On the way to a benefit with Bella, she sensed my mood and asked me what was wrong. I told her the whole long saga, and was surprised to discover that I didn't get much sympathy from her at all.

"You don't understand," I said, "it's a nude centerfold in full labial detail—and it has my face and head."

"And my labia," Bella deadpanned.

I burst out laughing.

Marilyn Marcosson Bella had an amazing level of intensity—and the ability to organize and get people to do things. That's why they made her a deputy whip. She understood better than most that you give and you get. So when she went on the Public Works Committee, she was in hog heaven. She could be very good at trading votes. The whole program where you could turn in highway money to get mass transit was one of her things. You know all the sidewalk curbs that were cut into ramps for the handicapped? That came from Bella and the Public Works Committee.

Charles Rangel In Washington, you become an expert with your own committee, and the personalities on the committee. And you could be just as ignorant as an outsider as to how some other committee operates; really committees operate so much on the personality of the chair. So much of legislation is personality, and the support—how you can persuade someone to help you, because you know you'll be able to help them, or, in my case, how helping the city of New York helps all urban communities that have the same problems, and so you know who to go to.

Jerrold Nadler Bella was a brilliant congresswoman. She had really good legislative skills. The Interstate Transfer Amendment was one of her great accomplishments. In those days we were still building the interstate highway system, with an act that passed under Eisenhower in 1955. The Congress made a map. "We're going to build Highway 95 here, and 83 there," and so forth. And the Congress would revisit that map every two years. You'd add things to the map, you'd take things off the map, whatever. And for every segment, there would be a cost estimate. In New York, we had the Westway project that was supposed to take the West Side Highway from the Battery to Forty-second Street and turn it into an interstate, which means lots of lanes. Not only that, it was also this huge real estate boondoggle with like six hundred acres of landfill, lots of new high-rises—and a park. Whenever you want to build something, you'd say, "They'll build a park next to it." This was the number one priority of the governor, the mayor, and we on the West Side were all opposed to it for a lot of different reasons. And the environmentalists were opposed to it. There was this epic struggle.

She was the only Democrat from New York, I think, on the Transportation Committee—then it was Public Works; it's now Transportation and Infrastructure, and I'm on it. In other state delegations, everybody wants to be on the committee to bring the pork home, but in New York, people are not interested for a lot of political reasons. For New York City Democrats, the glamorous thing to be on was education and labor and things like that. But the transportation committee controls a lot of money, and she understood that.

Marilyn Marcosson The Public Works Committee was going to schedule hearings, and Bella went to the staff director and said, "You gotta have hearings in New York." It was a way to help get more money for the city. When they came for the hearings, she and Martin and the chairman of the Public Works Committee, a guy from Alabama, and his wife went to see *Hello, Dolly*. She took them backstage to meet Carol Channing, who was an old friend. Years later the chairman would still talk about how they met Carol Channing. She was good at working with her peers.

Jerrold Nadler With the 1973 Highway Bill, what the Interstate Transfer Amendment did was fantastic. Her amendment said that if a city or state had a segment of highway mapped and budgeted, but not yet built, they could petition Washington saying we don't want this anymore, and the amount of money would be given to the city for transportation in the corridor of that highway. So this meant that you had Westway budgeted for two billion dollars at that point, and you could say, "Never mind. Give us two billion dollars to upgrade the subway system." Now she passed that amendment quietly, with no great fuss. For another ten years that was one of the big weapons we had against Westway. We said, "Trade it in." We said, "Would you rather have a highway here that the local people don't want, or go out and buy more subway cars for Queens, and Brooklyn, and Manhattan so everybody benefits?" Eventually it was a victorious argument. By its terms the Interstate Transfer Amendment expired in the late eighties. When we won the battle against Westway, we traded it in just before the deadline and got the two billion dollars—590 million of which was spent to build the current route 9A from the Battery to Forty-second Street, and the rest of which went to the capital budget for the city subway system and helped repair the whole subway system. The trade-in had worked for thirty-one states and cities before that. We were the last one before it expired. This was at a time, remember, when the highway lobby wanted to pave over the whole country. People were just starting to recognize that maybe you should build a light-rail system instead of a highway. It worked all over the country. I remember it as an example of something of major importance that didn't get a lot of publicity at the time. It was a legislative step rather than a broad statement of principle, but she saw the opportunity. She did a lot of things like that. That's the one I happen to know about.

Eric Hirschhorn I left the Hill in the middle of 1973 to work for a law firm in New York. Of course, I still was doing a lot of Nixon impeachment stuff for Bella—I was doing it all long distance. Then I came back in September 1975 to be chief counsel on the subcommittee on government information and individual rights. We did the Sunshine Act and had oversight over the Privacy Act and the Freedom of Information Act. We did some high-profile intelligence investigations that were an echo of what Frank Church was doing in the Senate.* It turned out that the communications companies were simply saving copies of everybody's cables and handing them over to the FBI every night. They'd come in with a basket and take them away. It was before listening got as sophisticated as it is today, where it's all done by computers.

Edward M. Kennedy I worked in particular with Bella on one piece of legislation, which is not unimportant. It was the Freedom of Information Act,† which is the basis of much of the information that the ACLU has gotten recently on detainees in Guantánamo. We got it passed [after overriding President Ford's veto]. She understood the whole penchant for secrecy that is so evident today and the importance of open government. These are themes that rise and fall in different periods of our history, and

*A Senate committee named for its chairman, Senator Frank Church, a Democrat from Idaho, was created in 1975 to investigate the domestic surveillance activity of the FBI and other federal intelligence agencies. Among other things, the hearings resulted in restricting guidelines issued by the attorney general, which, in the wake of September 11, were substantially altered and loosened by Attorney General John Ashcroft in 2002.

†First passed in 1966, the FOIA was strengthened in 1974, after the Watergate scandal, to force greater compliance by federal agencies.

she understood it at that time. Of course, she was the first to call for Nixon's impeachment, but the broader issue is about openness in government, and how people are going to be able to see how government can function. This was a passion that she had. If we got an openness in government, that was truth to power. But if you had secretive government, you were going to have trouble breaking through the abuses of government in power. Even as a freshman congressperson, Bella knew the rules, knew how to try and move a system that doesn't move, and still doesn't move. She stirred the House in such a way to push her view, irritate, antagonize, cajole, persuade, inspire, and lead.

Bill Moyers In 1974 President Gerald Ford's chief of staff, one Donald Rumsfeld, and his deputy chief of staff, one Dick Cheney, talked the president out of signing amendments that would have put stronger teeth in the Freedom of Information Act. As members of the House of Representatives, Congressman Rumsfeld actually cosponsored the act and Congressman Ford voted for it. But then Richard Nixon was sent scuttling from the White House in disgrace after the secrets of Watergate came spilling out. Rumsfeld and Cheney wanted no more embarrassing revelations of their party's abuse of power, and they were assisted in their arguments by yet another rising Republican star, Antonin Scalia, then a top lawyer at the Justice Department.

Marilyn Marcosson A couple of years ago, Bella's good friend Barbara Bick arranged a little get-together and invited a bunch of the Washington staff people. I said to Mim, "I am amazed at the level of responsibility that you gave us. We were working on ERISA.* We were working on equal credit. How did you trust us

*The Employment Retirement Income Security Act of 1974 set minimum standards to protect the rights of private-industry employees in pension plans.

to do that?" Mim was very gracious. Whatever ability I have to write a clear English sentence, I owe a lot of it to Mim. She said, "We were just so impressed with how smart you guys were, so we let you run with it." But I think it goes the other way. It was their guidance. It was a period of *incredible* activity, just the number of issues: the Clean Water Bill, the Highway Bill, the Equal Credit Act, ERISA, the Child Care Act, the end of the war in Vietnam, the Resolution of Inquiry on Nixon's pardon, the bill to fund the International Women's Year meetings and the Houston Conference. By taking the far forward position, Bella allowed others to move up and look more moderate.

We had fun, too. Bella sometimes played on our office softball team. She would pitch, of course. There was much discussion about what we were going to name the team. Bella's Bombers was one idea, but we thought that was too militaristic. I still have the T-shirt—the name was the Mad Hatter's Batters.

Harold Holzer She took a lot of pride in her athletic stuff. I remember when the House had a volleyball team, she went up to Connecticut and had her dressmaker, Charita, make her a special volleyball outfit. It was not the most flattering thing I've ever seen—blue and white with striped pants, striped culottes and polka dots on top and a special sailor hat. Oy! It was an unfortunate outfit, but it was so cute that she tried.

All my life I've been a private citizen. Now suddenly I'm in the papers all the time and on television, and I'm instantly a public personality. I enjoy it, but it's tough, because I'm not used to it . . . The only time it upsets me is when they say, "We're countin' on ya, Bella." Too many strangers say that to me. It makes me feel as though I've created a monster, and that I'm not going to be able to live up to their expectations.

9

Running and Losing—and Regrouping

Chronology

1976 Bella gives up her safe seat after three terms to become the first woman in New York State to run for the U.S. Senate. She loses the Democratic primary by less than 1 percent to Daniel Patrick Moynihan, who holds the seat for the next twenty years.

1976 Jimmy Carter wins the presidency, unseating Gerald Ford.

1977 Bella becomes the first woman to run for mayor of New York City, in a race with eight other candidates. She loses in the primary to Ed Koch, who becomes mayor.

1978 Bella loses a special election to Bill Green to fill the vacancy caused by Koch's resignation from the House of Representatives.

1979 U.S. Embassy personnel are taken hostage in Iran, not to be released until 1981.

1980 Ronald Reagan unseats Jimmy Carter, winning the presidency.

1986 Bella runs again for Congress—this time in Westchester County (where her family lived for many years). Just before primary day, her husband, Martin, suffers a massive heart attack and dies. She considers dropping out of the race, but goes on to win the primary; she narrowly loses the general election.

1992 Congressman Ted Weiss dies the day before the Democratic primary in New York. Bella considers running for the seat but supports Ronnie Eldridge instead. Jerrold Nadler ultimately wins the seat, which he has held ever since.

Martha Baker If I worked for Women Strike for Peace, I was working for Bella. It was the same thing: whatever you needed to do, that's where you were. So we lived through the whole Senate campaign.* I was at the very first meeting in '75, when she talked about entering that race, in a huge apartment on the Upper West Side. Some were very excited, and some were very scared. Many people who loved her and supported her were afraid she'd lose her seat, her seniority, and her clout, and then where would we be? But Bella was determined. She said, "Look, there's no change unless we have these breakthroughs," and certainly she was right. When you saw how well she did upstate, it was so clear that at a flick of a finger it could have turned the other way. It was a huge gamble, but it wasn't like she didn't understand what was at play. She did.

*The 1976 race for the U.S. Senate in New York involved a multicandidate Democratic primary to decide who should face the first-term conservative Republican, James Buckley. Buckley was vulnerable, having won the seat with only 39 percent of the vote when running on the Conservative line against a Democrat (Representative Richard Ottinger) and the Republican incumbent (Charles E. Goodall), who split the liberal vote. Along with Bella, the front-runner in the '76 Democratic primary was Daniel Patrick Moynihan, who had resigned as UN ambassador to make a late entry into the race as a centrist candidate. To his left, along with Bella, were Paul O'Dwyer, New York City Council president, and Ramsey Clark, who had lost a race for the Senate two years before to Jacob Javits.

I share my feelings, I share my despair, I share my hopes, I share my tears and my joys. Most politicians don't do that, they just talk, talk, talk. And people care about that. People want someone who cares, and I naturally exude that. That's why in some races, particularly ones that I lost, like the U.S. Senate, I had the support of conservatives. In fact, I was beaten by less than 1 percent because my liberal vote was divided, not my conservative vote.

Judy Lerner A lot of friends said, "Don't let her do it. If you have any influence at all, don't let her do it," and sometimes that made me angry. I said, "She has the right to be the senator from New York State." Her abilities were so great and her understanding of the foreign affairs and national issues was so much greater than the average congressperson's that she really belonged in the Senate, and it was a time when there was a good chance that she would make it.

Doug Ireland I was opposed to her running for the Senate, having gone through the first campaign to send her to Congress and then that terribly bitter '72 campaign against Bill Ryan. I would tell her, "This is not a congressional seat any longer. It's an annuity. You can represent this district until you die, and you will accumulate enormous seniority." Since the Voting Rights Act of 1964, things were beginning to change in the Democratic Party. One saw the withering away of the domination of the southern Democrats, whose longevity had given them a death grip on the committee chairs in the House. Bella was one of the greatest coalition builders ever to be in the House of Representatives. By this time, because of her charm when she turned it on and her undeniably brilliant legal mind, she had gotten the reputation as an extraordinarily effective congresswoman. She was able to build coalitions with some very conservative people on various issues, including some of those old southern Democrats.

Harold Holzer I never believed the people who said, "Don't leave a safe seat," because we learned in '72 that redistricting can happen, and no seat is safe. And there were no women in the Senate.* That was our great commercial. "What's wrong with this picture," and there was a picture of a hundred men looking out of the Senate. "A stag Senate is a stag-nation." That was Mim's slogan.

Ronald Dellums When Bella got ready to run for the Senate, we had lunch in the House dining room, just the two of us. I said, "Why are you running for the Senate?" "Why do you ask?" she said. And I said, you run for the Senate because it gives you a larger platform? Well the issues are the same and you already have a platform. You run because you have six years in a Senate term? You're Bella Abzug! It's just a matter of going home every two years and saying I'd be happy to go back to Washington, and they'll send you back because they believe in your politics and they trust your acumen. You run for the Senate because it gives you greater access to the media? The press loves to write about Bella Abzug. You have an enormous platform that is not rivaled by many senators. I said, "Bella, they can have a button with just a silhouette of a woman with a hat on, and people will say, 'Oh, Bella Abzug.' Everybody knows you, and you've learned to use that celebrity seriously." She was real ticked off. I said, "Bella, I'm your friend, and what friends owe each other is not to B.S." Then I committed the absolute cardinal sin. I said, "Suppose you lose." She got totally upset. "I can't think about losing! What do you mean even bringing it up?" I said, "I'm not suggesting that you're going to lose. I'm just saying, be anticipatory; look at the

*The only mid-twentieth-century women to serve a full term or more in the U.S. Senate were Republican of Maine Margaret Chase Smith (1949 to 1972) and Democrat of Oregon Maurine Brown Neuberger (1960 to 1967). Both first came to Congress to fill vacancies left by the deaths of their husbands.

possible scenarios. Can you survive that?" She totally blistered me out.

Harold Holzer Maggi Peyton and I spent almost every weekend traveling around the state with Bella. From '75 through '76, we went to sixty of the sixty-two counties in New York, and back many times to the big ones, such as Erie and Albany. It was not easy schlepping her around, spending at least one day a weekend in small planes. She dressed impeccably. She had a dressmaker and a hat maker. She was in Ultrasuede before anyone else. We had to travel with a hatbox. The truth is, when she made Maggi and me mad, we would give a little punch to the hatbox. She'd open it later and say, "What happened to these hats?" But it was worth it. She did very well upstate. In those parts of New York, Bella did the best when she was regarded as a celebrity and a strong leader, because when it got down to specific issues, they didn't agree with her on a lot of things. Not everybody agreed on the war, not everybody agreed on the Equal Rights Amendment, or things that we cared about then. Not everybody agreed on abortion—a woman's right to choose. But when it came to someone who was charismatic and strong, someone who would be entertaining and thrilling to have as a leader, that's when we did best. We used to take her celebrity friends upstate with us—Candice Bergen, Marlo Thomas. I saw a sea change when Bella began introducing Candice Bergen instead of Candice Bergen introducing Bella. I thought that we had moved up a notch in the world of celebrity recognition!

In one of these remote areas, an older woman came up to Candice Bergen and said, "How is your wonderful father?* I enjoyed him for so many years. And how is Charlie?" I said to Candice, "Is it customary for people to ask how the puppet is?" She

*The ventriloquist and vaudeville star Edgar Bergen.

said, "Yes, because there's a whole generation of people who heard my father on the radio who think Charlie McCarthy's a real person." I said, "Oh, okay. That's our group, I guess."

Maggi Peyton Years later I worked with some young men, one Italian-American, one Greek or Arabic, and they were so impressed that I had worked with Bella. They told me stories about how their mothers loved to tease and annoy their fathers, saying, "I'm going out to work with Bella. I'll be at campaign headquarters." She got tremendous support from women who were homemakers, not highly educated but looking for something new for their children, or for their daughters. Bella once got a wonderful letter from some nuns in upstate New York. Even with her pro-choice stance, they sent her twenty-five dollars or something.

Barbara Bick Bella would take me to all these parties she had to go to. It was fabulous for me. I saw some incredible apartments, Lee Radziwill's for instance. Bella had a need to be reassured—she wanted to be able to look across the room and lock eyes with someone familiar. Beforehand, she'd ask me, "Is this the right hat?" She had a terrible temper, but she had great loyalty, and that's why people forgave her when she shouted at them. It was just fun to be with Bella. I met so many people I would never have met. I always felt I got more out of Bella than Bella got out of me. On the other hand, Bella needed someone that she could trust 100 percent, someone on the same wavelength with her. I would never get paid for anything, though. Once you became her employee, you switched your position.

Judy Berek In 1976 she had a campaign going on and I got married. And I very quickly got a divorce; in fact it was a stupid mistake to get married. I used to tell people that it was the best wedding and the worst marriage. And one of the things I did as I was going through the process was lose a lot of weight, and so I looked good. And I went to some huge political dinner, I mean it was one of these fifteen hundred people dinners, and I saw Bella, and she said to me, "Marriage agrees with you," and I said, "Marriage has nothing to do with it; I'm getting a divorce." And as she was talking to me someone else came up to me and said, "Marriage made you look terrific," and Bella looked at the person and said something—she had stopped him already—and she spent the entire evening standing there with her arm around me like a human fly swatter. It could have been the worst night of my life. And she had work to do at that party; she didn't need to be standing there with one person, but it was the point at which I knew that deep down inside she was a mother.

Barbara Bick Faye [Wattleton] and Bella were very close. They would go to movies together in New York. And Carl Bernstein was a big man in Faye's life for a while. She was crazy about him. Bella kept asking, "What can you see in that pipsqueak?" Here's Faye, enormously tall and gorgeous. But that never bothered Carl; I'll say that. He did like powerful, intelligent women. He was also a very good friend of Shirley MacLaine.

Mim Kelber She liked to counsel women on the men in their lives. Bella considered herself a maven at that. She wasn't happy when Ronnie Eldridge married Jimmy Breslin.

Marlo Thomas Bella wanted me to marry Phil. She nagged me terribly. I called her "Tanta Bella," because she was always, "Well, why don't you marry him? There's someone better than that?" She wanted me to be married. Her wedding present was the first to arrive—a Delft china fruit compote thing, beautiful. I always think of her when I take it out.

Henry Foner Working for Bella's campaigns was a labor of love. I was able to involve a lot of members of the union,* particularly women members. They came out in droves to canvas or whatever was required. I have pictures in our union paper of Bella speaking at our meetings.

Judy Berek At District 1199 we were thrilled because we wanted Bella in the Senate. We were very enthusiastic about her race.

Gloria Steinem When she was running for the Senate, I was helping to organize fund-raisers in the suburbs of New York City, the same places that sprouted lawn signs and gave money for the anti-Vietnam candidacy of Eugene McCarthy. Bella had been against the Vietnam War long before McCarthy was—not to mention that she was running a race she might actually win—but the response to her was not the same. Where the silver-haired Minnesota poet raised thousands, Bella raised hundreds. Where he got cocktail parties and elegant dinners, she was lucky to get a brunch.

This seemed so unfair that I finally raised it at a campaign meeting. Didn't it make her angry? Didn't it surprise her? "Of course not," Bella said. "I'm everything these people moved to the suburbs to escape."

Harold Holzer Things happened that would have stopped any ordinary person in her or his tracks. Nothing stopped her, no demonstration, no heckling, no criticism, no editorial board. She was straight ahead. I remember once we got to a small town, I think it was Oneida, and when we got there this policeman, a state trooper type, with a wide-brimmed hat and a leather strap, a gun in his holster, said, "Ms. Abzug, ma'am, I just want you to know

*Henry Foner was president of the Fur and Leather Workers Union.

that we've received a violent death threat, and I urge you to take your hat off as we go in from the airport, because you're too recognizable." Bella said, "Honey, I'm not taking my hat off for you or for anybody else." And this went on, and finally Maggi and I, who, incidentally, were in the line of fire, we said, "Bella, please take your hat off." So she took her hat off.

We got to her hotel and we said, "Do you take this seriously?" She said, "Are you kidding? I've had death threats all over the world. I don't care about this." So she went to bed. Next morning, Maggi and I went down to breakfast to plan the day in advance, and we were marveling at her bravery. We were sitting at the table in the dining room, and the maître d' comes over and says, "You have a call," and brought a phone. These were in the days before cell phones, so it was pretty unusual. Maggi gets on the phone. I'm listening. And Bella said, "And you have left me to be murdered in my bed." She said, "Get up here this minute."

So we got up just as room-service breakfast was being sent to Bella. She said, "How dare you two leave me. Am I sending you to go off and have breakfast on your own? You're to be here." We said, "We asked you whether you were nervous about this. Are you?" And she said, "Absolutely not." And just then she lifted up her orange juice, handed it to Maggi, and said, "Here. Taste it."

Doug Ireland The moment when we lost the Senate campaign can be put down to a moment of temper. I would call it atypical, but it was a moment of temper.

I thought that the liberal left progressive vote was going to be too split for Bella to be able to win in the primary against Pat Moynihan. The problem was that we had both Paul O'Dwyer—a historic figure of New York State progressivism who had been the Democratic Senate candidate in 1970 after his leading role with the antiwar forces at the Chicago '68 convention—and Ramsey Clark, who had run in '74, gotten creamed, and decided to run again. My strategic head said to me, with three people dividing up the progressive vote, Moynihan was going to win. The miracle is that we came as close as we did. We tried very hard to get Ramsey out of the race, and at one point, I thought we had succeeded when the polls were showing that he was barely breaking out of the single digits and that his votes were almost all coming from her base. In the end Ramsey, whom I never liked and don't have much respect for, decided to stay in.

But the moment when we lost that Senate campaign was two weeks before the primary election. Bella was campaigning up in Westchester, and some young stringer for the Associated Press asked her, "If you are defeated by Pat Moynihan, will you support him in the general election in November?" Now this is one of the issues we discussed at the very beginning of the campaign. I told her very early on, "Look, I don't really give a good crap whether or not you support Pat Moynihan. You simply cannot say in public that you won't support him if he wins." It had been a very hard-fought and bitter primary, but we had the momentum, we were out in front in the polls, and I thought that it was more than likely we were going to win. I had already begun putting together a post-primary unity operation. I'd gotten hold of Steve Smith, the Kennedy brother-in-law, who agreed to chair a unity effort and we were talking about how we were going to pull the party together behind her after the primary was over. But all this was blown out of the water when Bella told this young AP stringer in a moment of pique at Pat Moynihan that she would not support him if he ran in the general election in November. This killed our chance of getting the endorsement of *The New York Times*, which I thought we had. This was the thing that pushed Punch Sulzberger over the line. That endorsement was worth a good five points in New York City and in the suburbs.

I had taken the weekend off, because I was just exhausted, and I knew the fall campaign was going to be very tough and that we had this extraordinary job ahead of us of putting the party back together if she won. I decided to give myself a three-day weekend off to just recharge my batteries for the next phase. And so I'm relaxing out there, and I get a call telling me that this story had moved over the AP wire. I forget who called me, but I said, "We just lost the election." I knew that that was the death knell.

Harold Holzer Bella worked long hours. I once told the press that she works fourteen hours a day. She said, "How dare you tell them that. I work sixteen hours a day! Correct it!" We had a good operation, though. And Maggi and I would do anything for her. We traveled for a hundred weekends in two years, and we still regret that the one weekend we didn't go—the weekend Mim and Lynn Abraham went with her instead—was when she said if Moynihan wins, she wouldn't support him. I hope I would have stopped her. I would have said, "Tell them you didn't mean it. Just go back and say, 'That's not what I meant.' " Then the worst story is that she fumbled.

Maggi Peyton The day before had been horrible. A private plane couldn't land where it was supposed to land so we went to the wrong airport. Bella was really tough on me, and Harold was annoyed, so we decided not to go the next day. Maybe if Harold had been with her . . .

Daniel Patrick Moynihan That's the kind of attitude—if you can't have it your way there will be no way—that has gotten us to the point where we are one of nine states in the Union that doesn't have a Democratic senator . . . There's got to be a certain element of party loyalty.

What I did say was, I could not actively campaign for a person who was not yet, had not renounced the politics of Nixon and Ford.

Harold Holzer I remember all the bad days, like the day that the publisher intervened and *The New York Times* endorsed Moynihan after the editorial board voted eleven to two to endorse Bella. That was a bad day. I used to go to Ninety-sixth and Broadway every night at 10:30 to get the *Times*—that doesn't happen today—and I'd complain if I didn't like the positioning of a picture or if there was a mistake. I was famous on the night desk for complaining and kvetching.

John Oakes My dad [John B. Oakes, *Times* editorial page editor, 1961–1976] and I were driving back from the Vineyard, where we spent the summers. He had gotten the call just before we left saying that Punch [Sulzberger, *Times* publisher and Oakes's cousin] had pulled the Bella endorsement. He was very upset, and at some point he pulled over to the side of the road where there was a phone box and called in his letter to the editor—in effect a letter to himself. When he got back in the car, he said to me, "Remember this day; it is the first time that the publisher of *The New York Times* has killed an editorial." His letter ran the next day.* I always thought of that as the first chink between him and Punch.

Maggi Peyton Some years later, I was putting together the primary-day operation for Joe Rose, who was running for the State Senate against Fred Ohrenstein.† Rose's mother said to me, "You know that Daniel Patrick Moynihan will support my son. I was the one that got the endorsement for Moynihan. I went to

*The letter, which ran on September 10, 1976, read in part: "As the editor of the editorial page of *The New York Times* I must express disagreement with the endorsement in today's editorial columns of Mr. Moynihan over other candidates in the New York Democratic primary contest for the U.S. Senate."

†In 1988 Joseph B. Rose unsuccessfully challenged Manfred Ohrenstein, a state senator and Senate Democratic leader.

Sulzberger, and I produced that endorsement. He went down and changed it in the middle of the night." There was a lot of the establishment Jewish money that didn't go to Bella. They thought of her as a "fishwife," an embarrassment.

Joyce Miller I felt very warmly toward Bella, but personally, I was very unhappy when she made the decision to run for the Senate. I thought, "Stay in the House. The southerners stay and get to be head of the committees." But she was determined, and she had the support of much of the labor community. Our union [Amalgamated Clothing & Textile Workers Union] supported her. Of course, a large part of labor supported Moynihan. One thing the trade union movement always had was loyalty. We could yell at each other in a closed room, but when we went out to face the public, we were on the same side. So the day Bella blew it as far as labor was concerned was when she said, "If Moynihan wins, I will not support him." I'm still angry about it. She had no business opening her mouth. Ed Gray of the UAW had given her tremendous support, and he called her. All she did was swear at him over the telephone. Now, on the one hand, perseverance and holding on to things gave Bella strength. I recognize that and I admire it. But there are times when *not* being stubborn is the way to go. I ran into her on the third floor of the Amalgamated headquarters, and I said to her, nicely, "Bella, please. People are very upset. You're making a terrible mistake. The labor movement is loyal to the party. Don't say you won't support him if he wins the primary." And she said, "Absolutely not. I won't support that son of a bitch."

Jerrold Nadler Dick Dresner came out of our clubhouse—he became a major pollster and eventually a partner with Dick Morris. In '76 Dresner was a consultant for the Moynihan campaign even though our club was supporting Bella. I was running for the

State Assembly and handing out cards that said, "Vote for the Abzug/Nadler Team." I won my race and she lost by nine thousand votes statewide. Dresner claimed to me later that he deliberately baited her. He got Moynihan to say certain things designed to set her off. I can't vouch for the accuracy of that, but he claims the credit for it.

Doug Ireland Now as it happens, by the time primary day rolled around, we were able to get the momentum back. Dick Dresner told me a couple of months after the primary that their own daily tracking polling showed that we had gotten the momentum back and they thought we were going to win. If I had been able to find another hundred thousand dollars for television ads in Buffalo, we would have won. But we were tapped out. That was one of the reasons I got out of electoral politics—what that election showed to me was that politics had become so capital intensive that it was not really possible to use electoral politics as a forum to teach people anything. You had to find another way, and I wanted to get back to writing.

We had carefully constructed an attempt to soften the "Battling Bella" image that had been around her neck ever since I got my old pal Jimmy Breslin to write the first major magazine piece on her in *New York* magazine during the '70 campaign. For a statewide campaign, we needed to soften that. You have to remember how visible she was at that point. I mean she was all over television all the time. She was on *Saturday Night Live*! It was incredible. But there was an image around her that we needed to soften, which I very consciously did in the way the ads were filmed, the photographs that we used. I got a top-rate theatrical photographer to take the most wonderful pictures of Bella, showing her smiling and cute. It was one of those days that Bella was mad at me for something. The photographer was trying to adjust her makeup and the hair. She didn't like all this fussing around her, and she was being nasty. We started taking the pictures and the expression just wasn't right and I'm saying to myself, "We've gotta make this broad laugh, how do I do this?" I said, "All right, Bella, look, when he takes the picture think of firing me." And she broke into a guffaw, and we got the picture and it was the best picture ever taken of her. We used it throughout the campaign. I had all these ways I used to diffuse her anger, after so many years of knowing her. I used to say, "Oh, Bella, just shut up so people will think you're just another pretty face."

Henry Foner That was a tragic night—when Moynihan defeated her by a percentage point. And I got a call at three o'clock the following morning from Paul O'Dwyer. I was then a vice chairman of the Liberal Party, and he asked, "Do you think you can get Alex Rose to put Bella on the Liberal line?" He was feeling remorse. I never heard from Ramsey Clark, but Paul O'Dwyer felt terrible that he was one of the people who split the vote. He was asking the impossible because I think that Alex Rose was involved in getting Moynihan to run in the first place. Besides, it was pointless to run her on the Liberal line against Moynihan. Wow! I have memories of that night. It was such a terrible realization that just one percentage point . . .

Donald S. Harrington There was quite a wrangle inside the [Liberal] party about it. Alex Rose felt very strongly that while Moynihan was not an ideal candidate from the Liberal point of view, he was the only one who could beat Buckley—that Bella could not beat Buckley largely because this is a Catholic state and Buckley is Catholic and Moynihan is Catholic. So a whole group of us went to [Alex] and said, "Look we just don't trust him." And after Bella had lost the primary we told him, "We'd like to offer Bella our line." Alex's response was, "Well, I don't agree with you." But . . . Alex bowed to us and said, "The only thing I'll say is I will not oppose it; . . . you've got to remember: it's not only that you may reelect Buckley, but you may cost Carter enough votes that he loses New York State and loses the election. You wouldn't want that to happen." We finally felt that wasn't enough of a danger, but when I called [Bella] and sounded her out she said the moment had passed. [This was about two weeks after the primary.] She felt that if we had come to her a day or two after the primary that then she would have said yes.

Maggi Peyton I was heartbroken. She said to me, "Maggi, you have to know when a campaign is over." She figured she couldn't pull it off on the Liberal line.

Ronald Dellums Sometimes Bella would talk to me like my mother. She would lecture me from time to time, but I got to understand that was part of who Bella was and not to take offense. It was her way of caring about you enough to stop and say, "Okay, get it together." So in one sense she kept everybody honest, and I deeply appreciate it. If I had any lament it would have been, "Don't leave the House, Bella. I need your help." I was able to do what she wasn't able to do, which was to see it out for the next twenty-two years in the House. But it would have been fantastic to be the chair of the House Armed Services Committee with Bella still in Congress. And the interesting thing is she spent the rest of her life trying to figure out how to get back.

Martha Baker She was a wreck after that race. And from there we bounced right into the mayoral campaign, and that was gruesome—running against Ed Koch. Koch had done a number on Bella when they were both in Congress. There was a big fight about funding weapons and planes for Israel. Bella was a tremendous supporter of Israel, but Koch put out a letter [in the name of some group] that was sent to every major Jewish organization saying that she didn't support Israel. He's really a vicious man, and he hurt her tremendously. When she ran for mayor, he buried her on the death penalty—she was strongly against it and he was strongly for it—and with the Jewish community. Here's Bella with her background in Jewish learning, and he was spreading stories like, "Oh, she exaggerates her commitment to Israel, she exaggerates her connection to Jews." We would walk around Forest Hills, where a lot of elderly Jewish people live, and she would greet them and they'd ask her to talk in Hebrew to see if she really could, because they didn't believe it. That's how ugly it was.

Jerrold Nadler She came to me in early '77 and said if she ran for mayor would I support her.* I said, yes I would, but added, "Bella you shouldn't run for mayor. You'd be out of your mind to run for mayor. You can't win." She said, "What do you mean I can't win? Look at the polls." The polls showed her at 34 percent at that point. I said, "Bella, look at your name recognition. It's 98 percent. That means 64 percent of the voters know who you are and aren't for you. Thirty-four percent is your ceiling. Look at Koch. He's at 17 percent with 25 percent name recognition. When he's at 50 in name recognition, he'll be at 34 percent. When he's at 75, he'll be at 50 percent." I said, "It's the wrong office for you." And she said, "What do you mean it's the wrong office?" I said, "Look, people look at offices differently. You are a loudmouth. That's how people look at you. And that's good. It's good for the city, in certain offices. You express yourself. You're a fighter." That was her image. That's fine for the Senate; it's not fine for mayor or governor. For mayor or governor you want someone who's responsible, who'll do the budget right. You want a responsible executive, not a loudmouth. I said, "You can't run for mayor. Just calm down, wait a year, run for attorney general. You

*The 1977 Democratic mayoral primary pitted Mayor Abe Beame against Bella, Mario Cuomo, and Ed Koch.

can run against the utilities. For that, people want a loudmouth. You'll get elected, and you walk into the Senate two years later." But she was seduced by the polls, and unfortunately my reading of the poll was correct. Koch kept getting stronger. There was no guarantee that would happen, but the potential was there. The 34 percent she had was, if not a ceiling, clearly close to the ceiling. When you're that well known, and running against relatively unknown opposition, the people who aren't for you in the polls are saying, "I really want to see somebody else."

Robert F. Wagner The governor* would have to think about what kind of person you're going to have as mayor—to pull the town together. And she didn't seem to be a person who pulls people together, except a certain group that are attached to her. She didn't exhibit any knowledge of city government . . . She's a type that doesn't attract me at all. There are so many women now in the political field who are just as bright, just as dedicated, but so much more nice and like a woman . . . so much more attractive, and I don't just mean in the physical sense. They're much more attractive as people who can get things through, who are not constantly haranguing . . . I enjoy her company. I think she's amusing and interesting to talk to, but not as a public figure. She represented that district very well. They're a volatile district on the West Side. They have a lot of people over there who are screamers and yellers, too. That's all right, but confine it to there.

Maggi Peyton Did Jerry [Nadler] tell you he was the only person that endorsed her, the only elected official to endorse her when

*Governor Hugh Carey of New York pushed his secretary of state, Mario Cuomo, into the race for mayor; he couldn't stand either Beame, whom he blamed for failing to warn him of the extent of New York's financial problems, or Bella, who he was convinced would alienate the investment banks needed to secure the city's fiscal health. See Jonathan Mahler, *Ladies and Gentlemen, the Bronx Is Burning*, 182–83.

she ran for mayor? I spoke to a woman who had been somewhere recently with Mario Cuomo. She asked him, "Why did you get into that mayoral race?" He said, "They were afraid that Bella was going to win, and they put me in." And our tracking showed the Italian women were for Bella until Cuomo became a candidate. They figured all the angles. I think they probably would have preferred her to be the senator than to be the mayor. As senator, you might be able to name a few judges, but you don't have the billion-dollar contracts the mayor's office gives out. That would have really upset their apple cart.

*How arya? I'm Bella Abzug. I think I'm gonna be your next mayor. So let's get to know each other.**

Harold Holzer Bella was always fabulous on the streets. [People would respond] "Give 'em hell, Bella." "You've got my vote."

Robin Morgan I remember during the mayoral campaign standing at her side and thinking, well, there goes Brooklyn. The Hasids had attacked her for being pro-gay, and she was defending gay rights. At first she answered very sensibly, and then she got pissed. They asked one, two, three, four, many times how she could support perverts. And she said, "What the hell is this? You want to talk about perverts? Look at all these men wearing fur hats and ear curls." You just knew, there it went. We'd just lost Brooklyn. She had called Hasids perverts for wearing ear curls.

Harold Holzer [It was also my job as press secretary] to get *People* magazine† to cover the fact that Shirley [MacLaine] put Bella on a special macrobiotic diet during the mayoral campaign in 1977.

*On the streets, campaigning for mayor.

†It was *US* magazine, not *People*, according to Jonathan Mahler, in *Ladies and Gentlemen, the Bronx Is Burning*, p. 285.

It was supposed to be really great to keep an even keel in the hottest summer, I think, in the history of New York—100 degrees for six days in a row. And every time it would get really difficult, Shirley would reach into this huge freezer compartment that she kept, and say, "Here, Bella, have some nuts. Here, Bella, have some nuts." She ate about four hundred pounds of nuts during that campaign. By the time *People* magazine did the story, Bella had gained twenty-two pounds on Shirley's diet.

Campaign pamphlet attacking Con Edison after the New York City blackout in the summer of 1977 Vote Bella: She's the Greatest Energy Source in America.

Ladies and Gentlemen, the Bronx Is Burning On Friday, July 15, Abzug became the first mayoral candidate to visit what was left of Bushwick [after the blackout]. After touring the decimated neighborhood, she stopped by Bed-Stuy's Eighty-first Precinct, which had worked alongside Bushwick's Eighty-third during the long night of looting. Looking smart in a polka-dot sundress and white straw hat, Abzug defended her increasingly unpopular position on giving cops the right to strike.

"But what would you have done if the police had been on strike during the blackout?" one distressed community resident asked.

"Mobilize the community organizations and get them into the streets," Abzug replied.

"The community *was* mobilized," another resident volunteered. "They were out looting."

Almost every day we can read editorials in our leading newspapers telling us not to expect much from Washington and not to expect much from City Hall . . . The people with this outlook say we will continue to lose jobs and population. They say let's encourage the poor to get out *of town and let's tear down their neighborhoods. Let's continue to attack the unions because we have to drive down wages . . . They say let's get rid of free tuition and the municipal hospital system, shut down child care centers, senior centers, libraries, and fire stations. They say let's fire teachers, guidance counselors, and security guards, and let's get rid of rent control. Let's slash subway and bus service and crush more people into the trains, and maybe we'll even make them pay more for that memorable experience. That's not my vision and I know it's not yours. You have invested too much of yourselves, too much sweat, time, and thought into our city to settle for a spiral of further cutbacks and reduced services that will only hasten the decline of New York.***

Harold Holzer She thought the city was out of control. She thought it was beyond our control to remind people of what Lincoln would call the better angels of our nature, to remind them of possibilities, to remind them that harmony was more important than punitiveness. God knows it was impossible to say that people who pillaged in some pathetic effort to express anger should be pitied almost as much as punished. There was no way to get through the mood, between the murders† and the heat and the blackout looting.

Shirley MacLaine The night that she lost the nomination for mayor was a nightmare. They called her and gave her the figures—she wouldn't even be in the runoff.‡ She was on the

*Campaign speech, June 1977, at Camp Tamiment in the Poconos, a New York working-class retreat.

†During the mayoral campaign, the city not only suffered from the heat and the blackout and attendant looting, but had also slid into fiscal crisis. And from July 29, 1976, to his arrest on August 10, 1977, David Berkowitz, the serial killer known as the Son of Sam, had been terrorizing the outer boroughs.

‡Koch and Cuomo took the first two places and met in the runoff, which Koch won easily. In the general election, Cuomo, with the help of ex–Abzug staffers, managed to mount a strong challenge running on the Liberal line, but Koch won. (See Mahler, 315–18).

phone, and the light was hitting her face, and it was absolutely still. Then this big tear, so silently, came out and rolled down. No expression. Just a paralyzed anguish about what was she going to do with her life.

Gloria Steinem She was like an orchestra conductor without an orchestra.

Harold Holzer Then the East Side congressional race in '78 was another horror show. We thought this was an easy race. Koch endorsed her, Moynihan endorsed her. She had Cuomo and Beame—every living and dead politician. When Koch won the race for mayor and left the Congress, there was a procedure for the Democratic nomination to replace him. Bella always said, "I do well in procedures." She and Carter Burden were virtually tied in this daylong process. She won the last vote, but Carter Burden refused to accept the result, claiming that some of Bella's supporters—women who were probably one hundred years old and ready to pass out—had pre-marked their ballots and gone home. And you know what? He had an interesting point, but Justice Max Bloom, who was the husband of the deputy head of the Liberal Party—which had already endorsed Bella—ruled in our favor. I still remember the decision. "The nomination stands," and we all cheered. The judge said, "Quiet, or I'll clear the court," and I thought, "That's the first cheer we've been able to get for Bella in four years." We had a victory party that night and then she lost to the Republican, S. William Green. There was an underground campaign that Green was doing. I should have saved the literature: "Bella Abzug: Queen of the Lesbos." Just vicious stuff—that she was going to have gay people rule society. It didn't even make any sense. Doug Ireland said, "Tell everybody Green's first name is Sedgwick," which it is! "Tell everybody it's Sedgwick. *Tell everybody it's Sedg-*

wick." You know the way Doug talks. We didn't do it; we should have.

I remember we were driving on Park Avenue toward the headquarters the night before the November election. I said, "Boy, that last group we went to was terrific." She said, "Honey, I've learned not to believe what you feel on the streets." In 1976, we had chosen the Summit Hotel to gather for Senate primary night, and at the end of the mayoral race, Bella's friend and supporter Zero Mostel died, another bad omen, and we were in the same hotel. So for the East Side race, we chose a different hotel headquarters. But when we got there, it was the same hotel with a different name. Bella said, "How dare you put me in this jinxed hotel again!" And she was right.

Eric Hirschhorn There was also an effort made to get Bella's successor in Congress, Ted Weiss, to take a judgeship and give the Congressional seat back. He said, "My mom didn't raise me to be a judge."

Helene Savitzky Alexander They pleaded with that little guy, Ted Weiss, because they wanted Bella to come back to Congress. But he had wanted that seat for a long time. When people would say to me, "Why does she keep trying," I said, "You know it's like an actress, she's looking for a role." She tried for the Westchester seat in 1986. But it took an awful lot out of her because she never took care of herself. She just never had time. There was always some other place to go.

Martha Baker I took some time from my job to help Bella up in Westchester. I was planning that if she gets elected we'd move to Westchester, to that area. I was already figuring out how this was going to work. Because if she was going to be somewhere, why wouldn't you be there with her, right?

Liz Abzug My mother used to say that when you run for elective office, "You have to know who you are, and you have to have a good bit of luck and be at the right time." Well I believe into the depths of my soul that she really did understand herself quite well. Whether she wanted to deal with all the elements of herself, I don't think she did. And that was where the problem came. She was running repeatedly, one race after another without any pause. I understand where she was coming from. But it kept her from being in touch deeply enough to correct the mistakes in the campaigns—where she was paranoid sometimes, or where she was brutal to people. I believe as someone who was an observer of her that she did herself a disservice by not taking more of a pause between some of those races. Take a little bit of a minute to breathe and think about it. It didn't help her strategically. It didn't help her correct the mistakes you make being a candidate under pressure. Because running for office is the most inhuman thing anyone can do to oneself. Yet she goes and runs all these races one after another. She couldn't pull back and get perspective. She was so intent on being part of the mix, and being part of the debate, and being there at the table.

Doug Ireland She was a very ambitious woman, don't forget. This was no shrinking violet, our Bella. She wanted to play with the big boys. She was as good as they were. She was smarter than a lot of them. She had contempt for most of them. She saw herself as more than their equal, and she wanted to play on the bigger stage. And no one would have questioned this kind of ambition in a man.

Liz Abzug When Ted Weiss died, I really wanted to run for that Congressional seat. I wanted to be in that designation process. Not her, me! This was after I lost my City Council race. I said, "I don't understand why you don't see that maybe this is the time that I should go for it." She could not do it. She said, "No, you have to run for something else first." My sister even said, "You know, I think maybe you should let Liz do this." She could not do it. Why? Because she couldn't let go of the idea of being back in the fire.

Jerrold Nadler Ted Weiss died the day before the primary in 1992, unexpectedly. He was running against a nothing candidate, and it was too late to get his name off the ballot. He won the primary posthumously, got 89 percent of the vote. I got 89 percent of the vote for my State Assembly race the same day. Every newspaper headline was "Ted Weiss Dies," and every editorial page said, "Vote for Ted Weiss." If you didn't vote for Ted, this lunatic candidate running against him would be the Democratic nominee, and therefore, in this district, the congressman. If Ted won posthumously, the Democratic organization—the county committee for the congressional district—would have ten days to select the nominee and fill the vacancy. So Ted wins the primary, and the county committee convention is on Wednesday the next week. The man isn't buried yet, how do you campaign? It was very awkward for everybody. There were six candidates, altogether: in order of finish, myself, Ronnie Eldridge, Franz Leichter, Dick Godfrey, Bella—except she dropped out at the convention and threw her support to Ronnie—and Ted's wife, Sonny Hoover Rice. When Sonny called me to say she was going to run, a thought went through my mind: "Oh, my God. This could be a very awkward shivah call." But Sonny wasn't a factor. The real competition was Ronnie. In the end, I got 62 percent of the vote. Had there been a primary instead of a county committee procedure, Ronnie probably would have won it. Ronnie and Jimmy [Breslin, her husband] could have raised a lot of money. They had all the glitterati with them, and the governor wanted Ronnie. By this time, it was hard for Bella to climb even five stairs, and she had been away too long.

Ronnie Eldridge I never got over Gloria calling me up and asking me not to run when Weiss died and I ran for the congressional seat. Gloria called me, on her behalf, to ask me not to run; to let Bella run for the last time. That just took me so aback. I was on the City Council. Bella had lost about four times. Leave me alone. Let me run.

Gloria Steinem I was a member of the County Committee, which I called the Dracula Committee, because it only lived when someone died. I felt I had the responsibility to call Ronnie and ask her not to run. I did this after a lot of consulting with people and soul-searching, but the truth was that Bella had the experience to be a force in Congress; Ronnie didn't. And I wanted to prevent two good women from running against each other. I hate conflict and it was a tough call. Neither Ronnie nor Jimmy Breslin spoke to me for a while—they may still be angry—but the fact was that Bella could hit the ground running in a way that Ronnie could not.

Liz Abzug After a lot of negotiation and craziness, my mother stepped out and gave her votes over to Ronnie.

Maggi Peyton In a campaign, Bella was hard on everybody. But most of the time it wasn't that you hadn't made a call, you hadn't sent a letter, or you hadn't got a check for something. It was that she wanted more, and she was right. I said to my husband, as the Senate race was winding down, "You know, if she wins this primary, I don't know if I'll be able to work for her anymore." But then you'd start the next day and you'd forget all about it. My mentors were women who were very strong. My aunts organized the teachers union, and two of them went into the legislature in New Hampshire after they retired. But to work for Bella was like a whole different dimension. We used to joke about how she had compassion for everybody except her staff. Yet it was the defining moment of my life.

Robin Morgan I think to her dying day Bella still harbored the hope, “If I get back in office . . .” It was one of her excuses for not working on her memoir. “I can’t tell the real truth because what if I run again?”

10

Mobilizing American Women Voters

Chronology

1975 The first UN International Women's Year Conference is held in Mexico City in June. Bella attends as a congressional representative. She collaborates with Representative Patsy Mink on legislation to hold a national women's conference preceded by meetings in every state and U.S. territory.

1977 Bella is named by President Jimmy Carter to head the National Commission on the Observance of International Women's Year, which replaces a commission appointed by President Gerald Ford.

1977 Having authored legislation to fund the process, Bella presides over the National Women's Conference held in Houston. Twenty thousand attend, and delegates debate a twenty-six-plank Plan of Action from November 18 to 24.

1978 Bella is appointed cochair, with Carmen Delgado Votaw, of President Carter's National Advisory Committee for Women, a body to carry out recommendations of the National Women's Conference. One and a half years later Carter abruptly fires her when the committee challenges his proposed cuts in funding for women's programs. A majority of the committee resigns in protest.

1980 Jimmy Carter is denied a second term as Ronald Reagan wins the presidential election.

Gloria Steinem Beginning even before the UN's International Women's Year [IWY] conference in Mexico City [1975], Bella had drawn up a piece of legislation and got other congresswomen to sign onto it, which called for a kind of constitutional conference for the female half of the United States. It mandated meetings in every state and territory to pick delegates and issues for a national conference in Houston. There, an agenda initiated by IWY commissions under Presidents Ford and Carter was discussed and finalized. It was a huge, huge undertaking and very important. It was her idea, it was her legislation, it was her leadership. It was also the most racially, economically, and generally representative national meeting this country has ever seen. For example, the Native American women there said they themselves had not come together from so many tribes and nations before.

Carmen Delgado Votaw The planning of all those state meetings really was a logistical nightmare. Remember, at the 1975 conference in Mexico City, the whole world was ahead of the United States. Almost everybody had had a preconference before they went to Mexico City, and the United States had not. So we were catching up. In 1977, we had to complete all the state meetings, and of course, the money from the government wasn't flowing fast enough.

Eleanor Smeal At the time, I was president of the National Organization for Women. Several characters in Washington were involved. One is Catherine East,* who played a big role in the formation of the women's movement in Washington. She was at the Women's Bureau and sort of the inside mole at the Department of Labor who helped to put a lot of things together. Catherine helped place Kathy Bonk, a young activist, at the Department of Justice, and Kathy was lent to the National Commission on the Observance of International Women's Year. They grabbed federal employees from everywhere to staff the commission, and feminists self-selected to be the ones transferred from the different departments. Many of the agencies were glad to get rid of these troublemakers, and they were just the people that the commission needed. Bella was the strategist. She got the legislation through and had the spirit to galvanize a first-class staff. Kay Clarenbach, the executive director, would smooth the waters, and she was very loyal to Bella. I remember one scene with Kathy Bonk—she was one of the kids in charge of PR. I don't remember what she did, but Bella had a fit. And Kay would always be there to keep everybody going.

Kathy Bonk Once I got so upset when Bella yelled at me that I didn't get my period for two months.

Eleanor Smeal I think initially Bella thought you would just advertise the state conventions and people would come, and they would be representative of women in the United States. But very early on, the right wing—the Phyllis Schlaflys of the world—organized and began to take over some of the early state meetings. They took over Indiana. In Hawaii and Nevada, thousands of people were turned out by the Mormon Church. They were busing people in and there was no way to know if they were all

*Catherine East was a staff member of the Kennedy Commission on the Status of Women in the early 1960s and also served on the staff of the National Commission on the Observance of International Women's Year. She died in 1996.

state residents. We got word that they're stacking the state conferences, so we had to go state by state and organize for a feminist slate. I'll tell you, that was a tough period.

Gloria Steinem These state conferences were part of my education about the power and politics of the Mormon Church. Buses of women would arrive with a man at the head of each who then seated them together and told them how to vote by holding up his hand with a glove on it. When we named what was happening, right-wing members of Congress forced Bella to apologize to the Mormon Church for telling the truth—and she had to.

Brownie Ledbetter We had a good delegation elected from Arkansas. Oklahoma had their meeting about a week or so before us, and women from there called me and said, "God, we were deluged. They'll come in with the damn school buses." So we started to figure out a strategy. We had plenty of local opposition, but we decided we could control the outsiders by cutting off the filing date to participate. The deadline came and went and about ten minutes later, the buses came roaring in. We said, "Sorry. Filing deadline." We still had a lot of opponents from home, though. All through the seventies, while we were working to ratify the Equal Rights Amendment in Arkansas, we had to contend with the WWWW—that's Women Who Want to be Women. The other one was HOTDOG, Humanitarians Opposed To Degrading Our Girls. They all had funny names like that, but they were Phyllis Schlafly's little bunch.

Carmen Delgado Votaw I was assigned to go to the Florida meeting, where Anita Bryant's people—the singer who represented Florida citrus growers and was organizing against gay rights at the time—were supposed to be a very big threat. They were going to pelt us with oranges. I made my speech, and there were no oranges! But they brought in all these people—they looked like little old ladies in tennis shoes. When the voting came on the ERA or the gay plank, or any of those they were trying to disrupt, they would put out their feet and trip people, trying to obstruct them from getting out of the pew to vote. They would have people stationed at every elevator to make sure it only went up, not down to the voting place. They would stand in the voting line and then get in line again—the idea was to make people stand in line to vote for two hours.

Eleanor Smeal At some point—I think after about fourteen states had met—we had an emergency meeting and said, that's enough of this. If they're organizing, we've got to counter-organize. From then on, the "Pro-Plan" forces won every conference. The right wing got about 19 percent of the delegates overall, but if you look at where they were from, they mostly represented the states that met before we organized. Truthfully, they shouldn't even have had 19 percent, because they didn't have the organized groups—even those like the National Conference of Catholic Women had a grassroots membership that supported women's rights. In Illinois, the organization of nuns was totally with us.

Letty Cottin Pogrebin I had that old red-baiting feeling, and I thought that some people were really questioning our loyalty as Americans. The opposition people who came in with the buses, who were so well organized—it wasn't like we think this and they think that. It started to be, "You are bad, evil, unpatriotic, un-American, un-Christian, baby-killing, terrible people, and we are everything good about America."

Joanne Edgar For the New York State meeting, a bunch of us from Ms. magazine went up to Albany as volunteers to help staff the event. We were worried, because we heard rumors that right-wing women were sending busloads to try and stack the state delegation. We stayed up all night in this huge government building, making hundreds of copies of the feminist plan and collating lists of delegates. But it was not only the staff volunteers who stayed up all night. So did Gloria and Bella and Mary Anne Krupsak, the lieutenant governor—all of us running the collating assembly line and planning for the next day's vote. Bella kept us laughing all night long.

In the middle of this, we got hungry. But nothing was open and we couldn't find a vending machine. Mary Anne came to the rescue, scrounging up some rather greenish roast-beef sandwiches that kept us going until breakfast. In the end, our teamwork paid off. We distributed our platform and list of delegates to everyone at the meeting the next day, and the group that went to Houston from New York State was solidly feminist.

Eleanor Smeal In February 1977, to prepare for the November national conference in Houston, President Carter appointed members to the National Commission on the Observance of International Women's Year to succeed the Ford appointees. I was one of the youngest members. He put some friends on, like Betty Blanton, who was married to the governor of Tennessee, and some Democrats he had to put on who weren't coming from any women's rights perspective. And people like Maya Angelou, whom I don't remember ever seeing at a meeting. He appointed Liz Carpenter, who had been Lady Bird Johnson's press secretary and very active in fighting for the ERA. She played a very useful role—as a link between the hard-core feminists and the more moderate commissioners—always siding with Bella's philosophy, but being a southerner, a little softer. There was Margaret Mealey from the National Council of Catholic Women—very moderate. But again, when push came to shove, she would go with us. The other person who plays a role in all of this is Midge

Costanza. She was the presidential liaison to the women's movement, one of six closest advisers to Carter.

Brownie Ledbetter My understanding was that Rosalynn Carter did not like Bella. She thought she was too rude.

Midge Costanza It wasn't that Rosalynn didn't like Bella. We all act based on our life experience. That's how we form our principles, our values, and the things we believe in. It's no different for Rosalynn Carter than it is for Midge Costanza. I was raised around New York State politics all my life. But look at Rosalynn Carter. In Georgia, political activism could mean something totally different. So what Rosalynn was saying was, "I don't believe she's the right image for us, because she will not attract women other than the political activists and feminists." Rosalynn was looking for somebody to appoint as the presiding officer who would come from another sphere. I said, "But right now, what we need is the strongest woman we can find. You have no idea the egos involved—not just individual women, but women's organizations. No one will be able to control this group, to bring about the International Women's Year conference in Houston as fast and good and right as Bella Abzug." I remember standing in the hallway, and staff members asked me, "Why are you pushing for Bella?" I said, "Because Bella pushed for us. She's the one who brought Wisconsin in for Jimmy. She is the right person for the job. If he named anyone else, they would be going to Bella for research." I stood there and I said, "I'm not budging. I am not budging."

Then, before the appointment was final, there was a routine vetting process. The FBI called me and said, "Are you serious? You want this background check done immediately? There's a whole room of files on Bella Abzug!" I said, "How dangerous can she be? She served in Congress." Then I thought about how I'm no big fan of Congress, so I said, "I take that back. But seriously, she must have had to go though a big check when she went into Congress. So can you just hurry it up?" I called Bella and said, "What the hell have you been doing?"

The Houston Conference

News Reporter In late September 1977 the torch left Seneca Falls, the site of the last Women's Conference back in 1848. Joining in for the last grand mile, down Allen Parkway [in Houston]: tennis star Billie Jean King and Olympic gold medalist Wilma Rudolph . . . Dozens of national press and Equal Rights Amendment supporters followed all the way downtown to the Albert Thomas Convention Center. Even less athletic types, like IWY leader Bella Abzug, jogged that last few steps, as the crowd cheered the two thousand women who brought the torch twenty-seven hundred miles to Houston.

Marguerite Rawalt [One anti-ERA congressman scoffed], "The girls are going to Houston for boozing and carousing," and Bella's retort: "I've attended many meetings, but I have never heard any woman ask for a call boy!" Wasn't that great?

Peggy Kobernot-Kaplan I was a marathon runner in Houston, and I heard that there was a need for women to go up to Alabama to run a sixteen-mile leg of this official relay . . . because Phyllis Schlafly, with the Eagles,* had been able to convince people in that area not to participate . . . And then they asked me to participate in the last mile, carrying the torch in. When we walked into the convention center and we had fourteen or fifteen thou-

*The Eagle Forum, a right-wing group.

sand people, women, cheering for us . . . it was an incredible feeling . . . an Hispanic woman on my right, and an African American woman . . . we walked up to the side of the stage and then we were to hand the torch to three First Ladies.

Robert K. (Bob) Dornan I watched this morning the corruption of young people in Albert Thomas Hall.* And the greatest tragedy of all was to see three former First Ladies of this nation, excuse me, two former First Ladies and the current wife of the president of the United States, all sitting properly with their hands in their lap, dressed according to White House protocol, and standing by their very presence, alongside of Abzug, approving of sexual perversion and the murder of young people in their mothers' wombs.

Rosalynn Carter I am proud to be a part of the National Women's Conference. Never before in our history has there been such a women's meeting: in numbers, in preparation, in diversity, in long-range effect . . . There have been a lot of disagreements and conflicts. There will be a lot of disagreements and conflicts. But I agree with my daughter-in-law Judy that we must guard against obscuring valid issues with defensiveness and anger. The glue that holds us together is the firm knowledge that our basic goals are the same. All of us cherish our freedom to live, to worship, to vote, to work as we please. We are all searching for ways to create a better future for our children. Here in Houston, we have that chance . . . It is a privilege we share these next few days.

Betty Ford We must keep focus on our goals in business, education, employment, and politics, or in the home. We may have

*Dornan, a former conservative talk show host and, at the time, congressman from western Los Angeles County, was addressing a counter-convention at Astro Arena in Houston. He was later unseated by Congresswoman Loretta Sanchez.

different interests, but we shouldn't be dismayed by the clash of opinion and ideas. It has been said the "evils" of controversy will pass, but its benefits are permanent.

Lady Bird Johnson (introducing the keynote speaker, Barbara Jordan) I once thought the women's movement belonged more to my daughters than to me, but I have come to know that it belongs to women of all ages. I am proud to say . . . that Texas was the ninth state to ratify the right to vote and the seventh state to ratify the Equal Rights Amendment.

Barbara Jordan This gavel was used by Susan B. Anthony, in 1896. Bella, may you preside in the true spirit of what this gavel means to American women, who are again on the move.

The road to Houston started more than a century and a half ago, when American women began organizing to win the rights of citizenship. The torch of freedom has been handed down from generation to generation of women, and the torch we see here today is a symbol of our past victories and our hopes for future ones . . .

Our conference is a first in many ways.

It is the first time the federal government has sponsored a National Women's Conference and the fifty state meetings and six territorial meetings that preceded this event. It is the first time the Congress and the president have mandated American women to identify and help remove the barriers that stand between us and full equality with men.

The mandate under which we meet does not tell us to consider whether women should seek to end discrimination, or should seek full equality, full citizenship, and full participation in society. Instead, it takes a stand for equality, a position that I believe has the support of a majority of Americans. The law under which we meet is rooted in the belief that men and women should share equally in the rights, responsibilities, and opportunities that our democracy offers . . .

After this weekend, the whole nation will know that the women's movement is not any one organization or set of ideas or particular lifestyle. It is millions of women deciding individually and together that we are determined to move history forward.

The women's movement has become an indestructible part of American life. It is the homemaker deciding that raising children, cleaning, cooking, and all the other things she does for her family is work that should be accorded respect and value. It is the young woman student asserting she wants to play baseball, major in physics, or become a brain surgeon. It is the working woman demanding that she get the same pay and promotion opportunities as a man. It is the divorcée fighting for Social Security benefits in her own right, the widow embarking on a new career, the mother organizing a day care center, the battered wife seeking help, the woman running for public office . . .

Let the sun shine on our deliberations, and let us celebrate womanhood and woman power.

Eleanor Smeal We did out-organize them during the state meetings. So in Houston, the audience was overwhelmingly ours. But we didn't leave much to chance even there. We organized every day to make sure our own vote got out. It was such a madhouse that you could have had your people going to lunch or something at a critical time. Koryne Horbal was Bella's person leading the pro-plan forces. I was sitting next to her, because a huge number of delegates were NOW members. And the two groups organized together to pass the Pro Plan. Anne Saunier chaired the most important sessions. She had chaired a recent NOW bylaws convention, and she knew Robert's Rules cold. She also got along really well with Bella.

Koryne Horbal We had gotten a small grant, the DFL [Democratic-Farm-Labor Party, Minnesota's Democratic Party] feminist caucus, to put a strategy together to pass the plan of action—I've been going through my papers and I just found a box of T-shirts from Houston that say, "Women's Agenda." We had done similar work in Minnesota every year—preparing a feminist state-of-the-state message and also a budget to release after the governor's budget address. One of the secrets to our success organizing on the floor was a DFL feminist caucus activist, Peggy Spector, who was an incredible strategist and knew all the vote numbers. Whenever people were discussing things in little caucuses, she was really good at finding out what was happening. At least four or five of our DFL organizers had become delegates at Houston.

Phyllis Schlafly The Commission on International Women's Year is a costly mistake at the taxpayer's expense. The whole thing was designed as a media event, a charade to go through the motions of those phony state conferences and national conference in order to pass resolutions that were pre-written and prepackaged a year and a half ago and published in June of 1976. And then after it was all over to tell the Congress and the State Legislatures that this is what American women want. By coming here today you have shown that that is not what American women want.

Martha Smiley The most unsettling part of it was the realization that there were women outside of this conference hall who are protesting our being inside, talking about issues like child care, health care, education, working rights, and equality, battered women. How could anyone, much less another woman, feel that that is an inappropriate conversation?

Gloria Steinem They were all the issues we now think of, from economic equity to reproductive freedom, some more controversial than others, some yet in the future, like health care.

Margaret Mead We have a chance, at last, to act as women in a way that women have not been able to act, virtually since the Paleolithic period . . . Men know a lot about dying but they don't know enough about living. It has been women's biological and social and cultural task through history to live.

David Broder The real significance of Houston was to bury the idea that so-called women's issues are a sideshow to the center-ring concerns of American politics.

Carmen Delgado Votaw Bella wanted the whole National Plan of Action to pass without any amendments. Because, boy, we had sweated it out. The commission had had all these committees. We had had all the people who were experts on the area take a look at it. And so she felt that anything that amended the plan was a threat, because then the delegates could become very active in trying to amend every resolution.

Eleanor Smeal But the nature of a huge conference like that is that there will be caucuses, there will be meetings. Because, whether we liked it or not, they had to do something. And some of the caucuses, especially the women-of-color caucuses, demanded changes. And actually, they strengthened it.

Gloria Steinem Bella and all of us were worried that this huge conference would break apart in the bright light of national publicity. But some delegations *had* to be protested—for example, one from a southern state had been stacked and taken over by the Ku Klux Klan. And some issue planks had to be expanded—to reflect, for example, the concerns of the various groups of women of color. All these different groups of women had not been able to meet together before and produce a real "minority women's plank." They did this at Houston in a day-and-night process. It was read by each different group in turn, passed by acclamation, and was the emotional high of the whole Houston conference.

***The Spirit of Houston* (the official report of the First National Women's Conference)** If there was to be a dramatic confrontation between women who were for and against change, it would come when the Equal Rights Amendment was considered. Delegates and photographers began positioning themselves in anticipation.

Equal Rights Amendment "Equality of rights under the law shall not be denied or abridged by the United States or by any state on account of sex."

Ann Richards I went over there late afternoon. Bella was eating, and I was terribly nervous. It would be like a Catholic being summoned to the Pope, to be invited by Bella Abzug to come and talk to her. She said, "I want to know more about you, Texas. Tell me something about you." I tried to give her a little bit of my history, and she said, "Well, I like you. Why don't you introduce the Equal Rights Amendment on the floor?"

The Spirit of Houston The Coliseum was tense and well filled when Commissioner Claire Randall, general secretary of the National Council of Churches of Christ, read the seven-word plank: "The Equal Rights Amendment should be ratified." Pandemonium broke out. There were signs, chants, songs, and microphones jammed with women impatient to be heard.

Ann Richards I rise on behalf of those few of us who are fortunate enough to be in the positions we are in but also for those who are speechless and voiceless, the divorced who may not get credit, the widows who are incapable of making a living . . . my own daughter, who cannot find women in the history texts of this country in the elementary schools. I also rise on behalf of the men, the contemporary men of America in thirty-five states, who had the guts to stand up and ratify the Equal Rights Amendment.

The Spirit of Houston Susan B. Anthony of Florida, grandniece of "Susan B. Anthony the Great," spoke for the resolution, "the fulfillment of her lifetime work, her fifty-one years spent living and dying for women. Failure is impossible."

Jean Westwood I am a Mormon woman speaking in favor of ERA. I grew up in Utah, where women had the vote when it was a territory. They had the vote as a state, and in 1896, with the help of the Mormon Church, Utah passed in their Constitution an amendment which said, "Women shall have equal civil, political, and religious rights with men." I have devoted my life in politics to seeing that this privilege is extended to all women.

The Spirit of Houston The ERA resolution was adopted by an enthusiastic and noisy standing vote that appeared to be almost five to one . . . For several minutes, the chair did not even try to restore order. It was clearly impossible.

Sarah Weddington (speaking in favor of the reproductive choice resolution) We would all agree that the best way to prevent the problem of unwanted pregnancies is contraception . . . We do stress that we are for sex education; we are for the availability of family planning information and services, [but] there are some who refuse to continue pregnancy and . . . we save our support for their choice.

The Spirit of Houston When the microphone monitor made a mistake and raised a white card calling for the close of debate, the outcry came not from the antiabortionists who would be cut off, but from the Pro Plan delegates. "These people have a right to be heard," Bella Abzug cried, leaving the platform and striding down the aisle to the microphone . . . After the speeches, the Resolution on Reproductive Freedom was adopted by a standing vote that appeared to be about five to one, the same division as in the national public opinion polls. The celebration was quieter than the demonstration for ERA the night before, with pro-choice delegates letting the songs and chants of the antichoice minority go unanswered. They seemed to recognize how deeply those opposing them felt about the resolution and respected their feelings.

Maxine Waters The women's conference in Houston was my real entrance into feminist national politics, and Bella became one of the most influential women in my life. I remember at Houston, when I was just getting to know Bella, she didn't like something that Gloria Steinem had done and she dressed Gloria down. She shouted at her. And I thought, "Oh, my God. What is she doing?" I couldn't believe it. I said to Gloria right after, "I'm so sorry!" She said, "Oh, that's nothing. That's just the way we talk to each other in New York." When you got to know Bella, she couldn't insult you because you knew her—you know what I'm saying? But if you didn't know her, you would think that she was the meanest, toughest woman in the world.

I was really gung ho at that conference. I ended up working with the minority women who put together a plank. And Gloria helped to write the plank with us.

Barbara Bick Bella had a two-story suite and it was all in white, up above over Houston. There was a big white baby grand piano and a gigantic Texas-sized bed. Bella was just exhausted and Liz Carpenter said "Bella, I have the most wonderful masseur"—

so this big giant of a man comes in, and he's got this really tiny little massage table, and he sets it up and then Bella gets undressed, and she's on it and he starts pounding her. And Bella's screaming, "Stop. Stop already. Stop." In agony, because he was pounding her, and Amy [Swerdlow] and Judy [Lerner] and I were rolling around the bed laughing. She just sent the masseur out.

Carmen Delgado Votaw The original resolution on minority women was too generic and too short. People thought it was trivializing. I went around with Gloria and a couple of other people—we spent, I would say, at least eight hours caucusing with the Native Americans, with the Mexican Americans, with everybody. [The *New York* magazine journalist] Gail Sheehy joined us, but we couldn't agree on the wording. The Native Americans wanted to talk about our relationship to mother earth. The Puerto Ricans wanted to say, we're citizens. We spent a long time with Dorothy Height, the head of the National Council of Negro Women. There were about twelve of us closeted for hours and hours. And Gloria was great because she didn't rush people. Then there was a fight as to who was going to read what parts of the plank. Coretta Scott King hadn't participated in any of the discussions about the text, but the symbolism of having her present the African American section was just wonderful. And when it came to the outpouring of "We Shall Overcome" from the convention floor, we knew all those hours were worth that.

Eleanor Smeal The other resolution that was controversial was the gay plank. It looked like there was going to be major opposition. From within the feminist caucus, a group called the Susan B. Anthony Caucus had formed, and it had labor women who opposed the passage of the sexual preference plank. They weren't against gay rights, but they were afraid that it would hurt the whole Plan of Action. So it was one of the turning points when Betty Friedan agreed to second the resolution on the floor. A whole group of us got her to do that. We thought it would be a dramatic moment.

Sexual Preference Resolution Congress, state, and local legislatures should enact legislation to eliminate discrimination on the basis of sexual and affectional preference in areas including, but not limited to, employment, housing, public accommodations, credit, public facilities, government funding, and the military.

Eleanor Smeal (speaking in favor of the sexual-preference resolution) This is a feminist issue, because discrimination against women begins at the basis of sexuality. There are double standards: one standard for males, another for females; one standard for heterosexuals, another for homosexuals. And all these double standards in the issue of sexuality work to keep women in their place.

Betty Friedan I am known to be violently opposed to the lesbian issue. As someone who has grown up in Middle America and as someone who has loved men too well, I have had trouble with this issue. Now my priority is in passing the ERA. And because there is nothing in it that will give any protection to homosexuals, I believe we must help the women who are lesbians.

Eleanor Smeal In the end, the resolution passed overwhelmingly. The only plank that was defeated was the proposal that there be a Cabinet-level women's commissioner. The NOW caucus opposed it, because even then, the specter of Ronald Reagan being elected was on the horizon. We feared that Schlafly would be that person.

Judy Lerner I was so tired when I left Houston. I got on the plane, and everybody was coming from the conference. A woman sat down next to me who came from a little town, maybe fifteen hundred people, Swayzee, Indiana. I asked her what she thought of it, and she said that abortion was against her religion, and homosexuality. "But the thing that gets to me," she said, "is battered women." She talked about a sister who was a battered wife in a little town, and I had the feeling that she might have been the one who was the battered wife. We talked, and I felt I could be honest with her. I said, "Isn't compassion for other women the thing you want?" When we got off to change planes, she hugged me. I thought somehow in this crazy dialogue it will sink in that she met somebody there who didn't wear horns, who was a mother like her.

Lindsy Van Gelder Houston transformed us all. We learned that we could excel at serious parliamentary procedure, and still indulge in singing "Happy Birthday" to speaker Margaret Mead, to knit and nurse babies during debates, to laugh with Bella as she banged the gavel to adjourn and wished us "Good night, my loves."

London Evening Standard For better or worse, mainstream feminism has evolved into the most broadly based movement for egalitarianism that America possesses . . . The women's movement is now a truly national, unified engine of change which could conceivably become the cutting edge of the most important human issues America faces in the next decade.

Liz Carpenter Every political figure has to make a decision whether he is going to be for us or against us. And that began to happen. We got on the political agenda of every elected official for good or worse.

Patrick J. Buchanan If Carter is thinking of a second term, he will thank them for their work, promise to study the agenda, give the girls some milk and cookies and send them on their way. Why? Because the National Plan of Action adopted in Houston points Carter in precisely the opposite direction from where the national majority is headed.

Eleanor Smeal The overwhelming sentiment was that the conference was a smashing success. We were on a high, and the momentum was with us.

Brownie Ledbetter The president didn't want to appoint a committee to advise on implementing the resolutions, but as a result of Houston, we got the committee formed.

Carter's Women's Commission

Midge Costanza After the *Spirit of Houston* report* was prepared, the next battle was, would Carter name a commission for women, or would he just say, "Give me the report. Let's work with Congress and see what we can do." The day before the report was to be presented to the president, Bella's on the phone, "What did he say about a commission? Where is he leaning? We're all waiting." "He hasn't given me an answer yet," I said. "How was I to know Menachem Begin was going to come to town?" It was a challenging day for Jimmy Carter, and there are maybe fifteen hundred pink slips that I'm trying to reach him. My office is next to the Oval Office, and I look out in the hall every twenty minutes, thinking, "Damn, why isn't he coming back?" Finally I see him. I wait about five minutes and knock on the door, and he says, "Come in." There's a chair next to the

**The Spirit of Houston/The First National Women's Conference: An Official Report to the President, the Congress and the People of the United States* was presented to President Carter at a ceremony in the East Room of the White House on March 22, 1978.

president's desk, and I don't sit in it. I plop in it. I'm worn out from hearing Bella and Gloria all day. I'm sitting next to the most powerful political figure in the free world, and I say, "Whoa, have I had a tough day." He turned with his grin and says, "Oh, really, Midget? Let me tell you about mine." I said, "All you had was Menachem Begin. I had Bella and Gloria." You know what he said? "I'll trade you!" He had a wonderful sense of humor. And he loved Bella. I know people don't think so. He had an enormous respect for her, and he loved hearing her responses to some of the stuff that he would mandate. He'd shake his head and say, "There's no one like her."

So when I went in to talk about Bella, I was talking about a friend of mine. I would be sharing that with the president of the United States, whom I was viewing as another friend. He knew how I felt about her. To me, there never will be another Bella Abzug. You couldn't if you wanted to clone her. You couldn't create what came from her soul and combined with her brilliance to produce the ability, knowledge, and policy wisdom that I wish even a minimum number of our world leaders today could present.

Brownie Ledbetter There were over forty of us as I recall, an enormously diverse group. It was run out of a little office in the Labor Department. Mim Kelber, Bella's lifelong collaborator, was there all the time. We went to work and did a ton of research. We had regular meetings, but Carter never acknowledged us. He never came and kicked it off like he did other presidential commissions, and with Midge Costanza gone,* we had no communica-

*Costanza, the only high-ranking woman in the Carter White House until Anne Wexler was appointed assistant to the president in 1978, resigned August 1 that year, writing in her resignation letter, "In recent months I have had to deal increasingly with the subject of approach rather than that of substance, spending valuable time and energy on discussions of whether I have spoken out too much, what my relations are to your other senior

tion from the White House. We thought Sarah Weddington would be helpful, but she absolutely was not our advocate. And they wouldn't let Bella be chair alone.* She had to share it with Carmen Delgado Votaw.

Sey Chassler We all had committee assignments—I was of course on the media committee . . . and each of the committees had lunch together in the Department of State office building, and Bella sat with each of the groups. She actually was a member of our committee, and I was the chair of it, so she was below me in that context. I put forward some ideas which she took note of, and then we all reconvened and we had to give our committee reports, so she went around the table, committee after committee, until she got to me, and then she said, "It's okay, Sey, you don't have to report; I already know what your ideas are." She wasn't sharing it with the rest of the group.

I didn't have any axe to grind with her. I mean, that's the way she wanted it, but it was typical of her. And you could really get hurt that way if you were in a power struggle with her. But on the other hand, she could be very, very persuasive, and that's why it was such a shock to us the day she got fired . . .

I think she was fired because she stood for a series of actions and needs that the president was not prepared to follow through on. They have to do with all of the basic women's issues—job rights, economic rights, educational equality, pro-choice, the Equal Rights Amendment, and even though Carter did [and continued to] campaign for the Equal Rights Amendment, the amount of commitment was rather low. I don't know if you remember that he was walking out of church one Sunday morning and a reporter asked him what he thought about the progress of

---

staff, or where my office is located." "Miss Costanza Resigns as Assistant to Carter, Citing Problems of Style," Karen De Witt, *The New York Times*, August 2, 1978.

*In *Gender Gap*, the book she coauthored with Mim Kelber, Bella wrote that it was at her suggestion that Carter appointed cochairs and named Carmen Delgado Votaw.

women's rights and what he said was, "I think women have gone about as far as they can for the moment." It was a slip but it was a very significant slip.

Carmen Delgado Votaw Bella and I talked to the president, saying this committee is very important. We have things to say to you, but you've never met with us. We'd like to have an appointment. And he agreed. But then we heard from Hamilton Jordan*, the meeting was to be for fifteen minutes—only time enough for having pictures taken, and we had substantive things to talk about.

Brownie Ledbetter The president finally invited us to the White House at four something in the afternoon the Wednesday before Thanksgiving. Most of us wanted to be home with our families at Thanksgiving. The commission members met, and we were really pissed. Bella wasn't there—she had a speaking engagement and Carmen was running the meeting. Ann Richards got up and said, "We need more than just a photo op!" About that time, I left the room to go to the bathroom, and by the time I got back, they had voted to turn the president down. And I must say, everyone felt good about it. Well, I hardly got home before Bella was on the phone saying, "How could you let this happen, for God's sake? He is the president of the United States!" She was just furious that we had made that strategic error. And that was in conjunction with releasing to the press criticisms of him on how he was dealing with inflation and his military budget and how that affected women. Bella was not present for that decision either.

Maxine Waters As the leader, Bella knew this was going to be detrimental to her. She went with the consensus that they must give

*President Carter's White House chief of staff.

us adequate time. But she told me that she felt that this was going to create a huge problem. She knew going in that they were coming after her.

Carmen Delgado Votaw When we talked to Carter, Bella and I said we didn't mean to be disrespectful, but that fifteen minutes wasn't enough time. So we got a second meeting—this time for half an hour.

The "Friday Night Massacre"

Brownie Ledbetter It was a Friday afternoon. I remember it was snowing. We were waiting in some outer room at the White House, because some labor guys were in there. And when they came out, we should have taken a clue. You could see it in their faces. They were dejected.

Carmen Delgado Votaw He had just met with the AFL-CIO, and he was very exercised about something. I was sitting next to him, and you could see his vein just going.

Eleanor Smeal I remember I was speaking on the ERA. I felt there was tension in the room from the minute we walked in. I was looking right at him, and I didn't like his body language. I couldn't figure it out, because we had had this very successful conference and we were going to push him to do things now.

Brownie Ledbetter When the president started his response to us, he was literally whining. "I appointed you. You're my commission. How could you do this to me? I supported you on ERA. I didn't agree with you on abortion, but I let you do your thing.

What do my inflation policy and my military policy have to do with women?"

Eleanor Smeal He was upset because a press release had gone out that was critical of the White House, and we were all White House appointees. He was blaming Bella for the press release, but I had known that Bella's husband, Martin, had had a heart attack, and she was with him in the hospital when those criticisms were released to the press.

Brownie Ledbetter Bella responded and it was brilliant. It was totally respectful, without the slightest bit of rancor. With great care, she explained what those policies had to do with women. It was beautifully done. When it was over and we came out, there was tons of press. Bella said the usual thing that you would say. We were delighted to meet with the president and we looked forward to working with the White House.

Eleanor Smeal As we left, I said, "My God. We've just been bawled out by the president of the United States." He was talking in a normal tone of voice but I felt we had been read the riot act.

Brownie Ledbetter I got in a cab with Ellie and Lane Kirkland,* who was the AFL-CIO representative on the commission, and they were going to drop me at the Labor Department office where I had my suitcase. I kept saying, "God, she was great. She was just brilliant." And Ellie was frowning and saying, "Brownie, something's wrong. I was sitting right beside Bella, and I was looking into his cold, blue-gray eyes. Something's not right." I remember walking up the steps to the Labor Department wondering what Ellie was concerned about.

*Lane Kirkland was secretary-treasurer and soon to be president of the AFL-CIO.

Sey Chassler Bella and I walked out of the White House together, and she, of course, was immediately surrounded by the press . . . She was saying, "The meeting I thought was quite good. We made some points with the president, and he has agreed to meet with us more frequently, and there will be a greater liaison with the White House with the commission and on the future of the platform of issues that the previous commission has produced." While talking to the press, she was tapped on the shoulder by someone who had come out of the White House to tell her that the president wanted to see her. So we said goodbye, and I took the plane back to New York. As soon as I got home I got a call from Gloria Steinem . . . to tell me that Bella had been fired, and of course most of us quit.

Carmen Delgado Votaw I got a piece of paper, and Bella did, as well, from Hamilton Jordan saying, "See me before you leave." I thought we'd go in together. He said, "No. I want to talk to you first." I went in, and he said, "Really it's untenable," referring to our criticisms of the White House. "We would like you to stay on the commission, but we're going to fire Bella." I said it was a decision of the whole commission, and Bella wasn't even at the meeting, so you couldn't pin it on her. Afterward, I waited for Bella. She told me she had been fired unceremoniously. I told her they wanted me to stay on, but I said I wouldn't. So we went back to the Labor Department and started calling all the commissioners. And Bella wanted to call the groups who had been involved in Houston to explain what happened. She was very inclusive in that. We reached really a lot of people.

Brownie Ledbetter When I got to the Labor Department office, there was nobody there but Mim and Bella, and Mimmie was in the outer room. She said, "Oh, Brownie, go in there." Bella was sobbing. She was on the phone with Hamilton Jordan, and I could hear the conversation. She was saying, "For God's sake, let me resign. Give me that bit of dignity." And he was saying, "No, we told the press." The press knew the whole time. They knew when we came out of the meeting. It was a real screw job. We got Bella back in that other room with Mimmie, and Koryne Horbal came in, and we all just hit the phones to call every single member we could find. And of course, we got 75 percent of the commission to resign. In effect we killed it. The Carter people thought they had done something clever and shown that Bella was too crude for the country. They were wrong, and it backfired.

Gloria Steinem We found out later that Carter's staff were telling him that he was looking "weak" and that he should do something to look strong and macho. Bella was sacrificed to that need for better PR. They thought it would work, because they assumed Bella was unpopular. In the end they were so wrong. Polls showed that more people disapproved of her firing than approved.

Jimmy Carter I have no quarrel with, no problems with the committee itself. I did select and appoint Ms. Abzug to serve as the chairperson of the committee last year, and it didn't work out well. The committee has never been well organized. Their functions have never been clearly expressed to me. There has not been good cooperation between the committee and the cabinet members or my advisers or me, and I felt it was necessary to change the chairperson, whom I had appointed personally. It's a prerogative of the president. And we'll do everything we can now under a fine, new chairperson of the committee [Marjorie Bell Chambers was named acting chair] to restore its effectiveness and to make sure that I and the women throughout the country, and particularly in this group, work to achieve those mutual goals which we share.

Marlo Thomas I heard that she was fired and then got a call from Bella saying she thought the best thing was that we all walk. I said, "Absolutely! If you've been fired I don't want to be on that damned committee." They felt we'd overstepped our bounds when talking about the budget. A budget wasn't supposed to be a women's issue. She was always walking uphill, bucking the tide in every possible way. Bella's also the kind of personality that if she wasn't walking uphill, she'd find the hill that could be walked up. It's what made her great. It's also what kept her alive, what she thrived on.

Eve Abzug That whole thing with Carter when she was fired—she was bitter. She did talk about that all the time. I think she was very sad and angry in a deep way, although it didn't stop her. It didn't stop her.

Carmen Delgado Votaw I live in Bethesda, and it was snowing. I'm not a very good driver when it's nice, and I was pretty upset by the time I got home. But I sat at my typewriter and typed my letter of resignation. I delivered it to the White House the next morning before going over to the Mayflower Hotel, where we had scheduled a press conference to announce the resignations.

Carolyn Reed The commission was set up to fail. I think what they figured was when they fired Bella—who's a very difficult person; there's no doubt about that—[since there were two cochairs] and there was no love lost between Bella and Carmen, Carmen would take over. What they did not figure on was Carmen's integrity, and the integrity of a lot of other women . . . I resigned on that very day . . . There was a name change. It was the National Advisory Committee for Women and he changed it to the President's Committee. I got several calls from Sarah Weddington's office, from Sarah herself, and some other people, to reconsider . . . I got a letter in May saying that they had accepted my resignation as of May so-and-so. I sent them back a letter that I wanted my resignation accepted when I gave it, which was on January 13.

Gloria Steinem I wasn't a member of that commission, but my friend Carolyn Reed, an organizer of household workers, was. She made the greatest of all the public explanations when she resigned. Carter's aide Sarah Weddington was semi-threatening people who quit. She was saying, "You can't give up a chance to influence the president." Carolyn told the press, "As a household worker, I've never confused access with influence."

Brownie Ledbetter There were about twenty women who stayed on. Erma Bombeck—this was just not her thing. When I called her she said, "Oh. I can't believe that, Brownie. Did he do that?" I said yes, and we're resigning. "Oh, I can't resign! He's the president of the United States." Ann Richards stayed on. And the thing that is so incredible about Bella is that, years later, when Ann ran for governor of Texas, Bella killed herself [campaigning] for Ann.

Sey Chassler There was a woman who represented Jewish organizations and there were women who represented American Indian organizations, Spanish, and black, and there was an oriental woman and as I recall most of them stayed . . . They had to stay, they felt, because this was the only access they had to the White House . . .

Erma Bombeck did not quit, and with good reason; everyone understood that Erma was out there talking . . . for the ERA . . . She had called me to discuss this and what she said was that her value was that when she arrived in a town she had nothing but good publicity and if she quit it would destroy that completely, and so she felt she had to stay.

Erma Bombeck Twenty-four words [the ERA] have never been so misunderstood since the four words "One size fits all."

At our post-firing press conference, Nancy Neuman of the League of Women Voters, one of the committee members who resigned to protest my dismissal, said, "When you have a tough day at the office you come home and kick your dog. They think women are vulnerable, like dogs." (My husband had a different view. "You're the only one I know," he said, "who can get fired from a nonpaying job.")

Karin Lippert Ms. magazine hosted a lot of events that were about firsts for women—the first woman in space, the first women's bank, you name it—and this was the first time a high-ranking woman representing all American women was fired by the president of the United States. We had the New York press conference in our offices. There was no time to organize it, but we were an activist group, available weekends, day and night, especially to Bella, who would not hesitate to call me during the night. I remember our sense of betrayal and outrage at what Carter had done. I also remember going to the *Today* show with her the next morning for an interview. When we arrived Bella was told that George Will had just been interviewed about the firing, and she said, "I want to see it!" The producer told her no. She said, "I want to see it!" and put this guy up against the wall—gently. She saw the clip before going on.

Carmen Delgado Votaw About six months later I was at the White House for a human rights gathering. A reporter I knew said in a loud voice, "I thought you were persona non grata at the White

House." Carter was standing there and he said, "No. She's persona grata here." He came to me and said, "It was very nice of you to resign before you went to the press conference." The niceties of office meant something to him.

Linda Tarr-Whelan I came to work for the Carter administration at the end of 1979, when the whole conflagration was over, when Linda Johnson Robb was chair of the President's Advisory Committee. The Carter administration was really interesting with regard to women. Carter and Mondale both were very personally engaged in ERA ratification. I set up for Carter a monthly sort of "kitchen cabinet" meeting with twenty of the top women leaders of organizations. Stuart Eisenstadt was head of the domestic policy campaign, and even back then was willing to look at a gender cut on all the domestic policies of the administration. It may be that they absorbed a lot of what the Advisory Committee had to say, even though they didn't want to hear it from Bella.

Eleanor Smeal I believe Bella's firing was the beginning of the end of Jimmy Carter's reign. Remember Clinton's campaign? The Sister Souljah strategy?* They distance themselves from someone they perceive as radical to make themselves look moderate. I think it had nothing to do with the PR release or refusing the first meeting. When Carter finds out she wasn't even there and he doesn't slow down—what's that about? They had decided they were going to be challenged by the right. They knew Reagan was moving. Carter felt he was too far exposed to the left with this commission. So he picked on the most vocal person,

*When a politician repudiates what is perceived as an extreme position in order to appear moderate and acceptable to voters: the expression comes from Bill Clinton's criticism of the hip-hop political activist, who, as part of a larger comment on the 1992 Los Angeles riots, was quoted in *The Washington Post* as saying, "If black people kill black people every day, why not have a week and kill white people?"

and he wanted to get big press doing it. What he didn't understand was that Bella, who looks like a radical person, had a large constituency. And I don't think they could surmise we would all quit. But he moved himself so far to the right that he helped bring on a challenge by Ted Kennedy at the 1980 convention. Kennedy took the last ten states in the primaries, and that slowed them down. Carter thought, what was he losing: a few people in New York? They didn't understand the spirit of Houston, which had gone throughout the country.

The same crowd who fires Bella then has this huge challenge by the left of the party, with Kennedy—at the first convention where there were equal numbers of men and women. The Carter people send word down that they are going to go against the ERA plank, and they're going against the abortion planks. We tell them we're going to win on the floor. We have the labor women, the liberal Democrats, the Kennedy delegates. There was a big NOW delegation, and NEA [the National Education Association] had a huge number of feminists involved. We decided not to withdraw and demanded a floor count. To make a long story short, those are the last votes in prime time. We win on a roll call against a sitting president.

Edward M. Kennedy When we started the 1980 presidential campaign, we had some challenges. After the Iowa primaries, I redefined the campaign and issues in a speech in Georgetown. And I asked for Bella's support. Bella and I had worked together on the Freedom of Information legislation, and we'd been very much involved in women's issues. She was very courageous because at that time, it certainly didn't look like it was going to be a winning cause, but she signed on and told me that she'd help. And she was right with us all the way. She went and campaigned in a number of different places and was very effective. We won the last series of primaries—New York and Connecticut, and California and New Jersey. I had enough of Carter's delegates that if they ever got rid of the faithful-delegate rule,* we could have been successful. She was indispensable on the platform. As I remember she gave the Carter people a fit, because she had all of these platform positions. Even after I conceded, they insisted on a roll call over things, which was sort of humiliating to them—you know, to get beaten again. She was my representative on the platform, and she was just enormously important. She fought hard and we had some very important successes on issues of health, on employment, on a number of women's issues.

Robin Morgan It's opera, drama. Jewish opera. I think the worst of it I ever had at Bella's hands was the Teddy Kennedy thing. Chappaquiddick had happened, and then he was going to run for president.† Gloria was under tremendous pressure to endorse. I think John Anderson was still in it, and at a certain point Gloria said, "What do you think? I'm under all this pressure to endorse Kennedy." And I lobbied intensely for her not to. "This we cannot live with. A dead woman's body. At the very least, just don't endorse." There was a press conference coming up and Gloria went to it, and did not endorse Kennedy. And then my phone rang in my office. It was Bella. And for forty-five minutes . . . finally I just held it away from my ear. "How dare you make Gloria change her mind?" I started out saying, "In the first place, Gloria's a grown-up. You lobbied in one direction, I lobbied in another direction." "How dare you? What do you know about it? You don't care . . ." It went on and on. Finally I put the phone

*The faithful-delegate rule, proposed by the Democratic National Committee in 1978 and adopted at the 1980 convention, required delegates to cast their first roll-call vote for the candidate to whom they had been committed.

†The Chappaquiddick tragedy happened in June 1969. An aide to Kennedy drowned in a car accident; Kennedy was driving and survived. The presidential campaign was in 1980.

down on the desk and went about doing my work, and periodically leaned down to the phone and said, "Un huh." She didn't speak to me for a while. And a few months later, at a party, my son Blake, who was at this point, five or six, who already had paper cuts on his tongue from licking envelopes for her campaigns, went up to Bella. He climbed onto her lap and said, "You mustn't be mad at my mother anymore, because this is tearing me apart." At which point she marched over to me, still holding him, and said, "Did you tell your son I was angry at you?" And I said, "Ah, well, you haven't been speaking to me since the Teddy Kennedy thing." She put Blake down and said to him, "Listen. I love your mother. I give her the respect of being angry at her."

Eleanor Smeal Nothing could fight what happened afterward in the right-wing sweep in 1980. Reagan came in with an anti–women's rights agenda, which I don't think the public was really aware of. But that's what happened. So we were slowed down. But I think the [Houston] conference was important. And it was important for what it did for women who participated. Twenty thousand women participated, first hand. It was important also because it set a mood internationally and worldwide. I think one of the most important things that have happened for women in the latter part of the twentieth century was the building of a global movement for women's rights, and this absolutely helped that.

11

Building an Agenda for Women— One Meeting, Conference, March at a Time

Chronology

1978 Faye Wattleton is elected president of Planned Parenthood, the first woman and first African American since the organization was founded in 1916 by Margaret Sanger.

1978 The National Organization for Women sponsors a huge march on Washington to persuade Congress to extend the deadline for ratifying the Equal Rights Amendment; the deadline is extended, but in June 1982, the ERA is stopped three states short of ratification.

1979 With Mim Kelber and others—including former congresswomen Patsy Mink and Yvonne Burke, Gloria Steinem, Brownie Ledbetter, California State Assemblywoman Maxine Waters, and the Gray Panthers founder, Maggie Kuhn—Bella cofounds Women USA Fund, Inc., to conduct voter education and registration projects and publish educational materials, including information about women's international efforts to fight pollution and poverty.

1980 Bella begins a daily commentary on CNN, which continues through 1981.

1980 The UN's second World Conference on Women is held in Copenhagen.

1981 Women USA, along with NOW and other groups, mobilizes a national Women's Rights Day of lobbying on Capitol Hill.

1983 Sally Ride, the first American woman astronaut, goes into outer space.

1983 Alice Walker becomes the first African American woman to win a Pulitzer Prize for fiction, with her novel *The Color Purple*.

1984 With Mim Kelber, Bella publishes *Gender Gap: Bella Abzug's Guide to Political Power for American Women*.

1984 Ronald Reagan defeats Walter Mondale and his running mate, Geraldine Ferraro, the first woman to run on a major party ticket.

1985 After the third UN women's conference, in Nairobi, Bella and Mim add an international project to the Women USA agenda, organizing colleagues from universities, think tanks, the media, and government into the Women's Foreign Policy Council, which compiled lists of women experts to be used by groups making policy and by the media as commentators on news events.

1986 Martin Abzug dies.

Liz Abzug After Carter fired her and the committee members resigned in protest, I think my mother was really at a loss to figure out what she was going to do in terms of having political clout, nationally or locally. She was saying, "What do I do with all my energy? Maybe I should look globally, because they're rejecting what I'm saying at the domestic level."

Faye Wattleton It sounds like a cliché, but Bella could walk into a room and know that room within minutes, if not seconds. She could know who in that room to avoid, who in that room she needed to get to, and what was the lay of the land. She had the rare capacity to integrate a landscape—not unlike the way Henry Kissinger can see the world on its broadest terms. (They were, by the way, cordial to each other.) She could see all of these movements and how they made sense in relationship to each other and apart from each other. You start with a fundamental gene for justice, and intolerance for injustice, and make sure you know that a little piece of it is in every brick in the building. Bella had that capacity to see how the peace movement was intricately tied to the women's movement, and how the environmental movement would never go anyplace if you didn't do something about women, and how the political process could be used for all of that. It's some inherent instinct you don't learn in school and you probably don't learn it on the road either.

Martha Baker When Mim got sick and couldn't work, she called me to ask if I would go and work with Bella in her office on Beaver Street. They had just started organizing the National Women's Rights Day—a lobby day in Washington, with NOW and Molly Yard and Barbara Mikulski, who was a congresswoman at that time. We never had that kind of relationship before. I was her staff person, but the worst thing was I didn't know how to type. Like Bella, I come from the era when, if you learned how to type, it meant that would be your job.

We had these old typewriters, and finally she got one with a correction key so you could fix small mistakes. Anyone can type a short letter, but she had some legal documents. Well, do you know who our typist was? Martin! He used to come in at the end of his day, and I would give him my typing. He'd say, "No. I don't want to use that typewriter. I'll use my own."

Leslie Bennetts Mary Tyler Moore, Gloria Steinem, and Bella Abzug went to see Representative Thomas P. O'Neill, Jr., speaker of the House. Dr. Benjamin Spock talked with Senator Ted Stevens. Former congresswoman Patsy Mink met with Senators Mark O. Hatfield and Robert J. Dole. But it was easy for the famous few to get lost in the crowd as three thousand women (along with the occasional man) turned out yesterday for Women's Rights Day in Congress. More than eighty national labor, religious, civil rights, educational, and other organizations sent members to join individuals who came to lobby their elected representatives in support of reproductive rights, Social Security reform, and a host of other concerns. The diverse groups included the American Women's Clergy Association, Catholics for a Free Choice, the United Auto Workers, Mormons for ERA, the National Conference of Puerto Rican Women, the National Council of Jewish Women, and the American Association of University Women.

Martha Baker Bella and I spent a few days in Washington organizing the national lobby event. That's when she started talking about doing Women USA. I got somebody I knew to design their logo and their stationery. I got someone to print it in green because it was environmental. We created this board. That's when I met Brownie, I guess.

Brownie Ledbetter We organized Women USA because the National Women's Political Caucus was becoming more of a membership organization, which we knew it would. But the trouble with membership organizations is they tend to turn on the moods of the members. So Bella wanted to organize this separate organization that could quickly mobilize around issues, and I thought it was a great idea. I remember going with Patsy Mink in Washington to get our 501(c)(3) status for the Women USA Fund so we could raise foundation money for educational projects and research.

Eleanor Smeal I think Bella in a way resented the Equal Rights Amendment campaign. Maybe "resents" is not the right word, but a group of people felt the ERA wasn't radical enough. Nevertheless, Bella came to D.C. to help us organize a massive and successful march in July 1978 to extend the 1979 deadline for ERA ratification to 1982. Bella came to help us because she saw us as not as informed and a lot younger—and we were. She was in the front line, marching, whatever her disagreement with our strategy.

Carmen Delgado Votaw In essence, it was the lowest common denominator. The Equal Rights Amendment was the one issue where you could get all the minority women and so on. There was real commitment to ERA.

Marlo Thomas At the end of the ERA campaign, Illinois was critical, one of three possible states where the legislature could assure ratification. And Phyllis Schlafly was scheduled to be a guest on the Phil Donahue show. Bella called me and said, "You've got to tell him to not put her on." I said, "You know, Bella, I can't tell Phil how to run his show. He's a political animal. I'll talk to him, but I've got to tell you, I don't have the power to stop him from doing his show." We were in Chicago, and I went to Phil. I said, "You know I have to tell you that I'm killing myself, as we all are, to pass the ERA. The vote is coming in Illinois, and for you to put on Phyllis Schlafly the week of the vote is really going to hurt us." He said to me, "If you don't understand why I have to put on Phyllis Schlafly the week of the vote, then you don't understand what I do."

I called Bella. She was furious. I knew that was going to be his answer. You can't tell someone who works in topical television to not show the other side of the argument. He had had Ellie Smeal and everyone else on, and now it was the other side's turn. And Bella found that absolutely unacceptable. I said, "Bella, this is what he does. I can't stop him from reporting the news." She banged the phone down.

Brownie Ledbetter Somehow my role in those days became to hire staff, which was hard because Bella was very hard on staff. And I would look for money and talk to the foundations. Bella said, "Well you went and talked, did you get any?" And I would say, "No, it takes months." She would say, "You don't know what you're doing!" Bella was used to calling up people with a lot of money from Hollywood and New York and getting it. She couldn't understand this process thing. It really irritated her.

June Zeitlin When I was working at the Ford Foundation, I tried to help Bella get funding for her projects. She was like, "How could you not give me funding?" She definitely thought she was entitled. She thought she should just have a meeting and get the money. Even though I was her funder, I always felt like I worked for her. But being her advocate within the funding community was easy for me, because I knew what she could produce. I think people respected her, but they were intimidated, because she wasn't someone they could control—someone who would do exactly what she wrote down in a funding proposal.

Brownie Ledbetter In one of our best projects, we targeted six congressional districts and got women in those districts to participate in discussions around about ten different concerns. If they came to understand the issues and think about them, then maybe they would organize politically around them. We had made a commitment in the funding proposal to pull the women together at the end and debrief, to find out what we could. But Bella didn't want to do the debriefing. She saw it as a waste of time. I thought we had an obligation to those women who had been isolated in huge congressional districts with no support. We owed it to them, if nothing else, to find out what their experience had been with the project.

We did end up with a debriefing session—we went to L.A. and had them all come there. Bella was furious the whole time. We stayed with the actors Joe Bologna and Renée Taylor, wonderful, close friends. And she was amazing with Bella. She would try to get Bella out of her funk. I remember one story: Joe was in this movie and they had a party when it opened. You know, Renée's a fabulous actress and comedian herself. But at one point this woman turned to her and said, "Ms. Bologna, what do you do?" And she said, "Well, first I peel the carrots, and then I add the raisins." She told stories like that all along.

Martha Baker We had Bella going around speaking everywhere. I would find someone to pay her to go to a particular city and match it up with a freebie, an organizing event where she'd speak as well. When Bella was out of the public eye, she didn't just wither and fade away. She didn't just do her thing hoping that everybody would take notice. She would organize to the point where they were forced to be involved and take notice. What I see today with women I know and love is that they don't get out of their little box. They think what they're doing is right, and they can't understand why everyone else isn't supporting them. How many national campaigns do you see going out of their way to focus on women? They know they need the women's vote, but they think if they focus on our issues it will hurt them.

The way Bella operated, no matter what you were working on, if something really important happened nationally or internationally, you would drop what you were doing on a dime to act on what needed to be addressed. She'd say, "We can't allow this to happen. Okay, let's get together next Saturday, because we have to take action." People would think, "Oh, I don't really want to, but I know she's going to do it so I'd better go along." So you'd have a strong, clear message coming from a lot of forces working together—women of color, women in the labor community, political women, movement women. I haven't seen that kind of action from the women's community in a long time.

Faye Wattleton As head of Planned Parenthood, I was sitting on a very powerful organization, and I think she respected that I was using it as a platform and didn't back down. But she did show jealous streaks. At the 1989 Washington march for reproductive rights, she wanted to be sure she had a better place on the agenda than I had. I just sat there and said, "Whenever I speak, it's going to be fine." Bella was always jockeying for the right position. Now, those are the survival instincts of a politician.

At the time of the '89 march, we were awaiting the Webster decision,* and Ellie [Smeal], as she often did, announced that we were having a march. And those of us at other pro-choice organizations said, "Excuse me. Were we asleep when you decided this? None of us have this in our budgets." But by that time she'd made a public pronouncement, so we're between a rock and a hard spot. If we don't participate, it looks like the movement is divided. Yet we're pissed. Ellie didn't have any money.† She couldn't pay for the porta-potties. We had at the time a very viable pro-choice coalition—we'd get together every month or every other month and debate message and strategy. Molly Yard was the head of NOW, and in the ring were Molly and Bella, who was then head of Women USA. Bella was saying, "How can

*In *Webster v. Reproductive Health Services*, in a five-to-four plurality ruling, the Supreme Court held that Missouri could ban the use of state employees and facilities to perform abortions. Three justices in the majority recommended revisiting *Roe v. Wade*, and Justice Antonin Scalia suggested it be overturned. The fifth, Justice Sandra Day O'Connor, pointedly refused to reconsider *Roe*.

†After her terms as NOW president, Eleanor Smeal had founded the Feminist Majority Foundation in 1987, but she was still very much involved in the leadership of NOW.

you do this without being respectful to us?" But we did manage to pull it together after several meetings and raise the money with a joint letter to all our members and donors. It was interesting, because when we merged and purged the lists, there was only a 20 percent duplication across the organizations—ACLU, NARAL, NOW, and Planned Parenthood were the big ones—so we were obviously reaching different constituencies. But really it was Bella and Molly Yard who fought it out to pull the march together. Those were golden days—those backroom battles.

Eleanor Smeal What's killing the movement today is e-mails. People don't even get on their damn phones. I have something that is very important going on right now, and we're trying to get an informal meeting of women's leaders. In the old days, Bella would be coming from New York. She would drag Gloria with her. Gloria sometimes thinks of herself as a writer, an observer, and Bella would push her into being a doer—to understanding her power as a women's leader, not as a celebrity.

But the truth of it is, everything is tamped down by e-mails. You can't get passion with e-mails. You can't organize that way. They're wonderful for telling people the meeting is set for two o'clock, but they are terrible for exchanging ideas. There's no emotion. You can't pick people's brains. I think it's a serious problem. Bella wouldn't be an e-mail person. She'd be a talking person.

She believed we could make a difference—that if we got together and decided on something, we could make it happen. Right now many leaders are so hesitant. They believe they have no power.

June Zeitlin I was at this Washington conference in June 2004, and Maxine Waters got up and said, "Nobody is doing the Bella Abzug work." She just went on and on. "If Bella were here we'd be in the Kerry campaign. We'd be out of the Kerry campaign. We'd be talking about this. We'd be talking about that." Someone had just given me a hatpin they had found, because it looked rather like a Bella hatpin, and I was wearing it. Afterward, I was so moved by what Maxine was saying, I went up to her and gave her the pin. She started crying. Imagine, someone who contributes as much as Maxine Waters could also feel this gap so strongly.

Ronnie Eldridge Bella was one strong, ambitious person, who really did believe that she could single-handedly change the world. And I think she was always angry that she wasn't given enough of a chance—that she couldn't go further.

Faye Wattleton Frustration was what drove her. On one hand, she had an irrational sensitivity—"Did you hear what she said about me? Why do you think she said those nasty things about me?"—and on the other, to be completely focused and shut out everything but what she wanted to accomplish. Maybe it's necessary for someone like Bella to have a somewhat—I want to say flawed—insight about one's own actions, because that helps you not to put on the brakes. She could be highly sensitive and very compassionate and nurturing, but maybe it takes that kind of flaw to say, "Damn the torpedoes. I don't care what anybody thinks."

Robin Morgan Bella was an extraordinary organizer. I remember so many times—the UN World Conference on Women in Copenhagen, for example, the second one, in 1980, after Mexico City. We already had worked together and knew each other well. Bella came up with the idea that we should make a caucus of Arab and Jewish women. I had some credibility among the Arabs, and she, of course, was understood as a major leader of the Jews. After lobbying these disparate groups, we had five or six women ready to talk, but where would it happen, and when? Bella said breakfast, and I said, but some of the meetings start at seven in the morning. People would need some time to themselves to start the day. She said, "No, you're missing the point. We get them together at 6:00 a.m. Nobody wants to talk at 6:00 a.m., so they're going to have to listen." And they did. We didn't solve the Middle East, but by the end of the meeting, everybody was crying because we made them tell stories about their lives as women. That magic happened, where people embrace and cry and exchange telephone numbers.

Nadine Hack For the end of the Nairobi conference in 1985,* I organized a closing unity rally. Three of us worked on it—a very young Donna Brazile,† a little bit older Kathy Bonk, and me. The world media had been focusing on all the fights—between the Palestinian women and the Israeli women, between the Soviet delegation and the U.S. delegation. But those of us who were there with seventeen thousand women on the University of Nairobi campus were amidst a sea of women's camaraderie that was just so palpable and extraordinary. Everything at the NGO forum sessions‡ was conducted very much in the African style—sitting in circles under the trees and you could just walk from circle to circle. I was drawn to a circle of Masai women—they were very visible in their traditional dress—and I sat down with five women who were all the wives of the same husband. They had walked eight hours from their village to participate and talk

*The UN's Third World Conference on Women.

†The Voters for Choice operative Donna Brazile later became the first African American to lead a major presidential campaign (Gore-Lieberman 2000).

‡The UN conferences were organized into sessions for official delegations and a concurrent forum of nongovernmental organizations. Typically, most of the feminist organizing took place at the NGO forum meetings.

about women's issues. I never in my life needed more proof that women from every culture have fundamentally more in common with each other than not.

So in the middle of the week, we had this idea of a closing unity celebration, which meant that for the last four days, Kathy, Donna, and I did not sleep. There would be one woman after another coming up on the stage, and we were careful to pick representative women and to say how important it was at this closing moment of the conference not to say anything divisive but to emphasize their shared, positive experience. There was this wonderful feminist from Egypt, and despite all the preparation, and despite her promise, when she got up onstage, she said something, a little barb, nothing huge like what you had been hearing equating Zionism with racism, but it was enough. Bella came up to me and started screaming, "I'm gonna go back to New York, and I'm gonna tell every Jew that you are a traitor to Jews!" I had not slept, and the atmosphere was so highly charged, that I was utterly traumatized. I wandered off and stumbled into some bar in Nairobi, and I was shaking and sobbing and trying to calm myself. Later that night, people came up and said they had been trying to find me—that the celebration was brilliant and they wanted to congratulate me. And I saw Bella that night, too, and we were right back to, "Hey, kid," as she called me. It was just in the moment that she had been righteously angry about something she had cared deeply about since her childhood. Bella is the same age as my parents, and as with my parents, the socialist Zionist movement was idealized. It enshrined the rights of all people regardless of race or religion, and that was the Israel we loved. We were both Jews who fully supported the rights of Palestinians at a time when that was not even close to being an acceptable position in the Jewish community.

Barbara Bick We stayed in different places in Nairobi—Bella had a big position so she was given a room at a big hotel. I was running around printing up posters for her meetings. Betty Friedan was there, and Amy Swerdlow and Judy Lerner. We would go out together to parties. They would compare their invitations and decide which was the toniest gathering. Then we'd pile into cabs. After about the third night, Betty Friedan turned and looked at me as I got into the cab and said, "Who is this person?" One night we went to a French restaurant, very small and very excellent. I was sitting next to Bella, and Betty said something that made Bella mad. Betty kept talking, and Bella was getting angrier and angrier. I saw Bella pick up her dish—it was heaped with chewed-up chicken bones—and she was slowly rising. We all went silent because she was going to throw it. Betty went white. Finally I was able to get my hand on Bella's arm and make her sit down. And everybody breathed a sigh of relief.

Judy Lerner I went to all the conferences except Mexico City. In Copenhagen Bella and I roomed together. In Nairobi there was a lot of tension about Israel and Palestine. We went to dinner one night at an Italian restaurant, and there was a group of Israeli women sitting in another corner. Betty and Bella had a fight—about who knows what. Bella is wearing a white suit. Betty gets up with a plate of spaghetti with red sauce and looks like she's about to throw it at Bella. The other women in the room begin to realize this was happening. And Bella said, "Sit down, Betty. What the hell do you think you're doing?" Betty sat down. I'll never forget that.

When Bella died, there was an overflow of people at the memorial service in a room downstairs. I went down because Betty hadn't come yet. Even with all this competitiveness and hostility, they really were interdependent in some way. So I went downstairs to get Betty and took her up and got her a seat in front. Somebody said to me, "What are you doing that for?" I said, "Because that's what Bella would have wanted."

Faye Wattleton I met Bella in 1985. The Sandinistas had just taken over in Nicaragua and Reagan sent Kissinger down to see whether U.S. policy was succeeding in Central America. There was not a single woman on the delegation. So Sissy Farenthold* found a rich person in Nevada [Maya Miller] to fund a women's delegation to Central America so that we could do our own assessment—we were there eight to ten days. I remember, because it was Christmas and we were still in Nicaragua New Year's Eve.

I first encountered Bella at the airport, with Martin tagging behind her. He was carrying on about, "I don't know why you're doing this. You know these aren't the kind of women that you should be spending a whole week with, none of them are as good as you are. I never can talk you out of these things." I thought, "Hmm, I'm not so bad." Of course Martin never thought that anybody was of Bella's caliber. So that was my first physical encounter with the "famous" Bella Abzug. We stopped in Miami for a briefing—in the airport hotel. Somehow, during that briefing Bella decided she wanted to room with me; she picked me out.

So we spent eight days on the road together. She had this ritual when getting up in the morning of sitting on the side of the bed, quietly, almost Buddha-like. She would tell people later, "I'd be sitting there, trying to figure out how to get going, and Faye would be at the mirror putting on her makeup." So we schlepped around three countries. In San Salvador we met with groups of mothers of the dead and missing, and those were really heart-wrenching experiences. I would see Bella cry. And in a prison, we saw three generations: a grandmother, a daughter, and a child. They had actually imprisoned the baby with the mother

*Frances (Sissy) Farenthold ran second in the balloting for Democratic vice presidential nominee at the 1972 convention. She was the first president of the National Women's Political Caucus, 1973–1975.

because they were deemed to be opposed to the government. On New Year's Eve of 1985 we were in Managua, Nicaragua, seated on the same pew with Daniel Ortega, celebrating Midnight Mass. Afterward we went to a nightclub, and we danced until two or three o'clock on conga lines. Bella led them.

Letty Cottin Pogrebin We were roommates on a trip to Israel, and she was amazingly difficult. "Get my pills. In this drawer." She completely forgot that we're supposed to be peers here, but I loved her so much. I have an image of her sitting in her chair with a pile of papers. She had such huge thighs that she didn't have a flat lap, so nothing would stay on. I was constantly picking up papers that fell off her lap. When she read in bed, I would take off her reading glasses after she fell asleep, because she was pushing herself to keep reading, keep going—like the Energizer Bunny.

Martin's Death

Judy Lerner Martin was very critical of [Bella's 1986 race for a congressional seat in Westchester]. He didn't want her to do it; he felt that she was going to take a beating up there . . . and they had a real disagreement. But once she decided to do it, he was there, supporting her and helping her in every way possible.

Maggi Peyton Eve Abzug and I were both working for Andrew Stein,* and I got a call that Martin had died and could I get Eve, and come over with her. So we went to the apartment on Fifth Avenue, and he was lying on the floor. He had come back from jogging, and I think he may have called downstairs and asked

*Andrew Stein was president of the New York City Council (1986–1992), the last president before the office was abolished.

them to get an ambulance because he wasn't feeling well. When they got there he had collapsed in front of the windows that faced out at Fifth Avenue. Bella came in—she had been up campaigning in Westchester—and it was just unbelievable. She knelt there and, what do the Irish say? She was keening, with the detectives and other people standing around. I went over and touched her, but she didn't feel my hand, or Liz's either. Someone said to me that he had been there for some time and they were going to have to move the body, and I had to get her up. But she still wouldn't move. It was tough.

Helene Savitzky Alexander There she was on the floor next to him. What a scene that was. Berating herself the whole time.

Barbara Bick I had just gotten back to Washington from Martha's Vineyard when I got the call that Martin had died, and so I took the next plane to New York. Bella had finally gotten up from the floor and she's sitting in a chair, all in black, and she's miserable. Shirley—I don't know if she had flown in from L.A. or what—but she swings the door open and runs across the room and plunks herself down on Bella's lap. She says, "Oh, Bella, he's where he wanted to be." And Bella pushed her off her lap.

Shirley MacLaine In those weeks after Martin went, we were all down in her place, sitting around. I was struck by how awful she looked. It was part of this awful reality but it was also an imposed drama. She was like an empress in tragedy as everybody came around. She didn't even think about washing her face or combing her hair. I said, "Let's go and get yourself fixed up." "No!"

Letty Cottin Pogrebin When we went to the grave it was just horrible, horrible, horrible. She was like a beached whale. She had no energy—a person you would usually think was like a furnace, she was a cold furnace. She wasn't one of those big-ego women with a milquetoast guy; she adored him. Her affection for him was as readily apparent as his was for her.

Liz Abzug I watched the depth of their relationship, the friendship and love between my parents—the playfulness. I have real memories of that. Right before he died, my mother was in from Mount Vernon, and she could barely make it back to the apartment, she was so tired from the campaign. We had dinner together, and my father said, "How beautiful she looks!" "Oh, give me a break!" I said. "She looks like shit!" He said, "No, really. I mean it. Look!"

Geraldine Ferraro It was fun to watch them together. Martin was in many ways like my husband, John. He kind of stepped back and enjoyed watching Bella be Bella.

Gloria Steinem I don't think that she ever, ever, ever got over the fact that Martin was no longer there. She was a slightly different person forever.

My reputation is that of an extremely independent woman, and I am. But I was dependent, clearly, on Martin. He would embrace me in his furry chest and warm heart and protect me from the meanness one experiences in the kind of life I lead.

Robin Morgan I remember the first day back on the campaign trail after Martin's death—after agonizing, should she continue, should she not. We went up in the car together to some kind of school in Westchester. It was going to be a press conference on education. We were in the kindergarten room. We went in. We were holding hands. She heaved her bulk down into these tiny little chairs, and I thought, "Oh, God, how is she going to get up?" They were winding up the introduction, and she turned to me. She wasn't crying but her eyes were glittering, and she said, very low, "I guess this is what they call being a trouper." And I said, "It sure as hell is." She got to her feet by herself, and she walked to the podium, and within seconds, she was on. By the time she finished her short first presentation before questions, people were crying and laughing. Just amazing.

Barbara Bick I traveled a lot with Bella. I went with her to Moscow for a meeting of the Women for a Meaningful Summit.* Then Bella and I went on to Leningrad. Martin and Bella had always said they were going to go to Russia together, and they never did. We traveled throughout Russia, just the two of us, and in any town we came to, we would meet right away with the women legislators. You just don't go to a place and be a tourist. No. She immediately made contact with the mayor and then had a special meeting with the council of women, whatever the local version was. They were real Russian women. The best clothes they had were housedresses. These were Party women who were seeing their power slip away after Gorbachev came in. And they didn't want their daughters to have to work. Well, Bella told them off! She would get these old Communist hierarchical women to talk about the role of women, in marriage, in politics, in careers. And they adored her.

Then we were in Odessa. We stood at the top of the steps that the baby carriage went down in the movie *The Battleship Potemkin*. And Bella talked to Martin. It was one of the places they had planned to visit together. I moved away so she could talk to Martin.

*Women for a Meaningful Summit, founded in 1985, was an American and, later, international network organized as forums to increase women's influence in the major foreign-policy debates of the time. The group met in Moscow in 1988.

Shirley MacLaine Bella used to come to channeling sessions with me quite regularly. And we argued afterwards about whether it could be possible. I said, "You came from the Orthodox tradition, you know the soul leaves at night and comes back." And she said, "Yes. That's the part that could be true." One night—it was Christmas Eve out at Malibu—and Jack Pursel, the one who channels Lazaris, was there. She got on her high horse, and she said, "Okay. If you came back and you decided that you wanted to be a human being like the rest of us, a physical presence, what would you do?" And he said—this is the channel talking—"Preferably, I would sit under a tree and watch the human race. I would observe what they are about and try to understand their emotions." "You mean you would do *nothing*?" she said. "You mean you'd fucking do *nothing*?" Like she's talking to a channel from God or something like that. The channel never moves. It so infuriated her. She screamed for an hour until all the people at my party left and went to a movie. And she's still screaming at this person who is in a trance, and Lazaris is saying, "There is no need to get upset. I simply want to observe the human race." After that I said to Bella, "You know your problem? You're like Mother Teresa. If he doesn't want to do anything for people, because it's up to the rest of us to do for ourselves and for each other, why can't you let him do that? Why do you have to be everybody's savior?" And that made her madder. She said, "Oh, all you New Age fuckheads. You never take a position. You have no spine."

Martha Baker The celebs were sometimes a pain in the ass. Shirley would call, and Bella would take the call when I was in the office and talk for hours. She'd write me a note, "Please go down and get frozen yogurt." That was our big afternoon treat—frozen yogurt, with wheat germ on top if she needed energy. You'd know that she was going to be on the phone for a good hour with Shirley pontificating. Oh, my God!

And she loved to gamble and play cards. She'd go once in a while to Atlantic City. When MGM opened in Vegas in 1994, Barbra Streisand was doing the show on New Year's Eve, and Shirley told Bella she was taking her mother. Bella said, "I would really like to go. Should I call somebody?" Somehow Bella got an invitation to go, but I remember Shirley gave her good advice. She said, "I'm telling you, this is a huge place. It's difficult to walk everywhere. If you are coming, I can't take care of you. I told my mother to get a wheelchair, and I'm telling you the same thing." And that's what she did.

Esther Broner Bella brought Shirley to BJ [B'nai Jeshurun synagogue], I think it was Rosh Hashanah though it may have been Yom Kippur. The service is long, and Shirley's sitting next to me, bored. Suddenly she stretches. She's very double-jointed. She stretches and hits the person in the row behind us. Finally, the cantor is singing, and she begins singing loudly. Bella says to her, "Very good, Shirley, nobody would know you never knew Hebrew." She's singing in a made-up language. And Shirley turns to us and says, "You know, I was a cantor in a former life." Bella was smiling so mischievously.

Spirituality and religious feelings are different. Bella once said that Shirley allowed her to access her own heart. Shirley allowed her to be partly an irrational, passionate person. But religion was very different for her. There was nothing New Age about her feeling about religion. If she burst into tears when reading from the Torah, those were the echoes of her grandfather—the childhood shul—and different from the being in outer space sort of thing.

After Martin died, some of us gathered with Bella. We crowded into a living room in the West Village, at Westbeth. She was sitting in a chair. We declared her the head of this circle—some people who knew her well, and others who knew her less. I invited them, like my friend, the actress Naomi Newman, who quoted lines from a play she wrote. I think I invited Naomi for ecstasy, to say the lines, "You go down, you get up, you fall down, you get up." And Bella would fall down and get up. It began a little more formally, and Bella was being careful not to say Martin's name, because it would make her cry. But then she did speak of him. She was so curiously dressed, all in red, red hat, red shoes. The room was warm, and we were close. It wasn't that anybody came up to pet her, or any California pet-in sort of thing. It was a more generalized kind of embrace, "We appreciate you, we incorporate you, we extol you, we mourn for you, we weep for you." Yes, she melted. Not everyone spoke, but it got warmer, more intimate. Some remembered Martin. My husband, Bob, and I had double dated with them in Paris, and he was so outrageous. The laughter was good. And she wept a little. Her temper could be out of control, but her weeping was not. Then people asked if she would sign posters we had from when she ran for Congress. She would sign, "I will never forget you, love of my life." I wrote her this little poem and excerpted it. Liz said she kept that with her. She was who she was, and we would help her to be who she was.

Now, every day the fire has to be lit all over again. I function. I completed the campaign after Martin died because he would have expected me to. I work hard, practice law, lecture, write. I'm involved in movements, organizational work, and I travel. But there's a great loneliness. I have a lot of friends and they've been great, but Martin and I spent our free time alone together. At the movies, theaters, concerts. Just the other night I said, I'm going to do what Martin and Bella did—go to two movies in a row. But nothing substitutes. I have two wonderful daughters, very close and warm and they're always calling and spending time with me, but it's different.

12

Loss, Poker, and Family Politics

Chronology

1986 The people's revolution in the Philippines overthrows Ferdinand Marcos and brings Corazon Aquino to power.

1988 George Herbert Walker Bush and his running mate, Indiana senator Dan Quayle, defeat Massachusetts governor Michael Dukakis and Texas senator Lloyd Bentsen for the presidency.

1989 The Berlin Wall is torn down.

1989 The Chinese government routs democracy protesters in Tiananmen Square.

1989 NOW and a coalition of groups organize Women's Equality/Women's Lives, a massive march on Washington for women's reproductive rights; an even larger March for Women's Lives in 1992 brings 750,000 protesters to Washington.

1990 Nelson Mandela is released from prison as apartheid ends in South Africa.

1992 Dan Quayle criticizes the TV sitcom character Murphy Brown for "mocking the importance of fathers by bearing a child alone and calling it just another lifestyle choice."

1992 Arkansas governor Bill Clinton and Tennessee senator Al

Gore defeat President Bush and Vice President Quayle to return the presidency to the Democratic Party.

1993 Bella and her daughters buy a house in the Hamptons, on Long Island, where they have many friends.

1996 The U.S. women's soccer team, led by Mia Hamm, wins the gold medal at the Olympics.

1997 Bella performs her Marlene Dietrich impersonation in public.

Eve Abzug After my father died, we finally bought the house that we talked about in the Hamptons in 1986. It was just expected, and it seemed necessary to spend a lot of time with my mother. When she was really sick toward the end, I have clear memories of helping her on with her sneakers and stuff, when she was fighting it less. That whole reversal of caretaking was both wonderful and sad.

Liz Abzug She really did rely on us in a whole different way after he died. She was always so independent, doing all her things, but after he died she wanted to spend a lot more time around us, and with us—having us dote on her.

Lesley Gore She stayed with Lois and me often before they bought the house. The amazing thing was you would have thought she'd be demanding and you would feel the presence everywhere, but it was like having a bird in the house; we almost never knew she was there. And many times we often shared one bathroom upstairs; we never knew she was there. As long as you cooked for her.

Lois Sasson And then, at twelve o'clock at night, we always had something sweet for her. When she was in the pool, she was better than a fish. She was able to tread water—we timed her once—for over forty minutes.

Martha Baker Who knew that Bella loved to go fishing? And she would clean the fish! She fished with this guy who was the boyfriend of one of our old woman friends; she had been living with this guy who was the head of the NAACP out there, and he would take Bella out in his little boat, a rowboat. And they'd go out on the water just the two of them, and then she'd bring home all these little fish and she'd clean them, and we'd cook them on the grill—she loved that.

Lois Sasson She had a black Jeep. She loved that Jeep. She hadn't driven for many years, but she knew how to drive. I'm not saying she drove it well, but in fact she did actually drive up to our house the first couple of weeks that she had it—and she beeped the horn, and we came out and there she was in the driver's seat. After that, mostly Liz did the driving.

Lesley Gore She was upset with me once for not driving her home. I thought that I had had too much wine to drink, and I was scared to get on the road, and I called a cab for her, and she didn't talk to me for five days.

Joan Nixon I volunteered as Bella's driver back in the mid-seventies. Once, there was a huge snowstorm when I was driving her back to her house. I got stuck in a snowdrift. I said, "I'm stuck, Bella. You can get out and walk." And she said, "Oh, no. I'll wait." So I rocked back and forth and finally delivered her to her front door.

Lois Sasson We went to a party together in the Hamptons, and I walked in with Bella; she smacks me on the arm, like she always does. "Hey, Sassy, look who's here," and I look up and there was

Ted Kennedy. I said, "Wow!" She said, "Watch," and she threw her arms back, and she said, "Ted!" And he turned around and he got through a hundred people, screaming, "Bella, Bella, Bella, Bella, Bella."

Letty Cottin Pogrebin Bella had her seventy-fifth birthday party at her house in East Hampton, and I couldn't believe it, but Betty [Friedan] was there. Bella said, "At seventy-five, I can afford to be nice." I remember the whole thing. Bella singing her favorite songs. Chatting with Betty, sitting by the pool. There were decorations on the toilet paper holder. I remember thinking, "Why would anyone put a toilet paper roll in a decorative thing like that?"

Eve Abzug We had bought Kathie Lee Gifford's house. It was really decorated—panda bears everywhere—and Mom wanted to leave it until all of her friends saw it. And even after every single friend was in that house, we still kept it that way—with parrots in the bowls.

Wendy Westbrook Fairey I had played poker in the city, and my friend Marilyn said, "Would you like to play poker at Bella Abzug's house?" And so I went and there she was. I was very surprised that it was a sort of yuppie Hampton house. There was an open living room/dining room/kitchen. And she was sitting at the table with her hat on. She always wore some hat when she was playing. She was fierce. We played various games. But she had a very big preference for a game called three-card monte, where you're dealt one card down, and you bet a dollar. One card up—it's a two dollar bet. And one card down, it's a three dollar bet. Just three cards. Since we played a quarter or fifty cents for most games, it was high stakes. And if someone bet three dollars on the third card, and someone raised, that would be a six-dollar bet, so that was very high stakes for us. To this day, when we play that particular game, we call it "Bella" and we say, "Let's play Bella." Sometimes we do it fifty cents, a dollar, a dollar fifty instead of one, two, three. And someone will say, "No, let's do a real Bella," and then we'll up the ante.

The other games were seven-card stud games, or games with common cards in the middle. And she'd say, "Eh! That isn't real poker." So you'd be intimidated to play her game. She didn't like to end it. We'd start at seven-thirty, eight, something like that. And at eleven or eleven-thirty people would want to stop. And she'd say, "Ah. You don't want to stop!" So we'd usually play another half hour, and she'd still be complaining. People brought food. She didn't provide it. There was a lot of sort of kowtowing. Like it was an honor to play with her, and we did things her way.

I did play with her a week before she went into the hospital the last time. She was all hooked up to an oxygen thing. And when she played, she took it off. She didn't make quite such a fuss about stopping. And then I left. But as I was leaving, there were two people staying to hold her and take her across the room. And it was really a very difficult task.

I never got to know her enough not to feel intimidated. I was just starting to play seriously, and it was always going too fast, and I was always worried that she would be scornful, which she was on a couple of occasions. But no one took it too seriously. There were people who knew her much better and really liked her. Those were the regulars. Her daughters would come in. They didn't play. But it was nice.

Liz Abzug I had some fights then with her at that period because this is when I'm coming into my own being, I'm "out"; I'm working very hard, I'm trying to make this decision to run for office. She was uptight about the fact that I would be running as an out lesbian. I had to confront her many times, many ways, and even confront my own issues to deal with that. I confronted her about her role in life and being the first person to actually introduce the gay rights bill and yet have this hypocrisy of not even accepting this very well with me. I think she was also very frightened on a personal level to have her friends know at first.

I had had several serious boyfriends that she knew, and was engaged to a man I lived with in college and afterward. He was very involved in our lives and the campaigns, and she kept asking me about him. I finally said, "This is my choice; I don't hate men, I love men. I've had great relationships with some men, as you well know!" But over and over she asked for the explanations, and "where did she go wrong?"

Finally when she was going to one of her conferences abroad, and she was giving me hell over all this, I said to her, "If you keep up like this and don't accept who I am, you ain't gonna see me, at all!" I said, "I'm not kidding. I am not kidding! I mean that!" And she said, "Oh, really?" And I said, "Oh, really! So make your choice; do you want to see me, and accept who I am and who I'm with, or do you not want to see me at all?" She went on the plane; she was hysterical, very upset, called my sister from the plane. And my sister's calling me and says, "She's calling me from the plane, she's so upset. What did you say to her?" And I told her. She wrote this long note to me from the plane, and said, "I'm really sorry I treated you so badly. I really love you. I think you're terrific. And I'm so sorry I've hurt you so deeply. And I'm going to try." And that turned the corner.

In a different era, not having been with my father, who she truly loved and he truly loved her, she probably could have been with a woman. I think she would not face her own demons, and I think this was a big conflict for her that she never resolved.

Robin Morgan What's interesting to me is that of all the issues, all the social justice issues and movements that Bella was in, the direction was from the gut out, whether it was as a woman, as a Jew, as a mother trying to ban the bomb—"children shouldn't drink bad milk and glow in the dark." This one, the politics had to go the other way. Intellectually she was already there, as she used to tell us interminably, "Before either you or my daughters fell in love with a woman, I was for gay rights." On the other hand, she literally could say to me at a certain time, "Both my girls, where did I go wrong?"

When she was in the hospital for the last time—by then she was sending the girls flowers on their anniversaries with their partners—I remember teasing her. I said to her, "Gimme a break, could we look at the pattern here? Most of your closest friends are lesbian or bisexual women. You hang with the Muffies and the Poofies in the Hamptons. You're up there in a tux singing Marlene Dietrich songs. Both of your daughters are lesbians. I loved Martin, and you had a great love affair, but let me just say, if I were a few years older or you were a few years younger, I'd give you a run for your money." She turned bright red and burst out laughing. So by the end she had a sense of humor about it.

Bella Does Marlene

Lesley Gore I was doing a show, in East Hampton at Guild Hall, a Labor Day Weekend show. They liked to close that venue in the summer with a rock 'n' roll act. It turned out to be the day after Princess Di died (in 1997). I decided I was going to do a show called "Lesley and Friends." Lois and I had invited a couple of friends out from New York who'd singled with me, and the bass player was my friend. So Bella said to me, "Well, I'm your friend, why don't you ask me to sing?"

Lois Sasson Wait, wait, wait. She calls up in the middle of the night, and she says, "You know what my mother really wanted me to do in life?" I said, "What?" She said, "Be an entertainer." We knew that she did this Marlene Dietrich, and she always wanted to wear a white tuxedo. But, like a stupid friend, I didn't realize how important it was to her, and I don't think she did either. Then the fortuitous gig came for Lesley, and she started with, "You know I could sell a lot of tickets."

Lesley Gore At first I thought that a woman who has done so much in her life, and has really nothing to prove to anyone, wouldn't want to put herself in a position where she's going to get up onstage and be critiqued by people. But she really wanted to do this, so we decided to not only have her do it, but to help her do it in the best possible way.

We couldn't actually find her a white tuxedo; we called a costume company out in Queens, and they picked out a couple of tuxedos and some vests and stuff for us, and Bella tried them all on. We rented a beautiful black tuxedo. With the white shirt. And they gave us a cape. She looked just divine.

Bella was terrific. She had a powerful voice. In fact, she sang very well. We rehearsed in New York with my band, and Liz helped to put together a little dance in the middle, and we rehearsed again out there. She did a wonderful imitation—it wasn't like Bella doing "Falling in Love Again"—she tried to do it like Marlene.

The first show was seven-thirty, with a second one at ten-thirty. I said to Bella, "This has been just great. If you don't want to do the second show, I totally understand if you're exhausted and want to go home." And she said to me, "What, are you kidding? I've got people coming to the second show." I think she was nervous, but she kind of sucked it in. It was this fantastic, "I am nervous, but I can do this, and I want to do it." It was really her desire that pushed her.

Lois Sasson We were scared for her, because in the beginning the audience didn't know how to respond. I mean here is Bella Abzug out of context. Lesley's very casually dressed, and Bella comes out in a tuxedo with a top hat. Nobody knew how to accept it at first. But within four minutes she got that audience—she had a walking stick, and there was buzz around her doing it, and she pounded that walking stick, and everybody was silent, and then she gave her delivery. And it was like she'd done it fifty-five thousand times.

13

Going Global

Chronology

1990 With Mim Kelber, Bella cofounds the Women's Environment and Development Organization (WEDO). It becomes one of the largest nongovernmental organizations at the UN, dealing with how development and environmental issues affect women worldwide—and the focus of the last years of Bella's life.

1991 The Persian Gulf War begins in January, triggered by Iraq's invasion of Kuwait in August 1990. The fighting is over by March.

1991 Meeting in Miami, WEDO organizes the Women's Action Agenda 21, which for the first time incorporates women's policy positions from local, national, and international environment and development communities into official UN documents. These documents are approved at the various UN environmental summits, the first of which was held in Rio de Janeiro in 1992.

1991 Anita Hill testifies at the hearing for Supreme Court nominee Clarence Thomas, precipitating a national conversation on sexual harassment.

1992 Bella is named chair of the New York City Commission on the Status of Women, which holds the first public hearing on breast cancer and the environment; during this same time, she herself discovers she has breast cancer and has a mastectomy.

1994 As an official U.S. delegate, Bella plays a key role in winning the recognition of women's concerns and roles in population and development at the UN International Conference on Population and Development in Cairo.

1994 Bella is inducted into the National Women's Hall of Fame, in Seneca Falls, N.Y.

1995 Having played a major role in UN international women's conferences in Mexico City (1975), Copenhagen (1980), and Nairobi (1985), Bella mobilizes an international coalition of women at the UN Women's Conference at Beijing—largely from her wheelchair.

1997 Bella addresses the World Conference on Breast Cancer in Kingston, Ontario, in July: "The world won't change until each of us is moved by the passion of people's needs—until we bring the reality of women's lives into our work in an integrated way—until we feel the joys and sorrows, the hopes and dreams, and until we turn into reality the dream that our daughters and sisters won't have the same fear of cancer that has haunted us."

1998 On March 3 at the UN, the night before entering the hospital for heart surgery, Bella receives an ovation following her address to the Commission on the Status of Women.

1998 Bella dies on March 31 at Columbia-Presbyterian Hospital, New York City.

1998 At her funeral service in New York City, April 2, an overflow crowd honors Bella.

1998 First Lady Hillary Clinton, D.C. House Delegate Eleanor Holmes Norton, and others pay tribute to Bella at a memorial service at the National Press Club, in Washington, April 9.

1998 The UN Tribute to Bella Abzug: A World Celebration, is led by Secretary General Kofi Annan, April 24.

Robin Morgan Once in a while in her later years Bella would realize that the work she was doing was as, or more important than, holding office, particularly when she began to shape the NGOs [nongovernmental organizations] at the UN. I mean, the NGOs pre–Bella Abzug, it was like, "Who the fuck are they? We're government. They're not important." But now at the UN, on every subject, not just women, the NGOs are a vast presence so that the organization gets worried that there's too much democracy. That's her astonishing legacy in international affairs.

Mim Kelber We founded the Women's Environment and Development Organization (WEDO) in 1990. A group of us had begun to talk about organizing to gain influence at the UN, and we finally got together a proposal and went to the Ford Foundation. We got nowhere. When Bella found out we didn't involve her, she was furious. So she went out and got the money. The whole idea for the Miami meeting* came from Perdita Huston† and a few others. We could raise tax-free money through the Women USA Fund, so WEDO became one of its offshoots. Bella came late to Miami, and she got sick and was in the hospital over-

*The World Women's Congress for a Healthy Planet (November 8–12, 1991, in Miami, Florida) gathered fifteen hundred women from eighty-three countries to craft an international agenda for women in the twenty-first century as a preparation for the UN Conference on Environment and Development in Rio de Janeiro (the UN Earth Summit, June 1992). The Miami congress collected testimony presented before a tribunal of five women judges from around the world and approved the Women's Action Agenda 21. The agenda was presented to and endorsed by Maurice Strong, secretary-general of the pending UN conference. He appointed Bella his advisory assistant for the Rio meetings.

†Perdita Huston, who died in 2001, was a feminist, journalist, and human rights activist who often consulted for the UN.

night. She really had nothing to do with the policy making. But once [the Women's Action Agenda 21] passed, she grabbed it.

Brownie Ledbetter That was the most amazing conference I have ever seen. The design of it was utterly fabulous. There was a lot of diversity—in nationality and ethnicity and the way they were used to functioning politically—so it was tough to organize. And there was resentment about who was this American woman telling us what to do. Bella was not always strategic in that way, but she was so incredibly good politically that the people who gave a damn came to see that.

*Bienvenu, mes soeurs—bienvenidos, hermanas—welcome to all our sisters who have come here for this first World Women's Congress for a Healthy Planet. We've worked for almost two years to bring you all here together, and you're a beautiful sight. Together, we're going to change the world—not for the worse but for the better.**

Dorothy Goldin Rosenberg In her keynote speech, Costa Rican presidential candidate Margarita Arias likened women's environmental work to their struggles to protect their own bodies from abuse. She reminded us that every advance in women's rights has meant a gain for all humanity. She encouraged women to develop new models of global leadership.

Michele Landsberg The five days were dense with both heroes and horrors. The participants cheered at the constantly invoked name of Rachel Carson, founder of the environmental movement, whose 1962 book, *Silent Spring*, sounded the first alarm about pesticides. And they cheered again when Marjory Stone-

*Welcoming speech at the Miami congress.

man Douglas, 101, waved jauntily from her wheelchair, acknowledging the crowd's gratitude for her fifty-year campaign to save the Florida Everglades. Wangari Maathai, founder of Kenya's Green Belt Movement, caused ripples of excitement everywhere she went. Beginning in 1977, Maathai has enlisted thousands of rural African women to plant ten million trees . . . Dr. Rosalie Bertell, the Toronto epidemiologist and antinuclear campaigner, electrified that audience with her quiet recitation of military assaults on the environment, from supersonic flights to nuclear testing . . . The military, she said, is the world's most dangerous ecological despoiler, yet it works in secrecy, while grassroots women struggle in the civic arena to "clean up the mess."

Wangari Maathai Bella was working very hard; all of us became terribly concerned because in the middle of the meeting she collapsed. They took her to hospital—she was literally exhausted. The following day she was back in her seat, conducting the meeting, looking as powerful and strong as ever. That was Bella, never giving up, never showing any sign of exhaustion. I never saw her being discouraged. She was always full of hope and ideas. She always asked, "So, what are we going to do about this?" I can't remember ever a situation where she said, "There's nothing we can do about that." I don't remember that coming out of Bella.

Dorothy Goldin Rosenberg The secretary-general of UNCED (the UN Conference on Environment and Development), the Canadian Maurice Strong, acknowledged the importance of the Women's Agenda—he could hardly avoid it. As the document was being read, women jumped to their feet cheering the resolutions containing the "sensitive issues" they demanded to be addressed at UNCED. The indomitable Bella Abzug shook her finger at him, saying, "Do you hear the women, Mr. Strong?" He promised to carry the message to the UNCED committee, and admitted that the rich nations are resisting such inclusion.

Brownie Ledbetter I roomed with Bella at UNCED in Rio, and somehow, I ended up typing her speech. We were all at the NGO park, but she made a speech to the official delegates. And she began, "Ladies, gentlemen, and other endangered species." It brought down the house. Every time Bella spoke at the UN, she had them laughing. She could cut through and get folks to open up so that they would hear what she was saying.

Susan Davis The Agenda 21 platform, the lobbying document for the Rio Earth Summit, gave WEDO its legitimacy. I had worked at the Ford Foundation, where June Zeitlin was my colleague, and I was hired to build WEDO and make sure Bella and Mim's work would last. And my very first day on the job, October 1, 1993, this African American man in a suit knocked on the door and stuck his head in and said, "Hello. I'm from the Internal Revenue Service here to audit you." It was a pretty scary first experience, but we managed.

Liz Abzug At the beginning she didn't know that much about global movements. She knew what she read, but she was not a specialist in that area. That's where her brilliance came in: she brought what she had learned in Congress, and nothing ever got lost.

Robin Morgan I remember asking her, "What are we doing in all these NGO caucuses?" And she said, "We're teaching them how to lobby. We're teaching them that by the time we get to the official UN conference, the document itself is already done and finished with. So they have to get into the prep meetings. We're teaching them all of this." And I suddenly saw, "Oh, my God, it's what she did in Congress!" She had found another structure—a system she could learn about and get into to change it.

Geraldine Ferraro The UN is very much a legislative body, even though they come out with resolutions rather than legislation. But those resolutions have impact. Bella understood that if you could get language that affects women in a resolution, it makes a difference. The message comes out very differently to most nations.

Brownie Ledbetter Bella would get a room at the UN and invite all the women, whether they were delegates, or staff, or NGOs. We would look at the documents in the morning, and in the afternoon there would be an unstructured workshop. And then each of us would lobby our own country's delegations to get changes reflecting our gender-based perspective.

June Zeitlin For women all over the world, leaders and grassroots activists, Bella was the icon of American women. The whole idea of bringing women together around a common agenda—women across all geographic, issue, race, ethnicity, and class lines—the strategy of organizing yourself as a caucus, in the way she organized the women's caucus in Congress, was revolutionary. NGOs and women had participated since the UN was founded, but in a supportive way, not pushing their agenda. She opened up the space at the UN. All the processes that are now standard operating procedure with NGO meetings—the different subgroups, caucuses, lobbying for language—people forget it was not always that way. Bella started it for women, but it benefited everybody.

Wangari Maathai She introduced into WEDO the idea of monitoring the governments and the United Nations to see how much they were implementing the commitments they had made in Nairobi, Beijing, and, of course, at Rio. If she were alive today, Bella would be very concerned about the slow movement toward the causes of organizations like WEDO, especially in Rio—I remember she organized a women's tent, where women from all over the world came and shared their experience. Miami was translated into the women's tent in Rio, which was very successful.

Jane Fonda The reason the Cairo conference on population was so crucial is because that was the first time women's NGOs were actually at the table. Bella asked me to come and speak to a group of women from developing countries. I was then a goodwill ambassador [for a UN family planning agency], but I was seeing population at that point in my evolution as an environmental issue. So I spoke to them from that point of view—and I got booed! Maybe that's why Bella brought me there. She knew that I needed to hear from women that the real conceptual framework of the conference—of everything!—was gender. I had never understood before.

Lifetime documentary During the [Rio] conference in 1992, Bella listened to [testimony regarding] toxins in the environment that might cause breast cancer. She didn't know that she herself was harboring the disease.

Faye Wattleton We were in San Salvador, and Bella was sitting on the side of the bed, as she did in the morning. She said, "Look at this blood on my gown. Where do you think I could have gotten that blood from?" I said, "I don't know. Do you have any cuts?" "No, I don't have any cuts." In my mind, the only place that it could have come from was her mammary ducts. I said, "Bella, you really have to have that checked out when you get back." I don't think she did it right away. I think it may have been a year or two afterward.*

I had a couple of biopsies, which confirmed the fact that I did have it and it was malignant.

Faye Wattleton She called me about her diagnosis and said, "Gloria is telling me she went to Boston, and she's got these doctors up there. But I don't know if I should have surgery, or whether I should do the hormones." I said, "Do you want me to go with you?" She said, "Yes, because you can tell me what the doctor says to me."

Gloria Steinem Faye and I went with Bella to doctors in New York. Then I took her to Boston, where I had been treated for breast cancer in 1986, to get a second opinion, and where there was a breast care clinic that was one-stop shopping—pathologist, surgeon, other specialists who saw you as a team instead of schlepping around to one at a time, as in New York. But it made even Bella laugh, I think, the impact on the doctors of our team arriving. This must have been a first in their careers. Not only did the doctors have a team, but so did the patient.

In Boston she and I also went to see her cardiologist: it made me remember that this was not only a woman facing breast cancer surgery, but one who had already had heart problems and a pacemaker.

Faye Wattleton I guess most women consider this such a private matter and traumatic moment, they would not invite all their closest friends to come join them. I was there because of my medical background, but Liz was asking questions, and Gloria

*Bella was diagnosed with breast cancer in 1993.

knew about the procedure. I was asking about the pros and cons of the surgery, and whether to do tamoxifen before or afterward. He was very patient and answered all our questions. He didn't seem to be annoyed, but I guess when you have a Bella Abzug as a patient, you take some time.

Amy Swerdlow I went to see her when she came out of her breast surgery [a double mastectomy in 1993]. The anesthesiologist walked in and said, "What were you muttering? Something about twenty?" She said, "Well, I was muttering I need twenty more years to accomplish what I have to do."

Robin Morgan She was in and out of the hospital so many times that we used to joke about putting together a "Bella Abzug Book of New York Hospitals." This one had a great view, but lousy food. This one good food, but bad service.

Gloria Steinem To visit Bella in one of her hospital rooms was *never* like going to a hospital. It was like a crossroads of family and visitors plus a national and global political organizing office. I've never seen anything like it before or since.

Martha Baker Bella was chair of New York City's Commission on the Status of Women, during the time David Dinkins was mayor (1990–1994), and we held hearings on breast cancer and the environment. Women from Long Island had a map tracking outbreaks. And we had a domestic-violence committee with Karen Burstein, who, as a sitting family court judge, got special permission to participate. We had a youth commission, too, for young women to develop issues of their own. I don't know if that's been done since.

WEDO News & Views Austin, Texas—A public hearing in the State Capitol February 22 and related events over four days will be held to examine testimony on the links between the breast cancer epidemic and environmental pollution stemming from toxic chemicals and low-level radiation . . . WEDO and Greenpeace will hold a two-day retreat for thirty women activists from around the country to plan the follow-up campaign and hearings in six other locations.

Susan Davis By the time I got to WEDO, in terms of the great UN conferences, Rio had happened and the Vienna human rights conference had just happened. We quickly had to organize for Cairo and Copenhagen and Beijing, and for Istanbul with the Habitat conference.* In Beijing, we organized around World Bank, International Monetary Fund, and World Trade Organization policies, and I think it was our work there that helped the women's movement be able to participate in the 1999 Seattle demonstrations at the WTO. This was part of an agenda to broaden the interests of women in the global movement. It was the same thing with environmental issues. We really couldn't move women on more technical issues in the environmental movement, like persistent organic pollutants, without getting a good hook, so that was part of our breast cancer campaign.

The environmental links to breast cancer gave us an entry point that all women can relate to. And it was easy to use the breast cancer metaphor for our malignant development model. That enabled us to organize the First World Congress on Breast Cancer in 1997. Relating things to your own life, your own body, is important, and to the struggle of those who are the least fortunate on the planet. Bella was advocating for a deep empathy, a kind of solidarity in organizing, to counter the "not in my back-

*The UN International Conference on Population and Development (ICPD), Cairo, Egypt, 1994; the UN World Conference on Social Development (WSSD), Copenhagen, Denmark, 1995; the UN Fourth World Conference on Women (FWCW), Beijing, China, 1995; the UN World Conference on Human Settlements (HABITAT), Istanbul, Turkey, 1996.

yard" approach. You had to organize not with blinders on but with eyes wide open. It's what endeared her to women of the world, because she took such an ecumenical approach, a broad humanistic approach.

Brownie Ledbetter Susan Davis was very important to Bella, but they had a strange relationship. It's the only time I'd ever seen Bella that vulnerable. She was tired, and sick a lot of the time.

Martha Baker It was one of these weird relationships where they used one another. Susan had a tremendous commitment to Bella, and certainly to the work. But the way you got the media was for Bella to be the speaker, so you do your work and get Bella out there to make the statement. But I guess there were times when that wasn't enough for Susan. I can't blame her for wanting her day in the sun. Sometimes I thought that she was abusing Bella and other times that Bella was abusing her.

Faye Wattleton Bella had never really run an organization where you had to write grants and do the bureaucratic stuff. That wasn't her thing. So she brought Susan in as executive director, and that was really an unfortunate decision. This young woman was so disrespectful; sometimes it was almost as if she had something on Bella. One time we were having a retreat for the board in the WEDO office and Bella was in the kitchen making the tea and getting out the food for people. I said, "Where is Susan? Why are you doing this?" And she said, "Susan won't do it. She told me that I'd better get in here and do it." To submit to this kind of behavior was just so uncharacteristic for the Bella that I knew, that I kept counseling her to get rid of Susan, but she was afraid to. She felt that she needed her to write the proposals and that she had the relationship with the donors. I said, "Bella, all that's nonsense. They're giving because of you." In a way, it was not terribly dissimilar to her relationship with Mim, but Mim seemed benign, trailing behind as Bella's friend. But Bella would always say, "You just don't know Mimmie. She's really tough." So maybe she felt intimidated by Mim on some occasions.

Martha Baker They were really Siamese twins. Bella and Mim played off each other, sometimes positively, sometimes very negatively. Not everyone could warm up to Mim. She put up a wall, and if she didn't really like you, she wouldn't put down the wall. Bella was just the opposite. Everything was out there, usually too much of it, too quickly, without any restraint. It was amazing what they managed to do together, almost like one person all those years—like an interesting married couple.

Maggi Peyton They were a perfect match, because I don't think Mim would ever want to run for office. Mim was shy in a way, but tough. She didn't worry about speaking up. She would fight with Bella, and Bella listened to her. Bella didn't have time to devote to the things that Mim did, like writing. And when Bella was with some of her superstar people, that kind of got to Mim. But Bella cared very deeply for Mim. She listened to Mim more than anyone else.

Mim Kelber There was no one like Bella at being able to negotiate. They accepted her as an equal. The rest of us were just women, but at the UN they considered her one of them.

Joan Nixon Bella was always talking about Mim. She was always saying that Mim should get equal recognition for all the things that she was getting recognized for.

Mim Kelber How did she propose to do that?

Joan Nixon Well, at the Belle of the Ball in 1997, WEDO gave a matriarch award to Mim for her seventy-fifth birthday, and then they made a scrapbook for Mim to give to her for her retirement.

Mim Kelber Yes, I remember. They honored me and then I found out they expected me to leave.

Gloria Steinem I worked with Bella much more, but Mim and I worked together a lot, too, because we were both writers. They were just two different people—one optimist and one pessimist, one who looked at the doughnut and the other at the hole—but each needed and loved the other. Of course, if you see the doughnut you get to eat it—and Mim just couldn't.

Wangari Maathai Bella and Mim Kelber were inseparable, and every time you think about Bella you think about Mim. When Mim died they sent me some of Mim's ashes, which I have buried in one of the forests we fought to save here in Nairobi. The forest is called Karura; it is next to the United Nations environmental program headquarters. Mim's daughter brought the ashes to Karura forest, and they are buried under a beautiful tree; that tree is doing very well and every time we see that tree we think of both Bella and Mim.

Beijing, UN Fourth World Conference on Women (1995)

Susan Davis Bella was a terrific strategist. We called together a global strategies meeting in November 1994, right after the horrible congressional election when everybody was completely depressed in the United States.* We had coming up in 1995

*Midterm elections featuring the Newt Gingrich Contract with America.

the World Summit for Social Development in Copenhagen in March and Beijing in August and the UN Fiftieth Anniversary Summit in September. Copenhagen and the UN anniversary were meetings where heads of state would represent their nations. Beijing, the UN Fourth World Conference on Women, was not; it was going to be ministers. So we had this conference to figure out how to get the media's attention and put the Beijing conference on the world map. We had no money for the meeting but Bella said, "Don't let that stop you. You just go ahead and organize and the money will come." There were about a hundred and fifty people there—all the leaders in the United States concerned with global feminism—and Robin Morgan wrote "A Woman's Creed," and we came up with "A Hundred and Eighty Days/A Hundred and Eighty Ways" countdown to Beijing. We also figured out a strategy to make sure Hillary Clinton got there. We delivered both Hillary and Al Gore.

Hillary was interested, and Bella told her staff, "If she wants to go, the way to do it is to prepare in advance. Go to Copenhagen first. Meet with the negotiators and the women's groups in developing countries, so when she gets to Beijing, she's not just one more First Lady who's there." And that's what she did. She went to Copenhagen and later to India with Chelsea. She was so moved by all of it, and the microfinance movement became one of her passions. When Hillary Clinton got to Beijing, she became one of the most adored people by women of the world because she spoke from a position of real substance. And Bella touched people as well. Traveling now in her seventies, she had to use the wheelchair. Even though she hated me for getting the damned thing, she gave in to it. She just couldn't get around long distances without it. That's, of course, my claim to fame. I'm the only person alive who really got to push Bella Abzug around. But it was just part of my job. If I had to get ten people in China to carry her up the stairs to get her into the Great Hall of the People, then that's what we did.

Judy Lerner That wheelchair, in Beijing. Every now and then we'd hear Susan having a fight with Bella, and I'd say, "I'll push your wheelchair." Barbara Bick was a big wheelchair pusher too. But Bella was going to persevere. She gave up her life for that. If she had been a little more careful, she might have lasted a little longer.

Amy Swerdlow I could see that she was moving slowly, not looking around, breathing poorly, hated to be in that wheelchair. She was very agitated about it, and that wasn't Bella. Bella knew how to storm into a room and storm out of a room and chase after people in a room, and she wasn't able to do that. But it didn't stop her.

Robin Morgan Huairou, where the Chinese government had moved the NGO forum to control it, was a mess. "Volunteer guides" were unfamiliar both with Huairou and any non-Chinese language. Maps turned out to be not to scale, and lacking entire buildings, a predicament compounded by the absence of directional signs—except those pointing the way to "Ladies' Shopping Places." Tent-area "paths"—thin concrete squares laid without fixative on bare earth—turned graham crackery with rain and sank in the surrounding gooey mud. I almost dumped Bella out of her wheelchair, which I was pushing at that particular moment, into the mud. But she laughed through it all and was still indefatigable, working the NGO forum as well as the conference itself in Beijing. And, of course, she became involved with the disability NGOs—who were outraged at crumbly paths; workshop assignments to second-floor, no-elevator venues; a tent that kept collapsing; and hastily assembled, steep ramps up to staired buildings. "For ski-jumping, not chairs," quipped one Filipina feminist on wheels. When they daringly staged the first demonstration outside the "designated protest area"—a small child's playground—Bella was with them, wheelchair and all. It was, as she phrased it, an energetic "roll-in."

Liz Abzug My mother was always helping people. To this day, I meet women who tell me stories. A radio commentator on WBAI interviewed me and said, "You don't know this, but your mother enabled me to go to China. I was a single mother, I was broke, and I really wanted to go to Beijing. She told me to come to the airport. She paid for my ticket."

Last Years

Anne Foner Cora Weiss had a book party for some man who had written a book about the UN and his experiences, and Bella came. I think she already had had an operation—she was thinner than I had remembered. She had been at that conference in Beijing, and she spoke. Well, first of all she was fairly subdued, but I was struck by how excellent and well-thought-out her talk was, not super militant, but really with a very balanced understanding of what was going on there. It wasn't only the substance of it, but how she was assessing all the political forces that made for it and what might come out of it—it was a tour de force really.

Faye Wattleton The last time I saw Bella, we went to a movie and to dinner at a Thai restaurant a half block away. It took a half hour for us to get down that half block. Her physical capacity was so compromised at that point, she couldn't breathe. But she was in great spirits. She was eating off my plate as well as her own. The time before, we went to a movie at the Carnegie Hall Cinema, where there's a theater in the basement. As we went down the steps I said, "Bella, how are you going to get up these steps?" She said, "Oh, there must be an elevator." So we come out of the movie and there's no elevator. It was both hysterical and pathetic. Every two steps up she would stop. She would beat her stick on the ground and say, "I'm going to call the city. This is an outrage. They have no facilities for the handicapped."

Esther Broner We would have a theme for our feminist seders and give out assignments. And Bella always did her homework. She would come prepared, and then of course, she'd put down the paper. At her very last seder with us she said, "I am so disappointed. Where is the feminist revolution? Why weren't you on the streets when they took welfare away from people? Why aren't you out there, all of you intelligent, activist people? Why didn't you care what happened?" It was a *cri de coeur*—bawling us out who she felt were so complacent. Her daughter Liz said, "Momma, I never heard you say this before." That was just the year before she died.

Judy Lerner I wasn't at the UN that last day she spoke [March 3, 1998]. But Bella was able to get up from her wheelchair and speak. Then the next day she was in the hospital.

Liz Abzug And [her doctor] said to me, "It's amazing she didn't drop dead at the UN . . . Most people I know, most of the women and men who are that age, in her condition, would have dropped dead right there and then." Incredible that she could talk for forty-five minutes and pull that off.

We celebrate the fiftieth anniversary of the Declaration of Human Rights. Some of you may not be too shocked to hear that I personally *have been fighting for human rights for sixty-five years and especially for the rights of women . . . Many of us made the pilgrimage to the Great Wall during the UN Conference on Women in Beijing in September 1995. But the role of women here today and the men who are our allies is to scale the great wall of gender apartheid. Because unless and until we scale that great barrier we will not eliminate the abuses of human rights that have dogged women every single day of their lives . . . And no matter how steep the passage and discouraging the pace, I ask you never to give in and never give up.**

Maggi Peyton At the UN speech, she said, "I haven't been feeling well." There were a couple of other instances where she kind of blacked out and went back and repeated things she had said. So I think that she decided to have the heart operation because she didn't want to be confined to the wheelchair anymore, and she felt she had things to do.

Shirley MacLaine Before she went in for the operation, she asked me if she could speak to Lazaris. I called Jack and asked him if he would channel Lazaris for her before she went to the hospital. He waited this long beat, and then said, "No, I'm not available." Later, I asked him, "What happened there?" He said, "Lazaris told me, she's going to make up her mind in the postoperative process whether she's going to go to Martin, because she's so furious with him for leaving, or whether she is going to survive. She hasn't made up her mind." And that's why he never talked to her because he didn't want to prejudice her against herself.

Robin Morgan She was scared those last months—one of the few times I actually saw her scared. We were sitting together in the

*Address to the forty-second session of the UN Commission on the Status of Women, March 3, 1998.

hospital a few days before that last surgery. I mentioned gently that it would be perfectly normal if even the intrepid Bella was feeling a little anxious, and she nodded. “You know,” she finally murmured, “they said the odds are eighty-twenty.” Silence. “Which way?” I asked. “Twenty percent of the patients *croak*,” she snapped. All I could conjure was, “Well, 80 percent odds of survival—pretty good. A sixty-point lead. When have we ever had such odds for winning an election?” She sat straight up, beaming. “That’s true!” she bellowed. “By God, that’s true!” And then she was off, ranting about the day’s political headlines. She was amazingly open to learning things up to the very end. Which is very unusual. People usually close down.

Maggi Peyton She made a point of calling Harold [Holzer] and me. I was very up about the operation, though there was something in her voice—I guess Harold may have felt the same thing.

Judy Lerner I saw her in the hospital. She looked beautiful before the operation. We shared opera tickets and she said, “I’m not going. Take my ticket.” I still have Bella’s seat. It’s an aisle seat, nineteenth row, orchestra. I keep them.

Robin Morgan Bella was only seventy-seven when she died, and in her case, I don’t mean “only” facetiously. She was intensely present up to the moment she was wheeled into the OR at 6:00 a.m.—sitting up on the gurney, one arm raised with a clenched fist, as we called out, “Give ’em hell!” Afterward, for weeks, she fought for life in the intensive-care unit. Standing there, talking and singing into her unconsciousness, I’d think of her shrewd aphorisms. The most merciless one she’d delivered two years earlier, when a small group was gathered at my home to watch the 1996 election returns. Democrats retained the White House but lost both houses of Congress to ultraconservative Republicans and suffered major blows in the gubernatorial races, including in New York. We were nervously eating more and getting gloomier as the night wore on, my son Blake especially. He'd spent hours of his childhood volunteering in idealistic, losing campaigns—three of them Bella's. Now, in his late twenties, he groaned, "Dammit, I want to *win* for a change. I'm so tired of this. It makes you lose hope." To which Bella replied, "Aww, no, honey. You gotta live in hope!" She paused a beat before landing the punchline: "That's why you die in despair." Then she threw back her head and laughed—we followed her lead.

Brownie Ledbetter I called the hospital at about ten at night, and Bella was mad. "I was asleep. I'm gonna be operated on in the morning." Of course, Bella would always call you at two or three in the morning. The next day, a fax came through, and a colleague came running in to me saying, "Brownie, look. Bella's better." Then, in less than a month, the phone rang and it was Lois. She had died.

About a week before, my husband and I were down at the beach, near Mobile. There was a picture below the fold on the Mobile *Register*. It was Mary Morgan, Ben Spock's wife. Ben had died, and Mary was in a black leotard with a black umbrella dancing on the top of the hearse with a New Orleans funeral band in front. Bella would have loved it. I never got to show it to her.

Faye Wattleton I had just returned from the Caribbean when Lois called. "Faye, get up to the hospital as soon as you can. Bella's almost gone." It was up at Columbia-Presbyterian. Lois was there. Mim was there, and Bella's sister, and Liz. Robin was there. There was no hysteria in the room. Some of us went over and talked to her after she was gone. We stayed a good while, and then the women came to wash her body. She belonged to a burial society.

It was a very cold March day at the cemetery, and we were all there taking turns at the shovel, piling dirt on Bella. It took about two hours, and it was very powerful for me: the rabbi's lesson at the grave was that we always look for recognition for the things we do, but this is an act for which you cannot be thanked, because she's not with you any longer.

Nadine Hack Everybody at WEDO and Bella's daughters wanted a memorial service in the UN General Assembly, even though the General Assembly hall had never before been used for a nonofficial UN event. Because of the years I spent as official liaison from the city (I was the New York City Commissioner for the UN Council under David Dinkins), I knew everyone to go to, and, following in Bella's footsteps, I would not take no as an answer. So we sat that day in the General Assembly for Bella's memorial—that was my last gift to Bella—where she had addressed that hall just eight weeks before.

Gloria Steinem Wangari Maathai got up and talked about taking Bella in Kenyan villages after the Nairobi conference, how Bella sang and danced with the women, and how they recognized her as a village woman. Then Wangari stood at that huge, long intimidating podium in front of the General Assembly hall, and she sang to Bella. I thought: "Bella, you've changed the molecules in this room forever. This is the most universal, head-and-heart thing that has ever happened here."

Kofi Annan Bella Abzug was a fixture at the United Nations during this past decade . . . She liked to say that since Noah we have done everything in pairs, except government. As I look around this hall, I can see the change she has done so much to bring about. As secretary-general I am committed to furthering that change at all levels of the United Nations. Bella Abzug was also passionate about safeguarding our environment . . . She made sure that Rio will always be remembered as the United Nations conference where women were recognized as full partners in our quest for environmental security and as a force to be reckoned with at the United Nations . . . There are many ways to celebrate the life of Bella Abzug. She was a fine lawyer, a loving wife and mother, a fearless politician, a loyal friend, a woman of vision and integrity . . . Like her, I believe in a partnership between nongovernmental organizations and the United Nations and in a "People's United Nations." In welcoming you here today, I see a gathering made possible largely because of Bella's efforts to open our doors. I pledge to do my utmost to guarantee that those doors remain open from this day forth. Bella's legacy shall endure.

Helene Savitzky Alexander A lot of people have said to me, "If Bella were around we would hear from her." Because there's no one out there talking for the people, and people are aware of that.

Ronnie Eldridge She would be organizing against preemptive strikes and for more internationalism, more communications with the Muslims. I think she would be out there trying to see how we can adjust to a different world in this century. If she were in the Congress, she'd be screaming about that. I'm not sure she'd come back to national politics. I think she'd most likely be doing more international stuff.

Faye Wattleton She would be speaker of the House. I don't have any doubt about that. If she had stayed in Congress, she would be alive today because she would have taken better care of herself and she would be speaker of the House. You were never unclear about what Bella meant when she said it, and people on both ends of the spectrum respected that. I don't believe that anyone could have bested her. She would make sure that she owned the public platform and she would have pushed them in a way she never had the opportunity to do.

Gloria Steinem [Bella was not just] the woman who fought the revolution. She was the woman we want to be after the revolution. [As John Kenneth Galbraith wrote in 1984], "In a perfectly just republic, Bella Abzug would be president."

Hillary Clinton As I travel around the world . . . I am always meeting women who introduce themselves by saying, "I'm the Bella Abzug of Russia," or "I'm the Bella Abzug of Kazakhstan," or "I'm the Bella Abzug of Uganda." Now what these women are really saying, whether or not they wear the hat of an advocate like Bella, is that they, too, are pioneers, that they are willing to take on the establishment and the institutions of their society on behalf of the rights of women, but not just that, on behalf of what families need, on behalf of peace, on behalf of civil society, all the many and varied causes that Bella stood for throughout her long and active life . . . She liked to say, "First they gave us the year of the woman, then they gave us the decade of the woman. Sooner or later, they'll have to give us the whole thing." She never stopped fighting for "the whole thing." So when women around the world say to me, "I am the Bella Abzug" from somewhere, I know what they really mean is that they'll never give up.

Notes

v *"I've been described as a tough and noisy woman . . ."* Bella Abzug and Mel Ziegler, *Bella! Ms. Abzug Goes to Washington* (New York; Saturday Review Press, 1972), 3.

1: The Early Years: A Passion for Social Justice

4 *"My parents had the foresight . . ."* Memoir, 20.

5 *"Papa was a serious man . . ."* Memoir, 2.

5 *"Papa was a big disciplinarian . . ."* Reminiscences of Bella Abzug, November 2, 1995–February 20, 1996, in the Columbia University Oral History Research Office Collection (hereafter Oral History), session one, 15.

6 *"I spent most of my free time . . ."* Memoir, 4, 5.

6 "ROBIN MORGAN . . ." Conversation between Morgan and Eve Abzug, July 26, 2004.

6 *"I would go on the subways . . ."* Memoir, 4, 5.

8 *"He was my babysitter . . ."* Memoir, 9.

9 *"I stood apart in the corner . . ."* Memoir, 9.

9 *"After I had become a congresswoman . . ."* Memoir, 10.

9 *"It was not until I was in my sixties . . ."* Memoir, 11.

10 *"I never saw a reason why girls . . ."* Memoir, 22.

11 *"My mother more than . . ."* Memoir, 14.

12 *"In my home always . . ."* Memoir, 24.

12 "MIM KELBER . . ." Interview with editors, fall 2003, and the New York memorial service, April 2, 1998.

13 "EVA LEDERMAN . . ." *Intimate Portrait: Bella Abzug,* directed and narrated by Lee Grant, copyright © 1999 Lifetime Entertainment Services, all rights reserved, courtesy of Lifetime Television.
13 *"If I got into trouble . . ."* Lifetime *Intimate Portrait: Bella Abzug.*
16 *"While I was going to Hunter . . ."* Memoir, 15.
16 *"We were anti-Franco . . ."* Oral History, session two, 8.
17 *"When I was in college . . ."* Oral History, session three, 4.
17 "MOE FONER . . ." Reminiscences of Moe Foner (October 25, 1984), on pp. 85, 88 in the Columbia University Oral History Research Office Collection, hereafter CUOHROC.
18 *"There's a whole group . . ."* Oral History, session two, 14.
18 "MIM KELBER . . ." New York memorial service, April 2, 1998.
19 *"I was not influenced . . ."* Oral History, session three, 9, 10.
19 "PHIL DONAHUE . . ." New York memorial service, April 2, 1998.
20 *"Toward the end of my time in college . . ."* Oral History, session three, 11.
20 *"[Our first date] was a pickup . . ."* "From the Heart: 'Martin, What Should I Do Now?' " Ms. Magazine, July–August 1990.
21 *"I must have had about six jobs . . ."* Memoir, 47.
22 *"Martin was in the army . . ."* "From the Heart."
22 *"So I go downtown . . ."* Oral History, session one, 57.
23 *"The law school faculty . . ."* Oral History, session two, 16.
23 *"There were many men and women like myself . . ."* Memoir, 63.
23 *"There was a crowd . . ."* Oral History, session two, 17.
24 "LYONEL ZUNZ . . ." New York memorial service, April 2, 1998.
24 *"While I was in law school . . ."* "From the Heart."
25 *"I was in the middle of writing . . ."* Oral History, session two, 17.
25 "LYONEL ZUNZ . . ." New York memorial service, April 2, 1998.
25 *"Because of the war's housing shortage . . ."* Memoir, 67.
25 "MARLO THOMAS . . ." New York memorial service, April 2, 1998.
26 *"People kept being drafted . . ."* Oral History, session two, 19, 21.
27 *"I always felt I was going to represent working people . . ."* Oral History, session two, 24.
28 *"I had a lot of trouble . . ."* Oral History, session two, 19.
28 *"Wherever I went representing my firm . . ."* Memoir, 70.
29 "FAYE WATTLETON . . ." New York memorial service, April 2, 1998.
29 *"If I had to work eighteen hours a day . . ."* "From the Heart."
30 *"So Pressman came in . . ."* Oral History, session two, 26.
31 *"He was a traitor . . ."* Oral History, session two, 26.
31 *"Lee Pressman had been horrible to me . . ."* Oral History, session three, 43.

31 *"When I was finished with them, I went to Europe . . ."* Oral History, session two, 37.

31 *"I wanted to be a lawyer . . ."* Oral History, session two, 54.

31 *"On the trip to Europe . . ."* Memoir, 80.

2: Civil Rights and Civil Liberties—and Raising a Family

35 *"In 1951 I moved to Mount Vernon . . ."* Oral History, session two, 38.

36 *"I used to take a month off . . ."* Oral History, session two, 31.

41 *"I wrote a letter to the school . . ."* Oral History, session two, 48.

43 *"We fought hard . . ."* Oral History, session two, 51.

44 *"My practice was wills, deeds . . ."* Oral History, session two, 39.

44 *"This guy was always sending me clients . . ."* Oral History, session three, 48.

44 "ROBERT F. WAGNER . . ." Reminiscences of Robert F. Wagner in the CUOHROC, May 1976, 16–17.

45 *"I also represented a lot of people who were victims . . ."* Oral History, session two, 39.

46 "TRANSCRIPT . . ." *Investigation of Communist Activities, New York Area—*Part VI, August 16, 1955.

46 *"There is nothing wrong with taking the Fifth . . ."* Oral History, session two, 46.

47 *"During the 1950s witch-hunts . . ."* "From the Heart."

49 *"I was working in a law firm . . ."* Oral History, session three, 13–31.

53 "Dear Rosalie . . ." Memoir outline, 13.

55 *"When I went to court, especially when I was pregnant . . ."* Memoir, 72.

55 "GERALDINE FERRARO . . ." New York memorial service, April 2, 1998.

56 *"I challenge the system . . ."* Oral History, session three, 32.

56 "JOE BOLOGNA . . ." New York memorial service, April 2, 1998.

56 *"Originally I felt that law was the instrument for social change . . ."* Oral History, session three, 33.

3: Building a Peace Movement

59 *"I didn't like Adlai . . ."* Oral History, session three, 51.

61 *"I can't really recall . . ."* Oral History, session four, 5.

61 *"They thought their cry . . ."* Oral History, session four, 5.

61 *"All I wanted to do . . ."* Oral History, session four, 9, 10.

62 *"I tried to get Women Strike . . ."* Oral History, session three, 53.

63 *"They often said . . ."* Oral History, session four, 24, 27.

64 "CORA WEISS . . ." E-mail, October 16, 2005.

66 "AMY SWERDLOW [W]hat is . . ." *Women Strike for Peace* (Chicago: University of Chicago Press, 1993), 135.

68 "*This Mother's Day* . . ." Speech delivered at a 1968 march, in Susan Dworkin, *She's Nobody's Baby: A History of American Women in the Twentieth Century*, ed. Suzanne Braun Levine (New York: Simon & Schuster, 1983), 162.

68 "ETHEL TAYLOR . . ." WSP coordinator in Philadelphia, quoted in Swerdlow, *Women Strike for Peace*, 125.

69 "*It was a very important* . . ." Oral History, session four, 70.

69 "*I have always enjoyed* . . ." Oral History, session four, 73.

69 "AMY SWERDLOW . . ." *Women Strike for Peace*, pages 134–35.

70 "*Once we had raised* . . ." Oral History, session four, 13, 16.

70 "*Well before anyone thought up* . . ." Oral History, session four, 17, 19, 28.

71 "*When I look at what* . . ." Oral History, session four, 2.

4: Transforming Local Politics

78 "*I worked to organize support for the district seat* . . ." Oral History, session three, 53.

81 "*I was very upset about the [Robert] Kennedy assassination* . . ." Oral History, session four, 58.

81 "*When Ronnie called about Lindsay* . . ." Oral History, session four, 580.

82 "*When Lindsay asked me what role I wanted* . . ." Oral History, session four, 61.

82 "*I was pretty upset* . . ." Oral History, session four, 63.

83 "*When I decided to run for office myself* . . ." Oral History, session four, 28.

5: Running and Winning: Building a New Coalition

86 "*I hadn't been a club person* . . ." Oral History, session four, 31.

86 "*When I ran for Congress* . . ." Oral History, session four, 28.

86 "*So many people asked me*," Oral History, session four, 50.

87 "*Gloria [Steinem] was always afraid* . . ." Oral History, session four, 52.

89 "*I was there in the streets, day and night* . . ." Oral History, session four, 42.

91 "PETE HAMILL . . ." *New York Post*, June 4, 1970.

92 "*They said I won by forty thousand shopping bags* . . ." Lifetime *Intimate Portrait: Bella Abzug*.

95 "*[March 28] I flew back to New York* . . ." *Bella!*, 89–90.

96 *"[April 2] I met [Barbra Streisand] . . ." Bella!*, 98.
97 "JIMMY BRESLIN . . ." "Is Washington Ready for Bella Abzug? Is Anybody?" *New York* magazine, October 5, 1970.
98 *"[T]he way people reacted . . ." Bella!*, 69–70.
98 "ED KOCH . . ." Reminiscences (January 5, 1976), on page 375 in the CUOHROC.
102 *"I'm not running against Bill . . ."* Lifetime *Intimate Portrait: Bella Abzug.*
104 *"There was a double standard . . ."* In Marlene Sanders, *The Hand that Rocks the Ballot Box*, ABC telecast, 1972.
106 *"I went to Susan Brownmiller . . ."* Oral History, session four, 46.
108 "LIFETIME DOCUMENTARY . . ." Lifetime *Intimate Portrait: Bella Abzug.*

6: An Outsider on the Inside

110 *"When I first came to Congress . . ."* Memoir outline, 40.
112 *"My first resolution was . . ."* Memoir outline, 36.
113 *"[May 13] Mary Perot Nichols . . ." Bella!*, 155.
114 "ED KOCH Bella and I just disliked one another . . ." Reminiscences of Ed Koch, December 19, 1975, on page 214 in the CUOHROC.
114 "I think that Bella is a radical . . ." Koch Oral History, January 5, 1976, 375.
114 "She is very smart, *very* smart . . ." Koch Oral History, January 5, 1976, 405–406.
121 "ROBIN MORGAN . . ." Eulogy for Mim Kelber, delivered August 17, 2004.
122 "[January 20, 1971] *As far as I can tell . . ." Bella!*, 11.
122 "[June 17, 1971] *Not only have I found ways to* tie up *the House . . ." Bella!*, 186–87.
126 *"If we are going to get anywhere . . ." Bella!*, 6.
130 *"Legislation to institute a universal child-care program . . ." Bella!*, 38–39.
131 *"Shirley Chisholm and I . . ." Bella!*, 156.
131 "ED KOCH . . ." Koch Oral History, January 5, 1976, 39.
132 *"I will tell you all the diets I've been on . . ."* Memoir outline, 17–18.

7: Building a Political Women's Movement

138 "EILEEN SHANAHAN . . ." Reminiscences of Eileen Shanahan, February 21, 1993, on page 115 in the CUOHROC.
141 "FANNIE LOU HAMER . . ." In Kay Mills, *This Little Light of Mine: The Life of Fannie Lou Hamer* (New York: Dutton, 1993), 276.

141 "SHIRLEY CHISHOLM . . ." In Mills, *This Little Light of Mine*, 277.
144 "MARLO THOMAS . . ." Lifetime *Intimate Portrait: Bella Abzug.*
146 "EILEEN SHANAHAN . . ." Shanahan Oral History, 108.

8: Becoming a Legislative Force in Congress

150 "EILEEN SHANAHAN . . ." Shanahan Oral History, 123.
151 "EILEEN SHANAHAN . . ." Ibid., 124.
152 "ED KOCH . . ." Koch Oral History, 386–88.
155 "ED KOCH . . ." Ibid., 395–96.
156 "*Outside of Martin and the kids . . .*" *Bella!*, 103.
158 "*New York Post . . .*" March 23, 1971.
159 "*I worked late again . . .*" *Bella!*, 71–73.
165 "BILL MOYERS . . ." "The Kingdom of the Half Blind," an address delivered on December 9, 2005, for the twentieth anniversary of the National Security Archive, a nongovernmental research institute and library at The George Washington University.
166 "*All my life I've been a private citizen . . .*" *Bella!*, 103.

9: Running and Losing—and Regrouping

169 "*I share my feelings . . .*" Oral History, session four, 40.
169 "JUDY LERNER . . ." Lifetime *Intimate Portrait: Bella Abzug.*
171 "HAROLD HOLZER, MAGGIE PEYTON AND I . . ." New York memorial service, April 2, 1998.
177 "DANIEL PATRICK MOYNIHAN . . ." Lifetime *Intimate Portrait: Bella Abzug.*
177 "*What I did say was . . .*" Lifetime *Intimate Portrait: Bella Abzug.*
181 "DONALD S. HARRINGTON . . ." Reminiscences of Donald S. Harrington, March 25, 1977, 179–81, in the CUOHROC.
184 "ROBERT F. WAGNER . . ." Reminiscences of Robert F. Wagner, June 1979, on pages 1146, 1156–87, in the CUOHROC.
185 "*How arya? I'm Bella Abzug . . .*" Jonathan Mahler, *Ladies and Gentlemen, The Bronx Is Burning* (New York: Farrar, Straus and Giroux, 2005), 130.
185 "HAROLD HOLZER Bella was always fabulous . . ." In Mahler, 130.
185 "HAROLD HOLZER It was also my job . . ." New York memorial service, April 2, 1998.
186 "CAMPAIGN PAMPHLET . . ." In Mahler, 282.
186 "*Ladies and Gentlemen, The Bronx Is Burning . . .*" Mahler, 362.
186 "*Almost every day . . .*" in Mahler, 134–35.

187 "HAROLD HOLZER . . ." In Mahler, 284.

193 "ROBIN MORGAN . . ." Conversation between Morgan and Liz Abzug, July 28, 2004.

10: Mobilizing American Women Voters

202 "NEWS REPORTER . . ." *Sisters of '77*, a film by Cynthia Salzman Mondell and Allen Mondell, a Media Projects production, PBS telecast, 2004.

202 "MARGUERITE RAWALT . . ." Reminiscences of Marguerite Rawalt, date unknown; subsequent interview dated September 25, 1980, session 16, 974, in the CUOHROC.

202 "PEGGY KOBERNOT-KAPLAN . . ." *Sisters of '77.*

203 "ROBERT K. (BOB) DORNAN . . ." *Sisters of '77.*

203 "ROSALYNN CARTER . . ." Address to the First Plenary Session, November 19, 1977, *Report to the President* in *The Spirit of Houston Report* (Washington, D.C., National Commission on the Observance of International Women's Year, 1978), 220.

203 "BETTY FORD . . ." Address to the First Plenary Session, in *Spirit of Houston Report*, 220–21.

204 "LADY BIRD JOHNSON . . ." Address to the First Plenary Session, in *Spirit of Houston Report*, 222.

204 "BARBARA JORDAN . . ." *Sisters of '77.*

204 "*The road to Houston* . . ." Opening the plenary session as Presiding Officer of the National Women's Conference at Houston, in *The Bella Abzug Reader*, 127–30; also in *Spirit of Houston Report*, First Plenary Session, November 19, 1977, 217–19.

206 "PHYLLIS SCHLAFLY . . ." *Sisters of '77.*

206 "MARTHA SMILEY . . ." *Sisters of '77.*

206 "GLORIA STEINEM . . ." Lifetime *Intimate Portrait: Bella Abzug.*

207 "MARGARET MEAD . . ." Address to the Fourth Plenary Session, November 20, 1977, in *Spirit of Houston Report*, p. 230.

207 "DAVID BRODER . . ." *The Washington Post*; cited in *Spirit of Houston Report*, 205.

208 "*The Spirit of Houston* . . ." Report, 147.

208 "ANN RICHARDS . . ." *Sisters of '77.*

208 "*The Spirit of Houston* . . ." Report, 148.

208 "ANN RICHARDS . . ." *Spirit of Houston Report*, 148, and *Sisters of '77.*

209 "*The Spirit of Houston* . . ." Report, 149.

209 "JEAN WESTWOOD . . ." *Spirit of Houston Report*, 149.

209 "*The Spirit of Houston* . . ." Report, 149, 152.

209 "SARAH WEDDINGTON . . ." *Spirit of Houston Report*, 162.
209 "*The Spirit of Houston . . .*" Report, 163.
212 "SEXUAL PREFERENCE RESOLUTION . . ." *Spirit of Houston Report*, 89.
212 "ELEANOR SMEAL . . ." *Sisters of '77*.
213 "BETTY FRIEDAN . . ." *Spirit of Houston Report*, 166.
213 "LINDSY VAN GELDER . . ." Ms. magazine, in *Spirit of Houston Report*, 205.
213 "*London Evening Standard . . .*" *Spirit of Houston Report*, 205–206.
213 "LIZ CARPENTER . . ." *Sisters of '77*.
213 "PATRICK J. BUCHANAN . . ." *Spirit of Houston Report*, 206.
220 "SEY CHASSLER . . ." Reminiscences of Sey Chassler, April 26, 1992, on pages 2, 60–63, in the CUOHROC.
220 "SEY CHASSLER . . ." Chassler Oral History, April 26, 1982, session two, 61–62.
221 "JIMMY CARTER . . ." Presidential news conference, January 17, 1979.
222 "CAROLYN REED . . ." Reminiscences of Carolyn Reed, April 15, 1981, 51, in the CUOHROC.
223 "SEY CHASSLER . . ." Chassler Oral History, April 26, 1982, 2–68.
224 "ERMA BOMBECK . . ." Ms. magazine, June 1978.
225 "ELEANOR SMEAL . . ." *Sisters of '77*

11: Building an Agenda for Women—One Meeting, Conference, March at a Time

231 "LESLIE BENNETTS . . ." Leslie Bennetts, "A Day of Lobbying for Women's Rights Issues," *The New York Times* Style News, February 6, 1981.
241 "JUDY LERNER . . ." Lifetime *Intimate Portrait: Bella Abzug*.
244 "HELENE SAVITZKY ALEXANDER . . ." Lifetime *Intimate Portrait: Bella Abzug*.
245 "GLORIA STEINEM . . ." Lifetime *Intimate Portrait: Bella Abzug*.
245 "*My reputation is that of an extremely independent woman . . .*" "From the Heart."
249 "*Now, every day the fire has to be lit . . .*" "From the Heart."

13: Going Global

263 "ROBIN MORGAN . . ." Conversation between Morgan and Eve Abzug, July 26, 2004.
264 "*Bienvenu, mes soeurs . . .*" *The Bella Abzug Reader*, 286.

264 "DOROTHY GOLDIN ROSENBERG . . ." *Peace Magazine*, March–April 1992, 8.

264 "MICHELE LANDSBERG . . ." From a series of columns in *The Toronto Star*, November 15–17, 1991; in *The Bella Abzug Reader*, 290–91.

265 "DOROTHY GOLDIN ROSENBERG . . ." *Peace Magazine*, 8.

268 "LIFETIME DOCUMENTARY . . ." Lifetime *Intimate Portrait: Bella Abzug*.

269 *"I had a couple of biopsies . . ."* Lifetime *Intimate Portrait: Bella Abzug*.

270 "AMY SWERDLOW . . ." Lifetime *Intimate Portrait: Bella Abzug*.

270 "WEDO NEWS & VIEWS . . ." A December 1993 report on launching the WEDO Project on Women, Cancer, and the Environment, reprinted in *The Bella Abzug Reader*, 322–23.

276 "AMY SWERDLOW . . ." Lifetime *Intimate Portrait: Bella Abzug*.

277 "LIZ ABZUG . . ." Lifetime *Intimate Portrait: Bella Abzug*.

278 *"We celebrate the fiftieth anniversary . . ."* *The Bella Abzug Reader*, 386–89.

282 "KOFI ANNAN . . ." Address at the United Nations Tribute to Bella Abzug: A World Celebration, April 24, 1998. Reprinted in *The Bella Abzug Reader*, 400–401.

284 "GLORIA STEINEM . . ." April 24, 1998, at the United Nations Tribute to Bella Abzug: A World Celebration (from Jewish Women's Archive www.jwa.org/exhibits/wov/abzug/torch.html).

284 "HILLARY CLINTON . . ." Address at the National Women's Political Caucus memorial service at the National Press Club in Washington, D.C., April 9, 1998. Reprinted in *The Bella Abzug Reader*, 399.

Sources

By Bella Abzug

The Bella Abzug Reader. Mim Kelber, coauthor. Edited by Mim Kelber and Libby Bassett. Privately published: copyright 2003 by Mim and Harry Kelber.

Bella! Ms. Abzug Goes to Washington. Mel Ziegler, coauthor. New York: Saturday Review Press, 1972.

"Celebrating Human Rights." Address before the forty-second session of the UN Commission on the Status of Women, March 3, 1998, in *The Bella Abzug Reader*, 386–89.

"From the Heart: 'Martin, What Should I Do Now?' " Ms. magazine (July–August 1990), p. 94–96.

Gender Gap: Bella Abzug's Guide to Political Power for American Women. Mim Kelber, coauthor. Boston: Houghton Mifflin, 1984.

Memoir, unpublished. Copyright © 2007 by the Bella Abzug Estate. All rights reserved.

Memoir outline, unpublished. Copyright © 2007 by the Bella Abzug Estate. All rights reserved.

Reminiscences of Bella Abzug, November 2, 1995–February 20, 1996. In the Columbia University Oral History Research Office Collection.

Reminiscences in the Columbia University Oral History Research Office Collection

Sey Chassler, April 26, 1982.

Moe Foner, October 25, 1984.

Rev. Donald S. Harrington, March 25, 1977.
Ed Koch, December 19, 1975; January 5, 1976.
Marguerite Rawalt, 1981.
Carolyn Reed, April 15, 1981.
Eileen Shanahan, February 21, 1993.
Robert F. Wagner, June 1979.

Government Documents

Transcript of the HUAC Subcommittee Investigation of Communist Activities in the New York Area. Part VI, August 16, 1955.

The Spirit of Houston: The First National Women's Conference: An Official Report to the President, the Congress and the People of the United States. Washington, D.C.: National Commission on the Observance of International Women's Year, 1978.

Books

Dworkin, Susan. *She's Nobody's Baby: A History of American Women in the Twentieth Century*. Edited by Suzanne Braun Levine. New York: Simon and Schuster, 1983.

Mahler, Jonathan. *Ladies and Gentlemen, the Bronx Is Burning: 1977, Baseball, Politics, and the Battle for the Soul of a City*. New York: Farrar, Straus and Giroux, 2005.

Mills, Kay. *This Little Light of Mine: The Life of Fannie Lou Hamer*. New York: Dutton, 1993.

Swerdlow, Amy. *Women Strike for Peace: Traditional Motherhood and Radical Politics in the 1960s*. Chicago: The University of Chicago Press, 1993.

Articles

Bennetts, Leslie. "A Day of Lobbying for Women's Rights Issues." *The New York Times* Style News, February 6, 1981.

Bombeck, Erma. "Hollywood Mobilizes for the ERA." Compiled by Letty Cottin Pogrebin, Ms., June 1978, 76.

Breslin, Jimmy. "Is Washington Ready for Bella Abzug? Is Anybody?" *New York* magazine, October 5, 1970.

Hamill, Pete. *New York Post* column (June 4, 1970).

Landsberg, Michele. A series of columns in *The Toronto Star*, November 15–17, 1991. Reprinted in *The Bella Abzug Reader*, 290–94.

New York Post, March 23, 1971.

Rosenberg, Dorothy Goldin. "Unsaid at UNCED: Women Dem and Inclusion of Military Issues at the Earth Summit." *Peace Magazine*, March–April 1992, 8.

WEDO News & Views. "WEDO Project on Women, Cancer, and the Environment: Texas Women Kick Off Campaign with a Public Hearing in Capitol." December 1993 report on launching the WEDO Project on Women, Cancer, and the Environment. Reprinted in *The Bella Abzug Reader*, 322–24.

Speeches, Statements

Annan, Kofi. Speech delivered at the United Nations Tribute to Bella Abzug: A World Celebration, April 24, 1998. Reprinted in *The Bella Abzug Reader*, 400–401.

Carter, Jimmy. Presidential news conference, January 17, 1979. Atlanta, Georgia: Jimmy Carter Library.

Clinton, Hillary. Speech delivered at the National Women's Political Caucus memorial service at the National Press Club in Washington, D.C., April 9, 1998. Reprinted in *The Bella Abzug Reader*, 399–400.

Eulogies delivered at the New York memorial service for Bella Abzug, April 2, 1998, Riverside Memorial Chapel.

Morgan, Robin. Eulogy given at a New York City memorial service for Mim Kelber, August 17, 2004.

Moyers, Bill. *The Kingdom of the Half Blind*. Address delivered for the twentieth anniversary of the National Security Archive, a nongovernmental research institute and library at The George Washington University, December 9, 2005.

Steinem, Gloria. Speech delivered at the United Nations Tribute to Bella Abzug: A World Celebration, April 24, 1998 from the Jewish Women's Archive http://www.jwa.org/exhibits/wov/abzug/torch.html

Documentaries

Intimate Portrait: Bella Abzug, directed and narrated by Lee Grant, © 1999 Lifetime Entertainment Services, all rights reserved, courtesy of Lifetime Television.

The Hand that Rocks the Ballot Box. Marlene Sanders, prod. ABC, 1972.

Sisters of '77, a film by Cynthia Salzman Mondell and Allen Mondell, a Media Projects production (www.mediaprojects.org). PBS telecast, 2004.

Acknowledgments

We are grateful to Bella's daughters, Eve and Liz, for their generous support of this project—making themselves available for interviews, sharing family photographs and, most crucially, giving us access to Bella's own words. We thank as well the many others—family, friends, colleagues, and sometime foes of Bella—who took the time to share their stories.

Thanks also to Bob Levine for seeing that this was an important undertaking and helping make it happen, and his colleague Kim Schefler for deftly managing the legal aspects.

To Jonathan Galassi, president and publisher of FSG, for believing in Bella; and our editor, Denise Oswald, for her intelligent and attentive participation in the shaping of the book.

To Karen Grenke for her devoted and smart attention to research, and Rose Heredia for meticulously and enthusiastically transcribing the interviews. Thanks also to Columbia University's Oral History Office—Mary Marshall Clark in particular—and to the Ford Foundation for supporting the Bella Abzug interviews.

And especially to our "family," who urged us on, contributed to the manuscript, and generally added joy to this already deeply satisfying project—Robin Morgan, Gloria Steinem, Harriet Lyons (who managed the photographs), Virginia Kerr, Joanne Edgar, Thom Loubet, Karin Lippert, and Patricia Bauman.

Index

Commentary in subentries refers to the life and activities of Bella Abzug unless otherwise indicated.